# Live Free or Die Lawfully

A devotional commentary on Galatians

# Live Free or Die Lawfully

A devotional commentary on Galatians

Joshua Wingerd

FYTR Publishing
2019

Live Free or Die Lawfully: A devotional commentary on Galatians

Copyright © 2019 by FYTR Publishing, Victorville, CA 92394
ISBN 978-0-9996342-1-9

www.lilfytr.com
www.lilwritr.wordpress.com

First Printing: 2019

All rights reserved. No part of this publication may be reproduced, stored in a retrieval system, or transmitted in any form or by any means—for example, electronic, photocopy, recording—without the prior written permission of the publisher. The only exception is brief quotations in printed reviews.

Unless otherwise noted, all Scripture quotations (Galatians references excluded) are taken from the Holman Christian Standard Bible, Copyright 2009 by Holman Bible Publishers. Used by permission.

All Scripture quotations throughout "EXCURSUS: Seeking the Seed" are taken from the NEW AMERICAN STANDARD BIBLE, Copyright 1995 by The Lockman Foundation. Used by permission.

Scripture quotations marked NRSV are from the New Revised Standard Version Bible, copyright 1989 the Division of Christian Education of the National Council of the Churches of Christ in the United States of America. Used by permission. All rights reserved.

Ordering Information:
Special discounts are available on quantity purchases by corporations, associations, educators, and others. For details, contact the publisher at the following email address:
wingerd.j@lilfytr.com

U.S. trade bookstores and wholesalers: Please contact FYTR Publishing at the email address listed above.

# Dedication

For Mo,
You may or may not remember giving me this advice,
But I'll never forget that I'm a "hard-wired legalist."
I'm still trying to "Stop it!"
Thank you for emulating Gospel-centered Christian ministry to me.

# Contents

Introduction ............................................................................................................. 1
Paul's Epistle to the Galatians ............................................................................ 5
Lesson 1: Galatians 1:1-5 ................................................................................... 13
Lesson 2: Galatians 1:6-10 ................................................................................. 21
Lesson 3: Galatians 1:11-24 ............................................................................... 31
Lesson 4: Galatians 2:1-10 ................................................................................. 43
Lesson 5: Galatians 2:11-21 ............................................................................... 53
Lesson 6: Galatians 3:1-5 ................................................................................... 65
Lesson 7: Galatians 3:6-14 ................................................................................. 75
Lesson 8: Galatians 3:15-18 ............................................................................... 87
Lesson 9: Galatians 3:19-29 ............................................................................... 95
Lesson 10: Galatians 4:1-7 ............................................................................... 105
Lesson 11: Galatians 4:8-20 ............................................................................. 115
Lesson 12: Galatians 4:21-31 ........................................................................... 125
Lesson 13: Galatians 5:1 ................................................................................... 135
Lesson 14: Galatians 5:2-12 ............................................................................. 147
Lesson 15: Galatians 5:13-15 ........................................................................... 159
Lesson 16: Galatians 5:16-18 ........................................................................... 169
Lesson 17: Galatians 5:19-21 ........................................................................... 181
Lesson 18: Galatians 5:22-24 ........................................................................... 197
Lesson 19: Galatians 5:25-6:5 .......................................................................... 211
Lesson 20: Galatians 6:6-10 ............................................................................. 221
Lesson 21: Galatians 6:11-18 ........................................................................... 231
EXCURSUS: Tough Love – liL fytr in Galatians ........................................... 245
EXCURSUS: Seeking the Seed – a treatise on Galatians 3:16 ..................... 251
References ......................................................................................................... 325

# Introduction

To the reader:

Biblical Christianity is a religion of unlearning what you have learned. People tell you that life is supposed to be about you and your happiness. You have been taught that if you are not happy, then something must be wrong with you or your life. You have been convinced that people are mostly good (even sins are labeled similarly now—"It's just a *little, white* lie"; "I was *just kidding,* not gossiping"; "My boyfriend and I are *living* together").[1]

But specifically, when it comes to Christian beliefs, the Bible demands that we unlearn what we have learned. We have been taught that salvation occurs via man's free will. We have been taught that after being saved by grace alone, the Bible is a whole list of things we must do if we are going to be Christians. We have been taught that the church is simply a recess for God before He gets back to fulfilling His promises to Israel.

The truth of the matter is that salvation is grace, and apart from God's active intervention, no one would be saved. The fact of the matter is that just like there are zero stipulations regarding who is allowed to believe, no one keeps themselves saved by following a list of rules. The truth of the matter is that the church was God's plan from day one, and God used Israel as the catalyst to bring Jesus into the world so that the church—made up of all nations—could be found *in Him*.

The following book exists as my journey of unlearning some seemingly fundamental things regarding Christianity.[2] It is essentially a

---

[1] A big thank you to my fellow Mingle friends (a Facebook group) who helped me brainstorm the items in this list.

[2] Interestingly enough, all three things mentioned above are discussed in the pages of Galatians. The utter grace of God in salvation is clearly present in 1:11-24 (among other places). The rule-free nature of Christianity is the primary focus of the entire book (especially 5:1-12). And the place of Israel in the plan of God is clearly delineated in 3:6-26.

commentary on Paul's letter to the Galatians. In addition to being a commentary, this book exists as a guidebook for you in your spiritual journey. Each chapter (Lesson) will begin with a section explaining the meaning of the biblical text, then turn to exalt the Gospel of Christ (because even Christians cannot get too much of the Gospel), then ask personal reflection questions (so that you can use this book for an individual/group study), and—finally—conclude by relating sample prayers inspired by the Lesson's Scripture text (because there is no better way to pray biblically than to pray the Bible).

Now, I mentioned above that this book exists as my journey of unlearning some fundamental things regarding Christianity. Let me tell you a little about that journey (for more on this personal testimony, check out Lesson 13).

I felt lost. I had moved 1600 miles away from my home church to go to Bible college, and I had taken a risk by asking a local pastor to help counsel me through a sin struggle. (Let me just say at the outset: If you are not fighting sin in your life, you need to be; if you don't fight it, it will snuff the fire out of your Christian life.)

The counsel I was receiving, though, was less than helpful. Christ was absent too much of the time, which is sad when we refer to ourselves as *Christ*ians. The counsel was: You're obviously not saved if you keep committing this sin. Now, I would agree with him on that point if I was trying to hide it, avoiding talking about it, or engaging in it every chance I got. But I wasn't. I had approached him for help, I confessed every time I had stumbled, and the rate of "failure" had dropped significantly since the day I was graciously saved by Jesus in July of 2010. Besides, the counsel was the opposite of the counsel I had received at my home church before going to college.

So, I was lost. That was when I decided to read through the whole book of Galatians one muggy, summer day in 2015. I had remembered my pastor back home mentioning something from Galatians one time, and I had remembered it being powerful. I wanted to find it again.

As I read, the book blew me away. Paul knew exactly what he was doing as he penned the words to the Galatians. He sought to convince his readers that if they didn't live free, then they would die under the Law. Thus,

## Introduction

the title of this book: *Live Free or Die Lawfully*. Virtually, no sooner than Paul has said, "Hi guys," he says, "If you add to Christ, you destroy the Gospel; if you add to grace, you destroy the Gospel; if you are seeking glory and recognition for yourself, you are destroying the Gospel. Stop it!"

And then I came to the first main point of the book: "<u>But having known that no person is made righteous by works of Law, but rather through [the] faithfulness of Jesus [the] Messiah, we have believed in [the] Messiah Jesus in order that we might be made righteous by [the] faithfulness of [the] Messiah and not by works of Law, because by works of Law no flesh [at] all will be made righteous.</u>"[3] (Galatians 2:16). Paul writes two times that works of Law will not make a person righteous. Paul writes two times that our only hope is the faithfulness of Christ. Praise Him for His faithfulness, especially since we are often faithless! And then in between all of that, Paul writes once that we believed in Jesus. This is the heart of the Gospel. We have believed. We must continue to believe. This is Christianity: It is most certainly not an easy religion, but it is simple:

- What must I do to be saved? **Believe!**
- What must I do now that I am saved? **Believe!**
- How do I know that I am saved? **Believe!**

And then, two and a half chapters later, I came to the climax of the book. Everything prior is building to it, and everything after flows from it: "<u>[The] Messiah set us free for freedom; therefore you all must stand, and you all must not be again entangled in a yoke of slavery</u>" (Galatians 5:1). And it was this verse that God used to open my eyes to my situation. The counsel I was receiving was placing a yoke on my shoulders. I couldn't take it. I needed Christ!

It is now a little over four years later, and I'm still learning how to walk in grace with Christ, but it was while sitting at that park bench that I

---

[3] All Scripture quotations from Galatians (excluding those found in EXCURSUS: Seeking the Seed) are the author's translation.

decided to put my college degree to use and exposit the book of Galatians on my blog.[4]

So, the book you hold in your hands is the result of my journey to seek only Christ. The original blog posts have been slightly edited, but the same desire present in the original posts is present in these pages.

I hope that you will join me on this journey and seek Christ alone as well.

    Soli Deo Gloria
    Solus Christus
    Sola Scriptura
    Sola Gratia
    Sola Fide
    Pro Ecclesia

Joshua Wingerd<br>October 20, 2019

---

[4] I currently blog at www.lilfytr.com. I would be honored if you'd check out more of my thoughts that I have posted there.

# Paul's Epistle to the Galatians

(Author's Translation)

**1** ¹Paul, an apostle—neither [sent][a] from people nor through [the agency of] a person, but [sent] through [the authority of] Jesus [the] Messiah[b] and God [the] Father, the One who raised Him from death—²and all the brothers who are with me.

To the churches of Galatia:

³Grace and peace to you all from God our Father and [the] Lord Jesus [the] Messiah, ⁴who gave Himself for our sins, so that He might release us from the present, evil age, according to the will of our God and Father, ⁵to whom be the glory forever. Amen.

⁶I am amazed that so soon you all are apostatizing yourselves away from the One who called you all by grace to a different gospel, ⁷which is not another, except some are troubling you all and wanting to change the Gospel of the Messiah. ⁸But even if we or an angel from heaven might evangelize to you all different from what we evangelized to you all, let [such a one] be cursed. ⁹As we have said before, I also now say again: If anyone evangelizes to you all different from what you all received, let [such a one] be cursed.

¹⁰For am I now trying to persuade people or God? Or am I seeking to please people? If I was still trying to please people, then I would not be a slave of [the] Messiah.

---

[a] Any words inside [brackets] are added by me to smooth out the translation and are not present in the original Greek. Cf. Kurt Aland, ed., *The Greek New Testament*, 4th ed (New York, NY: United Bible Societies), 1983.

[b] Literally, "Christ," and so throughout the translation. "Christ" is the English transliteration of the Greek translation of the Hebrew "Messiah." Even though Paul is primarily dealing with Gentile churches in the region of Galatia, the Gentile church is still dependent on the Jewish Messiah for salvation, and as such I decided to try to make the link to the Hebrew Scriptures more explicit in my translation.

¹¹For I make known to you all, brothers, that the Gospel evangelized by me is not according to [the desires and opinions of]ᶜ a person, ¹²for I myself did not receive it from a person, nor was I taught [it], but [I received it] through a revelation of Jesus [the] Messiah.

¹³For you all heard of my former way of life in Judaism, that I was excessively persecuting the church of God and was destroying it, ¹⁴and [that] I was advancing in Judaism beyond many contemporaries of my generation, being more zealous for my fathers' traditions. ¹⁵But when God (the One who set me apart from my mother's womb and called me through His grace) was pleased ¹⁶to reveal His Son in me (in order that I might evangelize Him to the nations) I did not immediately consult with flesh and blood, ¹⁷nor did I go up to Jerusalem to the [ones who were] apostles before me, but I went away into Arabia, and again I returned to Damascus.

¹⁸After three years, I went up to Jerusalem to get to know Cephas, and I stayed with him for fifteen days, ¹⁹but I did not see the other apostles, except James, the Lord's brother. ²⁰Now what I write to you all, behold, before God: I am not lying. ²¹Then I went into the regions of Syria and Cilicia, ²²but I was unknown by face to the churches of Judea in [the] Messiah. ²³They were only hearing, "The one who once persecutes us is now evangelizing the [very same] faith which he was once destroying," ²⁴and they were glorifying God because of me.

**2**¹After a period of fourteen years, I again went up to Jerusalem taking with me Barnabas and Titus; ²I went up according to a revelation, and I set forward to them the Gospel that I am preaching to the nations (but privately to the ones appearing [to be important]) lest I might be running—or had run—in vain. ³But not even Titus who [was] with me, being a Greek, was compelled to be circumcised. ⁴But [the circumcision dispute arose] because of false brothers, secretly brought in, who snuck in to spy on our freedom which we have in [the] Messiah Jesus, in order that they might enslave us, ⁵but to whom we did not yield in submission for an hour, in order that the truth of the Gospel might remain for you all. ⁶Now, to return toᵈ the ones who appear to be someone—whatever they were does not matter to me; God does not take [note of] a person's face—the ones who appear [to be someone] added nothing to me, ⁷but, on the contrary, after seeing that I had been entrusted with the

---

ᶜ "ουκ εστι κατα ανθρωπον is not accommodated to the opinions and desires of men, Galatians 1:11." J. H. Thayer, *Greek-English Lexicon of the New Testament* (New York: Harper & Brothers, 1889), WORD*search*.

ᵈ Literally, "away from."

Gospel to the uncircumcised even as Peter [had been entrusted with the Gospel] to the circumcised <sup>8</sup>(for the One who worked in Peter for an apostleship to the circumcised also worked in me to the nations) <sup>9</sup>and, after knowing the grace that was given to me, James, Cephas, and John—the ones who appear to be pillars—gave Barnabas and me [the] right hand of fellowship, in order that we [might be] for the nations what they [are] for the circumcised, <sup>10</sup>only [requesting] that we might remember the poor, which also was the very thing I was eager to do.

<sup>11</sup>Now, when Cephas had come to Antioch, I stood against his face because he had been condemned. <sup>12</sup>For prior to the arrival of certain men from James, he ate together with the nations, but when they came, he was withdrawing and separating himself, fearing those from [the] circumcision. <sup>13</sup>And the rest of the Jews joined with him in hypocrisy so that even Barnabas was carried away by their hypocrisy. <sup>14</sup>But when I saw that they were not walking in line with the truth of the Gospel, I said to Cephas in front of everyone:

"If you, being a Jew, live like a Gentile and not like a Jew, then how can you compel the Gentiles to Judaize? <sup>15</sup>We are Jews by nature, and [we are] not sinners like [the] Gentiles[e], <sup>16</sup>but having known that no person is made righteous by works of Law, but rather through [the] faithfulness of Jesus [the] Messiah, we have believed in [the] Messiah Jesus in order that we might be made righteous by [the] faithfulness of [the] Messiah and not by works of Law, because by works of Law no flesh [at] all will be made righteous. <sup>17</sup>Now if, while seeking to be made righteous by [the] Messiah, we might also be found sinners, then is [the] Messiah a servant of sin? May it never be! <sup>18</sup>For if I rebuild the very things I once destroyed, I show myself [to be] a transgressor. <sup>19</sup>For through Law, I myself died to Law, in order that I might live for God. I have been crucified together with [the] Messiah, <sup>20</sup>and I myself no longer live, but [the] Messiah lives in me, and the [life] which I now live in [the] flesh, I live by faith in the Son of God, the One who loved me and gave Himself up for me. <sup>21</sup>I do not set aside the grace of God, for if righteousness results from Law, then [the] Messiah died in vain."

**3**<sup>1</sup>Oh, mindless Galatians, what witch cursed you all[f], before whose eyes Jesus [the] Messiah was plainly set forward as being crucified? <sup>2</sup>I only

---

[e] Literally, "from [the] nations."

[f] "To bring evil on one by feigned praise or an evil eye, to charm, bewitch one . . . hence, of those who lead away others into error by wicked arts (Diodorus 4, 6): Galatians 3:1." J. H. Thayer, *Greek-English Lexicon of the New Testament*.

want to learn this from you all: Did you all receive the Spirit by works of Law or by faithful hearing? ³Thusly you all are mindless: After beginning by [the] Spirit, are you all now being completed by [the] flesh? ⁴Did you all suffer so many things for no benefit (if indeed [they were] for no benefit)? ⁵Therefore, [did] the One who ministered the Spirit to you all and who worked powerfully among you all, [do it] by works of Law or by faithful hearing? ⁶Even so, Abraham <u>believed God and it was registered to him as righteousness</u>.

⁷You all need to know then that the ones of faith, these very ones, are sons of Abraham. ⁸And the Scriptures, after foreseeing that God justifies the nations by faith, evangelized before to Abraham, "<u>In you, all the nations will be blessed</u>," ⁹so that the ones of faith are being blessed with the faith of Abraham. ¹⁰For as many as are [seeking righteousness] by works of Law are under a curse; for it has been written, "<u>A curse be upon everyone who does not continue to do every single thing that has been written in the Book of the Law</u>ᵍ." ¹¹Now, it is clear that no one is made righteous before God by [the] Law: "<u>The righteous person will live by faith</u>," ¹²but the Law is not by faith; rather, "<u>The one who after doing them will live on account of them</u>." ¹³[The] Messiah purchased us from the curse of the Law by becoming a curse for us, because it has been written, "<u>A curse be upon everyone who is being hung upon a tree</u>," ¹⁴in order that the blessing of Abraham might come to the nations through [the] Messiah Jesus, in order that we might receive the promise of the Spirit through faith.

¹⁵Brothers, I speak as a person: No one annuls or adds to a human covenant that had been previously ratified. ¹⁶Now the promises were spoken to Abraham and to his seed. It does not say, "And to seeds," as [though] to many, but as to one, "<u>And to your seed</u>," which is [the] Messiah. ¹⁷Now this I say: A covenant was previously ratified beforehand by God, [so] the Law having come—after four hundred and thirty years—does not cancel so as to destroy the promise. ¹⁸For if the inheritance [is] by Law, then [it is] no longer by promise, but God has graced it to Abraham through a promise. ¹⁹Therefore, why the Law? It was set down because of transgressions until the Seed to which it was promised might come, having been ordained through angels by [the] hand of a mediator. ²⁰Now the mediator is not [only] one, but God is one.

²¹Therefore, is the Law opposed to the promises of God? May it never be! For if a Law was given that was able to make [people] live, then righteousness would certainly be by Law, ²²but the Scripture shut up all things

---

g Literally, "who does not continue in everything that has been written in the Book of the Law to do them."

under sin in order that the promise might be given by [the] faithfulness of Jesus [the] Messiah to the ones who are believing.

²³But before the coming of the faith, we were being kept, shut up together [with all things], under Law as to the faith about to be revealed, ²⁴so that the Law has been our tutor toward [the] Messiah, so that we might be made righteous by faith, ²⁵and since the faith came, we are [now] no longer under a tutor.

²⁶For you are yourselves all sons of God through faith in [the] Messiah Jesus, ²⁷for as many of you all who were baptized into [the] Messiah have all been clothed with [the] Messiah. ²⁸There is not a Jew or a Greek, there is not a slave or a free [person], there is not male and female; for you all, yourselves, are one in [the] Messiah Jesus. ²⁹And if you all, yourselves, [belong to the] Messiah, then you all are Abraham's seed, heirs according to [the] promise.

**4**¹Now I say, for as long as the heir is an infant, he is not at all different from a slave, [though] being lord of all, ²but he is under guardians and stewards until the time set beforehand by his father. ³Thusly also us: We were infants, having been enslaved under the fundamental principles of the world, ⁴but then the fullness of time came, [and] God sent forth His Son (born of a woman, born under the Law) ⁵in order that He might purchase those under Law so that we might receive the sonship. ⁶Now because you all are sons, God sent forth the Spirit of His Son into our hearts, who is crying out, "Abba, Father!" ⁷So that you are no longer a slave, but a son, and if a son, also an heir through [the authority of] God.

⁸But then indeed, having not [yet] known God, you all slaved for things being by nature not gods, ⁹and now, after knowing God—or rather having become known by God—how are you all again turning to the weak and bankrupt fundamental principles to which you all want to be enslaved again? ¹⁰You all are keeping for yourselves days, months, seasons, and years, ¹¹[and] I am afraid for you all that perhaps I have labored on you all's behalf in vain.

¹²Become like me, because I also became like you all, brothers. I beg of you all. You all did nothing to harm me. ¹³You all know that despite weakness of the flesh I evangelized to you the first [time], ¹⁴and (despite you all's temptation on account of my flesh) you all neither regarded [me] with contempt nor spat [at me], but you received me as a messenger of God, as [the] Messiah Jesus. ¹⁵Then where is your blessing? For I testify to you all that if able, you all, after scooping out you all's eyes, would have given [them] to me. ¹⁶So have I become you all's enemy by telling the truth to you all? ¹⁷They are

zealous for you all, but not for good; instead they want to shut you all out in order that you all might be zealous for them. [18]Now [it is] always good to be zealous for a good thing, and not only when we are together[h]. [19]My children for whom I am again suffering birth pains until [the] Messiah might be formed in you all, [20]I want to be present with you all now and to change my voice, because I am confused about you all.

[21]Tell me, the ones who are wanting to be under Law, don't you all hear the Law? [22]For it has been written that Abraham had two sons: One from the servant-girl and one from the free-woman. [23]But whereas the one from the servant-girl had been born according to [the] flesh, the one from the free-woman [was born] as a result of [the] promise. [24]These things are allegorical, for these are two covenants: Indeed, the one from Mount Sinai bearing [children] into slavery is Hagar. [25]Hagar corresponds to Mount Sinai in Arabia—the present-day Jerusalem—for she is enslaved with her children. [26]But the Jerusalem above is free, who is our mother, [27]for it has been written,

> "Rejoice, [O] barren woman, who is not giving birth,
> Break forth and shout, the one who is not suffering birth pains;
> Because the children of the desolate one will be many more than [those of] the one who has a husband."

[28]You all, yourselves—brothers—are children of [the] promise, like Isaac. [29]But even as then, the one who had been born according to [the] flesh persecuted the one [born] according to [the] Spirit, so also [it is] now. [30]But what does the Scripture say? "Throw out the servant-girl and her son; for the son of the servant-girl will not inherit with the son of the free-woman." [31]Therefore, brothers, we are not children of [the] slave-girl, but of the free-woman.

**5** [1][The] Messiah set us free for freedom; therefore you all must stand, and you all must not be again entangled in a yoke of slavery.

[2]Behold, I, myself—Paul—say to you all that if you might get circumcised then [the] Messiah is of no benefit for you all. [3]Now I testify again that every man who is getting circumcised is obligated to keep the whole Law. [4]You all were cut off from [the] Messiah, the ones of you all who are trying to be made righteous by Law; you all fell away from grace. [5]For we ourselves are eagerly awaiting faith, hope, and righteousness by [the] Spirit. [6]For in [the]

---

[h] Literally, "in the presence me with you."

Messiah Jesus neither circumcision nor uncircumcision is any influencer, instead faith working itself out through love.

⁷You all were running well, [so] who cut in on you all to persuade you all to disobey the truth? ⁸The persuasion [is] not from the One who called you all. ⁹"A little yeast spreads throughout[i] the whole lump [of dough]." ¹⁰I myself have confidence in [the] Lord that you all will think nothing different, but the one who is troubling you all will bear the judgment, whoever he might be. ¹¹But if I myself, brothers, still preach circumcision, then why am I still being persecuted? Then the scandal of the cross has been abolished. ¹²I wish that the ones who are troubling you all might also emasculate themselves.

¹³For you all, yourselves, were called to freedom, brothers; only not the freedom of an occasion for the flesh, instead, [the freedom] to serve one another through love. ¹⁴For all of the Law has been summed up in one word, in this one, "You all must love your neighbor[j] as yourself." ¹⁵But if you all are biting and devouring one another, you all must watch out lest you all are destroyed by one another.

¹⁶Now I say: You all must walk by [the] Spirit, and you all will not at all fulfill fleshly lust. ¹⁷For the flesh desires [what is] opposed to the Spirit, and the Spirit [desires what is] opposed to the flesh, because these things are opposing one another so that you all might not do the very things you all might want [to do]. ¹⁸But if you all are being led by [the] Spirit, [then] you all are not under Law. ¹⁹Now the works of the flesh are manifest, which are: Fornications, immoralities, sensualities, ²⁰idolatries, sorceries, hostilities, discords, jealousies, rages, strifes, dissensions, heresies, ²¹envies, drunkennesses, carousings, and the things similar to these, about which I say to you all, as I said before, that the ones who are practicing these things will not inherit [the] Kingdom of God.

²²But the fruit of the Spirit is love, joy, peace, patience, kindness, goodness, faithfulness, ²³gentleness, [and] self-control; there is no Law opposed to such things. ²⁴But the ones belonging to [the] Messiah Jesus crucified the flesh with [its] passions and desires. ²⁵If we live by [the] Spirit, we should also order [our lives] by [the] Spirit. ²⁶We must not become conceited, provoking one another, envying one another.

---

[i] Literally, "a little leaven leavens" or "a little yeast yeasts." The noun and verb are both derived from the same root word.

[j] Literally, "the one who is close to you."

**6** ¹Brothers, if indeed a person might be caught in any transgression, you all who are spiritual must yourselves restore such a one in a gentle spirit, watching yourselves lest you also might be tempted. ²You all must carry one another's burdens, and thusly you all will fulfill the Law of the Messiah. ³For if someone might consider [himself] to be something, being nothing, [then] he deceives himself. ⁴But let each man's work show for himself, and then for his [work] alone he will have reason for boasting, and not for another's [work], ⁵for each one will have to carry his own burden.

⁶The one who is being taught the word must fellowship in all good things with the one who is teaching. ⁷Do not be deceived; God is not [able to be] mocked. For whatever a person might sow, this also a person will reap: ⁸"The one who is sowing to the flesh will himself, from the flesh, reap corruption, but the one who is sowing to the Spirit will, from the Spirit, reap eternal life." ⁹And we should not become weary while doing good things, for in [the] right season we will reap, not fainting. ¹⁰Therefore, as we have season, we should work for the good of all people, but especially for the ones of the household of faith.

¹¹Notice I wrote to you with large letters by my hand. ¹²The ones who are wanting to make a good showing in [the] flesh are the ones compelling you all to be circumcised, only in order that they might not be persecuted for the cross of the Messiah. ¹³For not even the ones being circumcised are keeping [the] Law themselves, but they are wanting you all to be circumcised in order that they might boast about [the] flesh of each of you. ¹⁴But may it never be for me to boast unless about the cross of our Lord Jesus [the] Messiah, through which [the] world has been crucified to me, and I [have been crucified] to [the] world! ¹⁵For neither circumcision nor uncircumcision is anything, instead a new creation. ¹⁶And as many as will walk according to this standard: Peace [be] upon them and mercy also [be] upon the Israel of God.

¹⁷For the remainder [of my life], let no one give me troubles, for I myself carry the marks of Jesus on my body.

¹⁸The grace of our Lord Jesus [the] Messiah be with you all's Spirit, brothers. Amen.

# Lesson 1

## Galatians 1:1-5

¹Paul, an apostle—neither [sent] from people nor through [the agency of] a person, but [sent] through [the authority of] Jesus [the] Messiah and God [the] Father, the One who raised Him from death—²and all the brothers who are with me.

To the churches of Galatia:

³Grace and peace to you all from God our Father and [the] Lord Jesus [the] Messiah, ⁴who gave Himself for our sins, so that He might release us from the present, evil age, according to the will of our God and Father, ⁵to whom be the glory forever. Amen.

# Greetings of Grace in Galatia

"It was a dark and stormy night."
"I opened my eyes and confusion hit me like a pick-up truck."[1]
"A long time ago in a galaxy far far away."[2]

Like any good piece of literature (I know the last quote isn't from literature, per-se), the introduction sets the pace. The more solid the introduction, the more likely someone is to keep reading. Biblically, the case is valid as well.

"In the beginning, God created the heavens and the earth" (Genesis 1:1).[3]
"The historical record of Jesus Christ, the Son of David, the Son of Abraham" (Matthew 1:1).
"How happy is the man who does not follow the advice of the wicked or take the path of sinners or join a group of mockers!" (Psalm 1:1).
"The revelation of Jesus Christ that God gave Him to show His slaves what must quickly take place" (Revelation 1:1a).

The opening statement lays out the point of the book in each instance. So, it follows, in the book of Galatians the introduction has been carefully crafted so that 1) we will be encouraged to keep reading the text, and 2) so that we will clearly understand the author's point before diving into the particulars that take six whole chapters to explain.

In starting, the first thing to do is to see who is writing. Verses 1-2a say,

---

[1] Joshua Wingerd, *Stranded*, Awakening, book 1 (Victorville, CA: Wingerd Writings, 2017), 1.

[2] *Star Wars: Episode VI – Return of the Jedi*, directed by Richard Marquand (Beverly Hills, CA: Twentieth Century Fox, 2013), DVD.

[3] As you will note throughout this work, all Scripture quotations have been underlined to bring attention to what is most important on each page. Non-underlined words can be disagreed with, but the underlined words are God's infallible, authoritative truth. Disagree with them to your own peril.

> Paul, an apostle—neither [sent] from people nor through [the agency of] a person, but [sent] through [the authority of] Jesus [the] Messiah and God [the] Father, the One who raised Him from death—and all the brothers who are with me.

The first word is Paul. Paul is the man who was a persecutor of Christians. He hated the cause of Christ. He wanted to stamp it out. He saw it as a heretical sect that was going to destroy Judaism. But all that changed, one fateful day, when Jesus appeared to him, on the road to Damascus, and commissioned him as an apostle. Paul, the Christian-hater, became Paul, the greatest-promoter-of-Christianity in history. Galatians is likely the first book he penned—the one that started the series of thirteen Pauline epistles that make up about 25% of our New Testament.[4]

The first thing Paul does is say what he is not. He is not sent out by people. He instantly takes us back to that day on the Damascus road and says, "I'm not writing from my own authority. I'm carrying a much greater message. These aren't my words. They come from Christ."

And when he says who did send him with this message, he gets caught up in a sort of theologizing. He says, "Jesus isn't the only one who sent me; God the Father sent me too—He's actually the One who raised Jesus from the dead." This is important for two reasons.

First, it shows the 1-80 that has taken place in Paul's life—he persecuted Christians because they worshipped a dead person; he hadn't believed the message of resurrection until the risen Jesus revealed Himself to Paul. Paul now worships and serves a resurrected Messiah.

Second, we see two-thirds of the Trinity here, and give it two chapters and we'll see the third person of the Trinity in 3:2 (the Trinity was present in one of the earliest books of the New Testament; not an invention of the church fathers!).[5]

---

[4] R. Alan.Cole, *Galatians: An Introduction and Commentary*, Tyndale New Testament Commentaries (Nottingham, England: Inter-Varsity Press, 1989), WORD*search*, 33. He doesn't hold to this view, but he did refer to it as a possibility. (I firmly believe James was the first book of the New Testament, followed by Galatians.)

[5] An argument could be made that the Spirit is referred to in 1:6. "The One who called you all by grace." As Paul will make clear later, the dichotomy is between flesh/Law and Spirit/faith. If they've been turned to Law, then they have been turned away from the Spirit, "The One who called [them] all by grace."

## Lesson 1: Galatians 1:1-5

In verse 2, Paul credits some other believers as having helped him write this letter. Too often we think that Paul was on his own with his theology of grace alone by faith alone apart from works, especially when we think of a verse like James 2:24: "You see that a man is justified by works and not by faith alone." But this verse says that other people agreed with Paul and helped him write this letter.

Thus, we must give Paul's words in this letter great heed because they've been attested by more than two witnesses (cf. Deuteronomy 19:15; Matthew 18:16; 2 Corinthians 13:1; 1 Timothy 5:19). We can't excuse legalism and the like under auspices of, "That was just Paul's theology." We must live in the freedom of the Gospel the way Paul declares in this letter. Many witnesses in his day and since would say that he was right on, and we have no right to say that they were wrong. To do so is to say that God is incorrect because these words are God's Word. But we'll dive into that whole situation in the ensuing posts.

Verse 2b-3 says,

> To the churches of Galatia: Grace and peace to you all from God our Father and [the] Lord Jesus [the] Messiah.

Paul is writing to a whole region of churches in this letter. And, interestingly, the first thing he says to them is "Grace and peace." Glance at verse 6, which we'll look at in Lesson 2, and you'll see why this is interesting. This is the only letter Paul wrote that doesn't contain an opening blessing (several verses of such) to the recipients. It'll be discussed more in Lesson 2, but the point is that Paul isn't forceful in this letter just because he can be; instead, he wants the people of Galatia to experience the grace and peace of God. They can't experience that when caught in the legalism in which they were trapped.

Finally, in verses 4-5, Paul describes Jesus in more precise terms. Jesus, the One who grace and peace come from,

> Gave Himself for our sins, so that He might release us from the present evil age, according to the will of our God and Father, to whom be the glory forever. Amen.

It is the death of Jesus that grants grace and peace. It is the death of Jesus that frees us from this present, evil age. It was God's will to rescue us. For this reason, God is the one who deserves the glory forever. Grace removes all chances of glory from us and instead places glory squarely in possession of the One who showed grace—God. When we try to save ourselves by Law-keeping, we try to steal the glory from God.

Maybe you're still trapped in this present, evil age. Turn to Jesus! He died for your sins. He can and will rescue you from them if you believe that He is who He claimed to be. Like Paul, make a 1-80 in your mind about Him, stop trying to save yourself by your good deeds, and let grace do its work.

Maybe you already know Him, but perhaps you still feel trapped in this evil age. Look to the cross. That's where the work was accomplished. Stop beating yourself up about your past.

Look forward to your future. Love God daily. Love people daily.

Loving people sometimes looks like writing them a harsh letter out of love for them, with their ultimate well-being in mind. This is what Paul has begun in these verses. This is what Paul will continue throughout the letter.

# Escape from this Evil Age!

It doesn't take much to see that the age we are living in today is evil. Just take a scroll through the news feed of your favorite social media platform and see all the anger and venom being spewed (even masked under amusing memes). Not only that, but it doesn't take long to see lust-inducing images as you scroll through social media (especially in the form of advertisements). And the easy access to news quickly reveals that we live in a fallen, violent, sinful world.

This is why Galatians 1:3-4 is so amazing. It is the Gospel! It explains why Jesus came:

> Grace and peace to you all from God our Father and [the] Lord Jesus [the] Messiah, who gave Himself for our sins, so that He might release us from the present, evil age, according to the will of our God and Father.

Paul wrote this book for the grace and peace of his readers. And the fact of the matter is that as long as you stay enslaved under the present evil age, you will never understand grace or have true peace.

But the answer to the problem is God. He sent His Son—Jesus Christ—to live a perfect life on our behalf and to perfectly follow the Law of God that

## Lesson 1: Galatians 1:1-5

we have all broken. And the reason why Jesus could do this for us is because "like Father, like Son." If His Father was God, then Jesus is God as well.

But it wasn't enough for Jesus to just live a perfect life on our behalf. He also had to die, taking the punishment we deserved. He entered the present evil age—taking our place—so that we could be removed from it.

He was nailed to a cross, crucified (cursed by God, cf. Galatians 3:13), and His life expired as His blood soaked into the Middle Eastern soil. He was buried in a tomb, but after three days, He rose from the dead, proving beyond a doubt that His sacrifice was efficient and, just as surely as He came back to life, so also we will one day entirely escape from this evil age by His power.

But only certain people will escape this evil age. It is those who say, "Jesus, I need Your grace. I believe that You are who You said You are. Please forgive my sins and remove me from this present, evil age." You don't have to say those exact words, but you need to place your faith in Him and continue to follow Him until the day you die.

Trust Him today!

# Reflection Questions

1. How does today's text show Paul's love for the church?
2. Do you have people in your life to validate your theological views?
3. Does the Gospel of Jesus Christ amaze you, or have you grown tired of it?
4. Do you live your Christian life for your glory or for God's glory?
5. Have you placed your faith in Jesus yet?

# Praying the Text

*Jesus,*

*Thank You for grace. Thank You for having Paul write this letter. Please help me never to grow tired of hearing Your Gospel. Help me to live for Your glory every day. It's not about me; it's about You. Thank You for loving me enough to give Yourself for me. Please help me to love You better than I currently do.*

# Lesson 2

## Galatians 1:6-10

⁶I am amazed that so soon you all are apostatizing yourselves away from the One who called you all by grace to a different gospel, ⁷which is not another, except some are troubling you all and wanting to change the Gospel of the Messiah. ⁸But even if we or an angel from heaven might evangelize to you all different from what we evangelized to you all, let [such a one] be cursed. ⁹As we have said before, I also now say again: If anyone evangelizes to you all different from what you all received, let [such a one] be cursed.

¹⁰For am I now trying to persuade people or God? Or am I seeking to please people? If I was still trying to please people, then I would not be a slave of [the] Messiah.

# Shaken and Stirred

Dr. Pepper is my favorite carbonated beverage. In fact, I had some for lunch today.[1] But Dr. Pepper can also be one of my biggest fears and pet peeves. You see, if someone shakes it up and I open it unknowingly, it gets everywhere, and I am no longer able to enjoy my beverage because I have to clean up my mess. Besides, the fear that the can may have been shaken up before reaching me can cause minor anxiety until I crack it open, hear the whoosh of carbonation, and see no liquid escaping. It is at that moment, and not before, that I can thoroughly enjoy my beverage.

And in this opening section of the book of Galatians, immediately following Paul's introduction, Paul explains that there is a mess for him to clean up in Galatia because someone shook the people up. And not only are they shaken up, but they have been shaken up to the point that they are unable to enjoy their freedom as Christians.

Right out of the gate, it is clear that Paul is trying to solve a huge problem. The word for "turning away"[2] can literally mean, "apostatizing," and the weight of the whole sentence is:

I am amazed that so soon you are all apostatizing yourselves.

Apostasy is rightly understood as decisively turning away from the Gospel; thus, as turning your back on Christianity; thus, as proving that you never really belonged to Christ. Interestingly enough, Paul leaves the verb in the present tense because he trusts that God will restore them through his letter. They "are apostatizing," not "have apostatized." This is very important. Paul wants to prevent further and irreversible apostasy.[3]

---

[1] Funnily enough, this Lesson originally began with the words:
Sitting at my desk, drinking a Dr. Pepper out of a can got me thinking about what happens if you shake a can of soda before opening it. It creates a huge mess that someone has to clean up (be responsible and clean up your own mess though!).

[2] Cf. *Holman Christian Standard Bible* on Galatians 1:6.

[3] In Christian culture today, we are too quick to declare everybody who might disagree with us on any little point of doctrine or practice a "heretic." And after labelling them that way, we treat them like garbage in the name of "Protecting the Flock." Social media is full of self-

So, we need to learn that apostasy is a process. It doesn't just up and say, "I quit on Jesus." Instead, it starts to excuse sin, or false ideas, or lack of love for God, and then eventually ends up where sin is pursued exclusively, God is hated, and false beliefs are accepted as true. Backsliding is the first step of apostasy (but throughout this Lesson I will refer to it as apostatizing). John Owen counsels and urges us to watch ourselves closely so that we don't get to the point of complete apostasy:

> [H]e who is spiritually sensible of the evil of his backsliding is unquestionably in a recoverable condition; and some may be so who are not yet sensible thereof, so long as they are capable of being made so by convictions. No man is past hopes of salvation until he is past all possibility of repentance; and no man is past all possibility of repentance until he be absolutely hardened against all Gospel convictions.[4]

The thing to note in Galatians 1:6 is that Paul is amazed. He is surprised. Apostasy shouldn't be prevalent amongst Christians. Unfortunately, though, in our day, it seems as if a good majority of those who refer to themselves as Christians are in some measure apostatizing from the Gospel. Paul would be astounded. Now, while it is true that no believer should ever consider himself immune to apostasy until safely in heaven, it is also true that our lives shouldn't evidence signs of apostasy. In context, this refers explicitly to false doctrine, but false belief leads to wrong living, as Paul will prove in chapters 5-6. Let's stand our ground against sin and deceit.

Paul's amazement was, in part, that they were so quickly and easily seduced away from the Gospel. He writes almost as if to say, "You didn't even object when the false teachers came in! You just bought their lies hook, line, and sinker." We need to know what we believe so we can stand up against this type of deceit. (There is a lot these days in the name of Christianity, Biblical

---

proclaimed doctrine police going around trying to make sure everything everybody posts lines up with their perceived opinion of what constitutes orthodoxy. A lot of them are just looking to fight and argue. Paul's attitude here should be our attitude as well. We will argue and fight when the Gospel is—when human souls are—at stake, but our arguing and "fighting" must be from a place of deep love and concern for them that God would change their hearts and bring them back to Himself.

[4] John Owen, *Sin and Grace,* Works of John Owen, Volume 7, 1689 (Carlisle, PA: Banner of Truth, 2014) Kindle.

## Lesson 2: Galatians 1:6-10

Studies, and Theology that would encourage Paul to write another epistle if he were here today; so beware!)

One line of thinking that we should be aware of in current evangelical "scholarship" comes in the area of Pauline studies. People spend more time trying to learn about Paul through his letters than they try to learn about Jesus through his letters. Paul preached (and wrote) Christ crucified. That was all. Some scholars will take the phrase that follows "turning away from" and say, "Paul is amazed that they are deserting him." This is foolishness of the terminal degree. Paul could care less if people deserted him. Paul's ultimate desire was that people follow Jesus; the specific minister of choice was no big deal (cf. 1 Corinthians 1:10-25).

The reason scholars even have a discussion here is because of intrusions into the text throughout the history of its transmission. There are 5 primary preservations of the phrase in verse 6, "<u>from the One who called you by grace</u>":

- From the one who called you by the grace of Christ
- From the one who called you by the grace of Jesus Christ
- From the one who called you by the grace of Christ Jesus
- From the one who called you by the grace of God
- From the one who called you by grace

Most English translations follow the first of the above list, which is fine because it is basically the best of both worlds. However, most of the time, the shortest text is preferred because it can explain the other variants. In this case, someone was probably trying to explain where grace comes from, and then different people tried expressing it differently (some as Christ, some as Jesus Christ, etc.). It's theologically accurate, but it also makes Paul the one they were deserting. The truth is that the only One who truly calls anyone by grace is Jesus (or His Spirit), whether his name is in the text or not, and if someone is apostatizing from the One who called them by grace, then they are apostatizing from Jesus. No man can truly be apostatized from. Paul wasn't out to please man, and he wasn't seeking to be pleased by men either (cf. 1:10).

Next, Paul explains to where they are being apostatized. This lasts from the end of verse 6 all the way through verse 7. It reads,

> I am amazed that so soon you all are apostatizing yourselves away from the One who called you all by grace to a different gospel, which is not another, except some are troubling you all and wanting to change the Gospel of the Messiah.

Paul explains that they've turned to a different Gospel, but then explains that there is no other Gospel. To believe anything but the Gospel of grace through faith is to claim another gospel (good news about the way to salvation), but to say salvation is anything other than grace through faith is not the Gospel at all. And the great thing about the whole book of Galatians is that it defines and explains what the ONE and ONLY Gospel is.

So, Paul points out that they haven't really turned to another Gospel, but he can't just leave it there. So he does something unique in all his letters. While Paul always has opponents, this is the only letter in which he goes after them explicitly. He gives a face to them. He says, "I disagree with these people, and I want everyone to know it." (As new believers who stumble upon a key point of theology, we are quick to call everyone else foolish and make a whole list of things we are against rather than things we promote.) Paul does it here, and since this is the Word of God, there is not necessarily sin in this approach. "Necessarily" is necessary because of the words Paul uses to describe the "some" he is writing against. They "are troubling you all and wanting to change the Gospel of the Messiah." This is key.

Most of the things we end up attacking others about are less than changes to the good news of the Gospel. Timing of creation, events of the end times, and whether alcohol and tobacco are right or wrong for Christians are not things to divide over. Paul draws a line in the sand for these people because they were changing the Gospel—a change to the Gospel ruins the Gospel and turns the result into something that is not the Gospel—and shaking up the Galatians. Since the Galatians were shaken up and confused, they wanted to find footing for themselves and wanted to look good in the eyes of these new teachers, so they gave in to the teaching. It created a mess, and Paul knew that they'd started the process of complete apostasy from the Gospel, and he was out to stop that. He was fighting for their salvation, not his own reputation. This is the difference between Paul's attitude in Galatians and our typical attitude on social media.

Paul is so adamant about the fact that this is the only Gospel that he says in verses 8-9,

## Lesson 2: Galatians 1:6-10

> But even if we or an angel from heaven might evangelize to you all different from what we evangelized to you all, let [such a one] be cursed. As we have said before, I also now say again: If anyone evangelizes to you all different from what you all received, let [such a one] be cursed.

Paul goes so far to prove that the Gospel he preached was the true Gospel that he says even he should be condemned to hell if he starts preaching anything else. The Gospel is what saves, the only thing that saves; if works are added to the Gospel, it can no longer save; if the message is in any way altered, it can no longer save; and since nothing but the Gospel can save, then it follows that anything that isn't the Gospel actually damns; and if the message damns, then Paul says the messenger should be damned too. And he is consistent enough to include himself in there because he is not promoting himself. He was sent out by Jesus to proclaim Jesus.

Paul loved others enough to try to keep them from being damned (cf. Romans 9:1-5). He was amazed at the fact that anyone would abandon the Gospel of grace for something else.

But, it's understandable why they would want to add works. We want some proof that we have been saved, so we do things to look at them and say, "Well, of course, God loves me. How could he not, when I do all these things?" However, that defeats the emphasis on faith in Christianity. The righteous one will live by his faith (Habakkuk 2:4), not works. This is the first step to a Christless Christianity, which is no Christianity (just Ianity). So let's love others like Paul loved them, and let's warn people about trusting themselves instead of trusting God. Paul loved the Galatians enough to tell them they had been deceived, but he also loved the purity of Gospel ministry enough to tell the false teachers they were wrong (cf. Titus 3:10-11; James 3:1). However, before getting back to either, Paul will elaborate on the fact that he didn't send himself or pull his Gospel out of a hat.

But first, Paul makes a transitional statement regarding his ministry. He says in verse 10,

> For am I now trying to persuade people or God? Or am I seeking to please people? If I was still trying to please people, then I would not be a slave of [the] Messiah.

God was his passion; humility was his method. Paul wants them to know that this letter isn't him blowing off steam. This letter isn't him just attacking people for fun. He isn't trying to get people to like him more. His goal is to please Christ. His goal is to persuade people to trust Christ alone and to refuse to trust in works. His goal is to get himself out of the way and let the Spirit of God do Its work. Paul loved God and wanted to glorify God, and that mindset led him to love people enough to want to see God glorified in them.

In conclusion, we've seen Paul appalled at apostasy and want to change people's minds. We've seen Paul horrified at false teaching and want to get them silenced. And we've seen Paul shocked at accusations of man-pleasing, and his desire to only glorify Christ.

Do we see people walking away from the faith (even if just maybe starting to dabble in some form of sin) and actually see it as a big deal and call them back to Christ (or even just remind them of the Gospel of Christ, including the bad news that initiates it)? Do we see people propagating something less than the Gospel and try to help them change? Do we try to please people or God? The answer to all of these questions will show us just how much we're living in love right now.

Maybe you don't know Christ. I speak of the Gospel, how there's only one, but I haven't laid it out in these pages yet. Here it is: You've done things that seek to bring you glory and ignore the glory due to God alone. That's idolatry of self, and it smacks God in the face. However, God loved you enough to send Jesus to the earth to live a life entirely for God's glory, to die on a cross in your place, and to rise again from the dead. All He requires is that you believe that truth, and if you do, grace has been made yours, and you can walk in the new way of life that Paul will describe in chapter 5 of Galatians. We're getting there, but I beg you today to put your faith in Jesus, watch out for apostasy, and love others well.

# The Only Way

In today's passage, Paul explains that there is only one Gospel. All other so-called gospels are frauds and deceitful, leading people to be cursed and damned. This is why Paul's tone throughout Galatians is urgent and heated at times. When souls are on the line, we don't have time to be careful about it.

## Lesson 2: Galatians 1:6-10

If you were blind and deaf and standing on a train track as a train barreled toward you, would me kindly tapping you on the shoulder or calling your name be loving or effective? No. You can't hear or see. I'll have to physically shove you out of the way of the train if you are to be rescued. Otherwise, it would be apparent that I don't genuinely love you and that I actually want to see you die.

This is what Paul is doing in Galatians. In Galatians 3:1, he essentially asks the Galatians, "Why are you acting blind?" His harshness is out of love[5] because *the* Gospel is essential. Turning away from the only Gospel is to say, "I want to go to hell." No one in their right mind should ever say this.

Jesus is the only way. He came to earth 2,000 years ago, He lived a perfect life, and then was cursed on the cross in our place, so that, if we are found in Him, we could be eternally blessed. He died, under the wrath of God, on the cross. But three days later, He rose again, because He hadn't done anything Himself to deserve death.

If you place your faith in Him, God will place you in Christ and see you with the perfection of Jesus, just like He saw Jesus with the vileness of your sin when He was on the cross (cf. 2 Corinthians 5:21).

Believe in Him today!

Any other message is seeking to lead you to hell. Jesus alone saves! Please trust Him today!

## Reflection Questions

1. How does today's text show Paul's love for the church?
2. Do you know someone (even yourself?) who needs to be called back to the Gospel?
3. What is the true Gospel?
4. Do you strive to live a life that makes you happy or a life that makes God happy?
5. Have you placed your faith in Jesus yet?

---

[5] Cf. EXCURSUS: Tough Love.

# Praying the Text

*Jesus,*

*Thank You for Paul's boldness to preach the Gospel and to fight for the Gospel regardless of what people might think of him. Help me to be just as bold as him. Make me every day to be more amazed by the beauties of the Gospel. I need more of You than I even admit myself. Please help me to seek You alone, and never my own glory. Keep me from apostasy. I love You; help me to love You more.*

# Lesson 3

## Galatians 1:11-24

<sup>11</sup>For I make known to you all, brothers, that the Gospel evangelized by me is not according to [the desires and opinions of] a person, <sup>12</sup>for I myself did not receive it from a person, nor was I taught [it], but [I received it] through a revelation of Jesus [the] Messiah.

<sup>13</sup>For you all heard of my former way of life in Judaism, that I was excessively persecuting the church of God and was destroying it, <sup>14</sup>and [that] I was advancing in Judaism beyond many contemporaries of my generation, being more zealous for my fathers' traditions. <sup>15</sup>But when God (the One who set me apart from my mother's womb and called me through His grace) was pleased <sup>16</sup>to reveal His Son in me (in order that I might evangelize Him to the nations) I did not immediately consult with flesh and blood, <sup>17</sup>nor did I go up to Jerusalem to the [ones who were] apostles before me, but I went away into Arabia, and again I returned to Damascus.

<sup>18</sup>After three years, I went up to Jerusalem to get to know Cephas, and I stayed with him for fifteen days, <sup>19</sup>but I did not see the other apostles, except James, the Lord's brother. <sup>20</sup>Now what I write to you all, behold, before God: I am not lying. <sup>21</sup>Then I went into the regions of Syria and Cilicia, <sup>22</sup>but I was unknown by face to the churches of Judea in [the] Messiah. <sup>23</sup>They were only hearing, "The one who once persecutes us is now evangelizing the [very same] faith which he was once destroying," <sup>24</sup>and they were glorifying God because of me.

# The Revelation of Jesus Christ to Paul

Secrets. They don't make friends, but friends do make them (or so the saying goes). It is interesting, therefore, to note what Jesus said to the disciples in John 15:15. "I do not call you slaves anymore, because a slave doesn't know what his master is doing. I have called you friends, because I have made known to you everything I have heard from My Father." Jesus didn't keep secrets from His friends. Jesus wanted his friends to be in on His business. So, when Paul twice uses the Greek word transliterated "apocalypse" in Galatians 1:11-24, he wants to show that he was one of Jesus' friends as well and that Jesus revealed secrets to him also. The Gospel is the secret that is the point of this passage.

Paul's goal here is to make it perfectly clear that he did not receive his Gospel from man. As such, his goal in all of this is to show that he isn't out to please people. I find R. Alan Cole's outline of Galatians particularly helpful at this point:

I. argument from experience (1:1-2:21)
II. argument from theology (3:1-5:1)
III. argument from results (5:2-6:10).[1]

And thus, we find ourselves in the epicenter of the argument from experience. And, lest anyone try to say, "We can't trust experience; experiences can vary, but God stays the same; so we must look to God alone as revealed in His Word," I would ask what the point of a Christian testimony is then? That's all Paul does here. He explains life before Christ, life as he met Christ, and life after and with Christ.

Verses 13-14 are Paul's statement regarding life before Christ. They read,

> For you all heard of my former way of life in Judaism, that I was excessively persecuting the church of God and was destroying it, and

---

[1] R. Alan.Cole, *Galatians*, 63, 126, 186.

[that] I was advancing in Judaism beyond many contemporaries of my generation, being more zealous for my fathers' traditions.

Two things are evident in these verses about Paul's past; two things are what he reflected on more than anything else about his past. First, he was a violent persecutor of the church. Second, he was a champion of Jewish theology and practice.

The first thing that came to Paul's mind regarding his past was his sinfulness. He was ashamed of the fact that he had harmed the church, the same church that he was now a part of. As believers (at least this is true in my case), we are quick to remember our sins. It might not necessarily be a problem (as Paul goes on to contrast this with the great grace of God, and thus glory in the grace of God), but it does say a lot about where our focus is. Does my focus on my sin lead me to praise God for His grace, or does it lead me to condemn myself for my mistakes? If the latter, I need to repent and turn my gaze back to Christ.

For free: if you don't yet know the Lord, I would urge you to reflect on your past. What are you doing that could be seriously harming a member of the body of Christ, or even a future member of the body of Christ (maybe you even are already a member of the body of Christ)? If you turned to Christ, or if that person turned to Christ, how would you feel about the way you've been treating them? Paul here feels intense remorse. He was actively persecuting the church and destroying it. In another passage it says,

> In fact, I myself supposed it was necessary to do many things in opposition to the name of Jesus the Nazarene. I actually did this in Jerusalem, and I locked up many of the saints in prison, since I had received authority for that from the chief priests. When they were put to death, I cast my vote against them. In all the synagogues I often tried to make them blaspheme by punishing them. I even pursued them to foreign cities since I was greatly enraged at them (Acts 26:9-11).

And in another place, he says, "Being zealous for God, just as all of you are today, I persecuted this Way to the death, binding and putting both men and women in jail, as both the high priest and the whole council of elders can testify about me. After I received letters from them to the brothers, I traveled to Damascus to bring those who were prisoners there to be punished in

## Lesson 3: Galatians 1:11-24

Jerusalem" (Acts 22:3b-5). Paul calls himself the worst of [sinners] (cf. 1 Timothy 1:15) because he was ashamed of his life before Christ. I guarantee that not a day went by that he didn't regret his actions against his brothers and sisters in Christ. So, my plea today is to think about others. If your life was dramatically changed, or even if someone else's life was dramatically changed, would there be things that you would regret about your life beforehand? If so, cast them aside and don't give Satan any more ammunition to use in accusing your soul.

And speaking of Paul's former zealousy for God leads to the second main point of his life before Christ. He was advancing ahead of all his contemporaries and was more zealous for his ancestor's traditions than anyone else. I'm sure he saw this partly as playing into the previous point, because his zeal for God led him to want to keep Judaism pure, and in his unconverted mind, Christianity was a pollution of Judaism. But at the same time, it shows his zeal for the Law. He was all about the Law. Philippians 3:4b-6 would expand on this at a later time: "If anyone else thinks he has grounds for confidence in the flesh, I have more: circumcised the eighth day; of the nation of Israel, of the tribe of Benjamin, a Hebrew born of Hebrews; regarding the law, a Pharisee; regarding zeal, persecuting the church; regarding the righteousness that is in the law, blameless."

Paul's point is that there is no way he made up this Gospel that he preaches. He was too schooled in the Law and too violent against Christians for him to join them on his own. So, he further elaborates on the divine intervention that occurred, initially introduced in verse 12: "For I myself did not receive it from a person, nor was I taught [it], but [I received it] through a revelation of Jesus [the] Messiah." In verses 15-16a, Paul describes his conversion. These verses read:

> But when God (the One who set me apart from my mother's womb and called me through His grace) was pleased to reveal His Son in me (in order that I might evangelize Him to the nations).

Paul is so adamant about the fact that his Gospel is not from humans, or based on human merit that the subject of this passage is God.[2] Paul is the object. It's

---

[2] I know there is a variant here, but the fact that the "One who called [him] through His grace was pleased to reveal His Son in [him]" proves that the One who called him was God the Father. So, whether God is included or not changes nothing and casts no shadow on the trustworthiness of the text.

clear in Greek as well. "The one who set me apart" is the subject, or "the one performing the action." "Me" is the object, or "the one who receives the action."

God had set Paul apart from his birth (if not before, cf. Ephesians 1:3-5). This means that before Paul had ever done anything good or bad, God had decided to set him apart for His work. The Greek word for "set apart" in this verse implies a setting apart for a specific use, which will come at the very end of 16a.

Paul highlights the grace of God when he says, "and called me by His grace," because by the time Jesus called to him on the Damascus road, Paul understands the reality that if it were up to him and his works, then he would have forfeited the fact that God had set him apart. However, the grace of God is shown in that all those He set apart *will be* called, justified, sanctified, and glorified (cf. Romans 8:28-39). There is no "what if" in God's sovereignty over salvation. Grace cannot and will not be forfeited.

God called Paul through the revealing of Jesus to him. Not only was Paul called through this revelation of Jesus Christ, but he was also given his Gospel at the same time (cf. 1:12). Jesus was revealed to Paul because God wanted to reveal Jesus to Paul. Paul didn't deserve to have Jesus revealed to him, just like you and I don't deserve to have Jesus revealed to us. When Jesus was revealed to Paul, He gave Paul a commission to service, described to Ananias, the one who restored his sight: "Go! For this man is My chosen instrument to take My name to Gentiles, kings, and the Israelites. I will show him how much he must suffer for My name!" (Acts 9:15-16). In the same way, every believer is called to be on mission for God. When was the last time you spoke to someone about spiritual matters?

But again, it is essential to reiterate that Paul nowhere had anyone explain Jesus to him. Jesus revealed Himself to him, and that was the source of Paul's Gospel. It will be even more clearly proved in the next 8 verses.

Verses 16b-24 are Paul's statement regarding life after conversion. They read:

> I did not immediately consult with flesh and blood, nor did I go up to Jerusalem to the [ones who were] apostles before me, but I went away into Arabia, and again I returned to Damascus. After three years, I went up to Jerusalem to get to know Cephas, and I stayed with him for fifteen days, but I did not see the other apostles, except James, the Lord's brother. Now what I write to you all, behold, before God: I am

> not lying. Then I went into the regions of Syria and Cilicia, but I was unknown by face to the churches of Judea in [the] Messiah. They were only hearing, 'The one who once persecutes us is now evangelizing the [very same] faith which he was once destroying,' and they were glorifying God because of me.

Paul explains some things here that are different from what we read in the book of Acts. Hopefully, by the time I've finished explaining it, you will see that they don't contradict. In fact, I hope you'll see that Paul's story in Galatians is unique from any other Christian's experience. Paul here writes that he didn't consult with anyone after meeting Jesus, which on face value seems to directly contradict Acts 9:19b-20: "Saul was with the disciples in Damascus for some days. Immediately he began proclaiming Jesus in the synagogues: 'He is the Son of God'." However, what does Galatians say? Paul simply writes that he did not go up to Jerusalem to confer with the other apostles but instead went to Arabia, and then he came back to Damascus for three years. It's safe to say that Paul traveled to Arabia between Acts 9:19a and 19b, and then stayed with the disciples in Damascus for three years.

Now, before explaining anything (purely conjecturally) about Paul's time in Arabia, it is crucial to make a point. There is a difference between Paul's situation and ours. We can't look at Paul here after we are saved and say, "I don't need to go join a fellowship of believers." Paul is making the point in Galatians that his Gospel was purely from Christ, and there was nothing that could have polluted it. In Acts, Luke is making the point that just like all believers should, Paul himself was part of a fellowship of faith. There is no contradiction, only a difference of emphasis. So please, if you haven't already, join a church! You aren't Paul. The canon of Scripture is closed. You need to fellowship with other believers, love them, and study the Word!

Arabia. Why does Paul go to Arabia? Since Arabia only occurs in the New Testament here and in 4:25, the only time we hear about Paul's trip to Arabia is right here in 1:17. So everything we can offer about what happened while he was there is pure conjecture. Some points seem to make sense, though, and I will share them here.

> In the second occurrence [of the word], Paul associated Arabia with the giving of the Mosaic law at Mount Sinai (Gal. 4:25). In an epistle where the law is depicted negatively with regard to justification and sanctification, it is natural to read 1:17 as colored by these themes.

While not denying the apostle's geographical movement from Damascus to Arabia and back, the impression is that Paul wanted believers to read that movement as part of his spiritual journey as well. In other words Paul united Arabia and Mount Sinai geographically in order to unite them theologically also. Shortly after Paul's conversion he departed ("I departed, withdrew") from Damascus (the place of grace and faith) to Arabia (the place of law). But he came back ("I returned once again") to Damascus (the place of grace and faith). Paul wanted the Galatians to follow his example and return to grace and faith and away from their law-centered living.[3]

It is an interesting viewpoint, and it sheds important light on the debate over Romans 7 (pre- or post-conversion Paul), and while it would say, "Paul didn't live a miraculous Christian life, he struggled with legalistic tendencies just like we do today even after salvation," it need not necessarily mean that. J. B. Lightfoot explains,

> Standing on the threshold of the new covenant, he was anxious to look upon the birthplace of the old, that, dwelling for a while in seclusion in the presence of " the mount that burned with fire," he might ponder over the transient glories of the " ministration of death," and apprehend its real purpose in relation to the more glorious covenant which was now to supplant it. Here, surrounded by the children of the desert, the descendants of Hagar the bondwoman, he read the true meaning and power of the law. In the rugged and barren region whence it issued he saw a fit type of that bleak desolation which it created, and was intended to create, in the soul of man.[4]

---

[3] John F. Hart, "Paul as Weak in Faith in Romans 7:7-25," *Bibliotheca Sacra* 170 (July-September 2013): 315-43. I am torn on whether or not to hold this viewpoint on why Paul discusses Arabia. I would not be surprised if Paul struggled against his legalistic tendencies (cf. Romans 7:7-25), but in a letter against legalism, it doesn't exactly seem like the best move to tell his readers that he's lived in their shoes.

[4] J. B. Lightfoot, *The Epistle of St. Paul to the Galatians* (Peabody, MA: Hendrickson Publishers, 1982), 88-89.

## Lesson 3: Galatians 1:11-24

So while some would say that Paul's time in Arabia is supposed to be a symbolic way of saying that for a time he fell into a form of legalistic Christianity; others would say that his time in Arabia was literal, and it was a time of meditation on the new task he'd been charged with. I have my doubts about supposing that Paul had a legalistic stint as a Christian, especially if it is Paul trying to find common ground with his readers, as the first quote above suggests. There is nothing in his tone throughout this letter that would indicate that he wants to say, "I've been where you are, but I got out; now it's your turn." The whole tone of his message in this book is, "Why are you so foolish?" So Paul traveled to Arabia literally, and he was likely reminded of the powerlessness of the Law to give life, which would be why he brings it up here. But again, this is all conjecture.

Paul then says in verses 18-20 that after three years in Damascus, he finally went to Jerusalem and spent about two weeks with Peter and also saw James, the brother of Jesus, while he was there. He makes it clear that this is the truth, that there was no one else he saw during this time, and the fact that he was only there for fifteen days would go to show that his three-year theology foundation wouldn't have been greatly shaken in such a short time. Even in visiting other church leaders after three years didn't change the fact that Paul received his Gospel from Jesus alone. He also makes it clear that the point of his time there was "to get to know Peter." He wasn't going there to share his beliefs (cf. 2:1-2), but simply to make a new friend. His Gospel, the one Christ gave to him, was not corrupted by people at any point.

Paul concludes his point of not being influenced by people by writing verses 21-24. He went away into Syria and Cilicia for fourteen years (cf. 2:1). Cilicia was a region more than 300 miles removed from Jerusalem, and also was the area in which Tarsus—Paul's hometown—was located. (Perhaps his first step, post-three years in Damascus, was to evangelize his own family and friends.) The region of Syria began about 100 miles north of Jerusalem and stretched another 200 miles before bordering Cilicia. So when Paul says, "I remained personally unknown to the Judean churches," he isn't lying. His first trip to Jerusalem was solely to visit Peter, and he stayed away from the churches. However, news of his transformation spread quickly. The man who had persecuted the church was now preaching the faith he had tried to destroy.

And lest anyone think that Paul preached a different Gospel than the other apostles and early Christians, think again. What Gospel did Paul preach? It was the same one that he had tried to destroy. The one Stephen preached in

Acts 7 was the one Paul preached as well. So, while Paul didn't get his Gospel from men, he did get it from Jesus, the same One who gave Peter and James and John their gospels. Jesus is consistent enough to give everyone the same Gospel; to say He gave Paul something different would be to say that Jesus doesn't believe in His people being unified, which would go against John 17, and would mean that Jesus prayed for things He wouldn't even work to achieve Himself, which would mean that Jesus didn't say what He meant, which would mean that He was a liar and a deceiver, which would mean that He wasn't sinless and couldn't die for our sins. So, when Paul says in verse 12 that he received his Gospel through a revelation of Jesus Christ, it is clear that Paul preached the exact same message that Peter and James and John preached, but maybe I'm getting ahead of myself. The proof of this will come in Lesson 4.

Paul concludes this point by saying that the people who heard about him praised God because of him. This was his life goal. He didn't want the praise for his transformation; that praise went to God alone. Galatians 1:5 says that it is to God that the glory belongs forever. This was Paul's motto, and it should be ours as well. What is your reason for wanting physically visible spiritual transformation in your life? Is it so you can pat yourself on the back? Is it so that others will pat you on the back? Or is it so that God will be seen as the gracious, glorious, powerful God that He is? Only the last option is viable. Let it be the story of your life. If our primary goal isn't glorifying and pleasing God, we will never rightly relate to people; Paul glorified God with his life and was able to impact all of Christianity for almost two millennia to follow. Let's do the same.

# Jesus Reveals Himself and Speaks through His Word

Maybe you're reading this, and you're thinking, "I'd believe in Jesus if He would appear to me as He appeared to Paul on the Damascus Road." Believe me. I've been there. I used to want nothing more than to hear God audibly speak to me. What I failed to understand back then was that the Bible is a written record of God's words to humanity. What is contained within the pages of the Bible is God speaking to us.

Look at what God says to us through Jesus' words to Thomas in John 20:29, "Because you have seen Me, you have believed. Those who believe without seeing are blessed." Jesus will probably never visually appear to you—this side of eternity—like He did for John, Thomas, and Paul. But He did make a promise to you. "You are blessed if you believe without seeing Me."

But what are you supposed to believe?

Jesus came to earth 2,000 years ago. He lived a perfect life. (I know it's hard to imagine what that looks like, but it's why it's part of our faith.) When we daily choose to satisfy ourselves, Jesus poured Himself out for others every day. And He proved His selflessness by dying on a Roman cross outside Jerusalem. Three days later He was raised from the dead, proving He had defeated death.

This is the message He commands you to believe without seeing Him. I plead with you today to believe it as well. Jesus promises a blessing to you if you do. That blessing is eternal life!

Believe in Jesus today!

# Reflection Questions

1. How does today's text show Paul's love for the church?
2. What is your testimony of salvation in Jesus?
3. Why is it important for Paul to emphasize that his Gospel came straight from Jesus?
4. Do you think Paul's trip to Arabia was an admission of a struggle with legalism? Or was it a literal trip? Why?
5. Have you placed your faith in Jesus yet?

# Praying the Text

*Jesus,*

*Thank You for saving me. Thank you for choosing me before I was even born. Please help me to bring You and Your Gospel glory every day of my life. I need Your grace immensely. I love You.*

# Lesson 4

## Galatians 2:1-10

¹After a period of fourteen years, I again went up to Jerusalem taking with me Barnabas and Titus; ²I went up according to a revelation, and I set forward to them the Gospel that I am preaching to the nations (but privately to the ones appearing [to be important]) lest I might be running—or had run—in vain. ³But not even Titus who [was] with me, being a Greek, was compelled to be circumcised. ⁴But [the circumcision dispute arose] because of false brothers, secretly brought in, who snuck in to spy on our freedom which we have in [the] Messiah Jesus, in order that they might enslave us, ⁵but to whom we did not yield in submission for an hour, in order that the truth of the Gospel might remain for you all. ⁶Now, to return to the ones who appear to be someone—whatever they were does not matter to me; God does not take [note of] a person's face—the ones who appear [to be someone] added nothing to me, ⁷but, on the contrary, after seeing that I had been entrusted with the Gospel to the uncircumcised even as Peter [had been entrusted with the Gospel] to the circumcised ⁸(for the One who worked in Peter for an apostleship to the circumcised also worked in me to the nations) ⁹and, after knowing the grace that was given to me, James, Cephas, and John—the ones who appear to be pillars—gave Barnabas and me [the] right hand of fellowship, in order that we [might be] for the nations what they [are] for the circumcised, ¹⁰only [requesting] that we might remember the poor, which also was the very thing I was eager to do.

# Confirmed and Commissioned

Have you ever been listening to someone tell a story—and understood everything the person was saying—but thought to yourself, "I'm missing the point," or maybe even vocalized, "What's your point?"

This is precisely the response Paul would have given to someone *casually promoting* a theology of circumcision for Christians. "What's your point?" "You're missing the point?" or any number of other responses would be fit if it were merely a *casual promotion*, but since it is actually a *deliberate attempt to deceive*, Paul has much harsher words. "False brothers." "Secretly brought in." "Might enslave us." (Galatians 2:4.) When one of Paul's Gentile associates was approached with the fact that he wasn't circumcised, he responded, "What's your point?" and both he and Paul went about their business unhindered.

Up to this point, Paul has made it very clear that he consulted no one for the content of his Gospel. Here, however, he turns the page and explains once and for all that he wasn't off doing his own thing. Paul's Gospel was confirmed as accurate by the original apostles—those who had followed Jesus during His earthly ministry—and in this way, he proves that they are all on the same team.

Paul begins by essentially saying, "Fourteen years later, I returned to Jerusalem. After 14 years of preaching to my countrymen, I made the 300+ mile journey south, back to Jerusalem." Verse 1-2a are his exact words:

> After a period of fourteen years, I again went up to Jerusalem taking with me Barnabas and Titus; I went up according to a revelation.

I cut it there to explain briefly some chronological points that need to be addressed here. There is great debate about when this visit (cf. 2:1-10) occurs in the life and ministry of Paul and the early church. Was it at the Jerusalem Council (Acts 15) or before (the famine relief trip of Acts 11:30)? I think, for various reasons, it is best to place this trip in Acts 11:30.

First, the situation in Acts 15 seeks to answer the question of circumcision of gentile converts—much like the book of Galatians does; if

Galatians were written after Acts 15 occurred, all Paul would have needed to say would be the letter written in Acts 15:23-29,

> From the apostles and the elders, your brothers, To the brothers among the Gentiles in Antioch, Syria, and Cilicia: Greetings. Because we have heard that some without our authorization went out from us and troubled you with their words and unsettled your hearts, we have unanimously decided to select men and send them to you along with our dearly loved Barnabas and Paul, who have risked their lives for the name of our Lord Jesus Christ. Therefore we have sent Judas and Silas, who will personally report the same things by word of mouth. For it was the Holy Spirit's decision—and ours—*to put no greater burden on you than these necessary things: that you abstain from food offered to idols, from blood, from eating anything that has been strangled, and from sexual immorality.* You will do well if you keep yourselves from these things. Farewell.[1]

Since, as today's passage will show, Paul and Peter and James and John were all agreed on the content of the Gospel, Paul wouldn't have needed to write his own letter if written after Acts 15.

Second, Paul seems to hint in verses 3-5 that the issue of circumcision wasn't the real reason for this trip to Jerusalem, but I'll explain that more in the following paragraphs. The discussion in Acts 15 was definitely focused on the circumcision issue.

Third, and most importantly—and most conclusively—is the reason Paul gives for his visit in verse 2. "Because of a revelation." Is this the same sort of revelation from 1:12 and 1:16? Did Jesus reveal to Paul directly that he was to return to Jerusalem a second time? I don't think so. If we look at Acts 11:27-30, we see,

> In those days some prophets came down from Jerusalem to Antioch. Then one of them, named *Agabus, stood up and predicted by the Spirit that there would be a severe famine* throughout the Roman world. This took place during the time of Claudius. So each of the disciples, according to his ability, determined to send relief to the brothers who

---

[1] Emphasis added.

## Lesson 4: Galatians 2:1-10

> lived in Judea. They did this, sending it to the elders by means of Barnabas and Saul [aka Paul].[2]

Is there any merit to using the word *revelation* to refer to a prophecy? Actually, yes. Paul uses it similarly in 1 Corinthians 14:6. "But now, brothers, if I come to you speaking in [other] languages, how will I benefit you unless I speak to you with a *revelation* or knowledge or prophecy or teaching?" (emphasis added). Leon Morris explains, "This word is often used in the wide sense, of God's revelation of himself, but there is also a narrower use for some specific matter that God reveals to one of the believers (cf. Gal. 2:2), and which he might then pass on to others (cf. v. 25). In this sense, revelation is closely related to prophecy (vv. 29-31)."[3]

Therefore, it is right to understand this trip to Jerusalem as the trip to relieve the churches of Judea during the famine. Paul didn't plan on having a circumcision discussion, but it was brought on due to the ethnicity of one of the people he brought with him. Part of Paul's plans while in Jerusalem this time was to share the content of his preaching with the Apostles, which he did. Verse 2b concludes:

> I set forward to them the Gospel that I am preaching to the nations (but privately to the ones appearing [to be important]) lest I might be running—or had run—in vain.

Paul wanted to make sure he wasn't preaching in vain. He knew that if his message was different from theirs that he would prove to be a sham.

Verses 3-5 explain a distraction that arose due to Titus being with Paul:

> But not even Titus who [was] with me, being a Greek, was compelled to be circumcised. But [the circumcision dispute arose] because of false brothers, secretly brought in, who snuck in to spy on our freedom which we have in [the] Messiah Jesus, in order that they might enslave us, but to whom we did not yield in submission for an hour, in order that the truth of the Gospel might remain for you all.

---

[2] Emphasis added.
[3] Leon Morris, *1 Corinthians: An Introduction and Commentary*, Tyndale New Testament Commentaries (Downers Grove, IL: InterVarsity Press, 1985), WORDsearch, 184.

Grammatically these verses are atrocious. In the Greek text, it is all one sentence, and our English translations do an excellent job attempting to smooth it out.

J. B. Lightfoot explains about the problems with these verses' grammar, "[T]he sense of the passage is well-nigh lost. The meaning of individual expressions is obscure. The thread of the sentence is broken, picked up, and broken again. From this shipwreck of grammar it is even difficult to extricate the main incident on which the whole controversy hinges."[4] In other words, it is very choppy and says a lot without telling us very much. It explains that the Titus-being-circumcised thing had nothing to do with the purpose of the meeting, but instead came up separately.

Some in the Jerusalem church must have found out that Titus was an uncircumcised Gentile and started urging him to be circumcised. He was so confident in his standing in Christ—apart from works of the Law—that he was not compelled to heed their urgings.

As Paul writes verses 4-5, describing in choppy, almost incoherent phrases the situation regarding Titus, I don't find it hard to imagine him relating it to the current situation in Galatia. "You guys want to follow works? That's because of false brothers who want to enslave you. I'm fighting for you for the truth of the Gospel. Listen to what I'm saying in the rest of this book."

Interestingly, Paul views keeping the Law as enslaving. We usually view sin as the thing that is enslaving—which it is—but Paul sees Law-keeping as enslaving too. It will come out clearly as Paul continues writing this letter, and I will spend time explaining it in chapter 5. Galatians 5:16-18 (Lesson16) is where it will be explored fully; it reads,

> Now I say: You all must walk by [the] Spirit, and you all will not at all fulfill fleshly lust. For the flesh desires [what is] opposed to the Spirit, and the Spirit [desires what is] opposed to the flesh, because these things are opposing one another so that you all might not do the very things you all might want [to do]. But if you all are being led by [the] Spirit, [then] you all are not under Law.

Verses 6-10 pick back up where verse 2 left off. Paul's meeting with the apostles about the content of his message. Verses 6-9 read:

---

[4] J. B. Lightfoot, *The Epistle of St. Paul to the Galatians*, 104.

## Lesson 4: Galatians 2:1-10

<u>Now, to return to the ones who appear to be someone — whatever they were does not matter to me; God does not take [note of] a person's face — the ones who appear [to be someone] added nothing to me, but, on the contrary, after seeing that I had been entrusted with the Gospel to the uncircumcised even as Peter [had been entrusted with the Gospel] to the circumcised (for the One who worked in Peter for an apostleship to the circumcised also worked in me to the nations) and, after knowing the grace that was given to me, James, Cephas, and John — the ones who appear to be pillars — gave Barnabas and me [the] right hand of fellowship, in order that we [might be] for the nations what they [are] for the circumcised.</u>

Paul reminds us again that he got nothing from people in this meeting. They <u>added nothing</u> to his message. They saw that he had been called primarily to the Gentiles while they had been commissioned mainly to the Jews. They saw that the same Spirit of God — Christ's Holy Spirit — was at work on both fronts. The Jerusalem apostles gave the right hand of fellowship to Paul and Barnabas, accepting them as their own, agreeing with their doctrine, and sending them out with their blessing.

"But wait!!!" you cry. "Why does Paul act all sarcastic about their importance if they are on the same team?"

Verse 6 reads in part, "<u>The ones who appear to be someone — whatever they were does not matter to me; God does not take [note of] a person's face,</u>" and it makes it seem like Paul has a problem with them. This is not it at all. Paul admits that they are important, or he wouldn't have used the word; he also wouldn't have called them pillars in verse 9 if they weren't the pillars of the church (cf. Ephesians 2:20; 1 Timothy 3:15; Revelation 21:14). His point is for the Galatians to not view any man as more important than he really is. He doesn't want them to think the words of the Jerusalem apostles are more important than his words; he especially doesn't want the Galatians to think the words of their new teachers are more important than anyone else's words. And to help solidify it in their minds, he reminds them that God doesn't show favorites. In God's sight, all people are equal. Paul wants them and us to remember this fact.

Verse 10 concludes by Paul sharing the one thing that someone might be able to claim was added by the Jerusalem apostles (though he says that it was in his mind already):

> Only [requesting] that we might remember the poor, which also was the very thing I was eager to do.

This would be clearly proven if this trip was the famine relief trip. Paul cared about the poor, wanted to help them, and made a long journey to bring them monetary relief.

And it is interesting to point out that in a meeting regarding the content and legitimacy of Paul's apostleship, an emphasis that is reiterated is helping the poor. There may be a reason why this is. The identifying mark for a believer is love (cf. John 13:35; Galatians 5:6, 13-14), and what better way to show selfless love than to love someone poor who has no way to pay you back for your love (cf. Luke 14:13-14)? Paul was very much a theologian—the theologian who had to contextualize the Jewish Gospel for Gentile hearers—and as such, he could easily be distracted from practical matters, such as caring for the poor. How often today do we get distracted from social Gospel activities (physical helps that cater to spiritual help being offered, listened to, and accepted; we can't leave the social Gospel at the word social, because without the Gospel it's just social damnation) to waste time arguing and debating different points of theology?[5]

And here's the spiritual side of the same coin: We are all poor—in fact, totally spiritually bankrupt—but God loved us enough to save us. If we know that truth about our past, then every non-Christian we meet fits this category of people we need to remember (the poor). So who do you need to remember today?

Paul has made it clear that people didn't add to his Gospel, that he is on the exact same page as the rest of the apostles, and that circumcision has nothing to do with the true Gospel. The true Gospel is a Gospel of freedom that frees people to love the poor. This is what marks Paul's life and the rest of this letter.

# The Poorest of the Poor

In our passage today, Paul explained that the reason for his stance on the issue of circumcision—even amongst the leaders in Jerusalem—was "in order that the truth of the Gospel might remain for you all" (2:5). This is huge.

---

[5] I know I am too often guilty of this. I would rather keep my head buried in books than utter audible words of evangelism to those who need to hear it.

## Lesson 4: Galatians 2:1-10

This is why I have penned this study. It is why every Lesson includes (as this section happens to be for Lesson 4) a specific tie-in and proclamation of the Gospel.

If we lose the Gospel, we lose the Christian faith. If we lose the Gospel, we become no different than Jews, Mormons, Muslims, or any other religion out there. The Gospel is the only good news in the world. Any other "good news" pales in comparison.

It is also important that Paul adds in 2:10, "Only [requesting] that we might remember the poor, which also was the very thing I was eager to do." You see, from its inception, Christianity has been the religion for the outcast and disenfranchised. This is why James wrote (in the first book of the New Testament to be penned), "Pure and undefiled religion before our God and Father is this: to look after orphans and widows in their distress and to keep oneself unstained by the world" (1:27). Within a few years, Paul penned Galatians and wrote about caring for the poor in 2:10.

Why would Christianity be primarily for the outcast, disenfranchised, poor?

Jesus came to earth, born of a virgin. He was born, not in a palace, but a stable. Later, Jesus Himself explained to someone trying to follow Him, "Foxes have dens and birds of the sky have nests, but the Son of Man has no place to lay His head" (Matthew 8:20), essentially saying, "This isn't for the rich and comfortable," because, as He later said, "I assure you: A slave is not greater than his master" (John 13:16).

Jesus identified with the poor in His life, and even in His death, He was executed among common criminals (cf. Matthew 27:38). Then He was buried in a borrowed grave (cf. Matthew 27:57-60).

But the Gospel is that Jesus didn't remain in the tomb. He rose to show that He had defeated death and sin. And if you trust Him, life may still not be easy and comfortable, but you will have riches that cannot be stolen (cf. Matthew 6:19-21)—eternal life.

Life on this planet may be rough, and money may be scarce, but you will know that this life is only a breath compared to an eternity of blessedness. Count the cost. I promise you it's worth it.

Believe in Jesus today!

# Reflection Questions

1. How does today's text show Paul's love for the church?
2. Do you have anyone to validate your claims of Christianity?
3. How many ways can you apply the phrase "God does not take of man's face" to your life?
4. Does your theological ministry lead to practical ministry?
5. Have you placed your faith in Jesus yet?

# Praying the Text

*Jesus,*
*Thank You for your practical concern for people. Help me to have a heart for the poor, just like Paul did here. But please, in my care for the poor, help me never to forget the Gospel. Food and money can only help people in this life; the Gospel has the power to save people eternally. Help me to have an eternal mindset. Help me to love You and others enough to share the Gospel with them.*

# Lesson 5

## Galatians 2:11-21

[11] Now, when Cephas had come to Antioch, I stood against his face because he had been condemned. [12] For prior to the arrival of certain men from James, he ate together with the nations, but when they came, he was withdrawing and separating himself, fearing those from [the] circumcision. [13] And the rest of the Jews joined with him in hypocrisy so that even Barnabas was carried away by their hypocrisy. [14] But when I saw that they were not walking in line with the truth of the Gospel, I said to Cephas in front of everyone:

"If you, being a Jew, live like a Gentile and not like a Jew, then how can you compel the Gentiles to Judaize? [15] We are Jews by nature, and [we are] not sinners like [the] Gentiles, [16] but having known that no person is made righteous by works of Law, but rather through [the] faithfulness of Jesus [the] Messiah, we have believed in [the] Messiah Jesus in order that we might be made righteous by [the] faithfulness of [the] Messiah and not by works of Law, because by works of Law no flesh [at] all will be justified. [17] Now if, while seeking to be made righteous by [the] Messiah, we might also be found sinners, then is [the] Messiah a servant of sin? May it never be! [18] For if I rebuild the very things I once destroyed, I show myself [to be] a transgressor. [19] For through Law, I myself died to Law, in order that I might live for God. I have been crucified together with [the] Messiah, [20] and I myself no longer live, but [the] Messiah lives in me, and the [life] which I now live in [the] flesh, I live by faith in the Son of God, the One who loved me and gave Himself up for me. [21] I do not set aside the grace of God, for if righteousness results from Law, then [the] Messiah died in vain."

# Freedom!!!

Happy Independence Day!!![1] While it is the Fourth of July today, we must never proclaim political freedom as more important than our spiritual freedom in Christ. And while Paul will write in Galatians 5:1, "[The] Messiah set us free for freedom; therefore you all must stand, and you all must not be again entangled in a yoke of slavery," Paul will introduce that concept quite clearly in today's passage.

To put Paul's message in perspective, let me give a political, historical example before Paul shares a spiritual example. The day is July 5, 1776, or maybe, better yet, September 4, 1783. Freedom has been declared, and the victory has been officially won. However, as a country, we decided, "You know what, it's hard being autonomous. We have way more responsibility now. Sure, we aren't being terrorized anymore, but now we have to figure out how to run this place. Let's ask King George to take us back." If, as a country, we returned to King George, then all the lives that were lost in the cause of freedom would have been in vain, England probably would have treated us even worse, and none of the freedoms that we enjoy today would exist.[2]

Let's pay careful attention to Paul's next—and final—argument from experience.

Paul wants to say a couple of things once and for all to conclude this first section (though the second one will definitely carry throughout the rest of the letter). First: His Gospel was not given to him by people. Second: The freedom of the Gospel is at stake in what the Galatians have started believing.

Verse 11 gives the situation:

> Now, when Cephas had come to Antioch, I stood against his face because he had been condemned.

---

[1] This Lesson was originally published as a blogpost on July 4, 2016.

[2] I can't help but think about the Israelites coming out of Egypt when I think about this example. I have a hunch that Exodus 16:3; Numbers 11:4-6, and Numbers 14:2-4 were going through Paul's mind as he pens this letter. Perhaps the only reason he didn't include them was because his Gentile readers would be unfamiliar with the story.

Cephas is Peter. Peter is the one with whom Paul got acquainted for fifteen days. Fifteen days were not enough time for Paul to change the theological foundation he had built over the previous three years. However, Paul's point throughout this section is that even if Peter had added anything to Paul's Gospel, Paul would throw it away if it was out of line with the truth of the Gospel.

Now when does this account take place in the scheme of things? I mentioned in Lesson 4 that verses 1-10 probably occur in Acts 11:30. The next thing we see in Acts is James, the brother of John, being martyred by King Herod. Afterward, Herod imprisons Peter, who is then miraculously released by an angel (cf. Acts 12:6-17). In Acts 12:17, "[Peter] departed and went to a different place." That different place could very well have been Antioch. Perhaps he wanted to give a face to the name likely being reported in relation to Jesus (cf. especially the stories related in Matthew's Gospel where Peter is the visible spokesperson; these stories would have been transmitted verbally at first). Or maybe he just wanted a vacation from Jerusalem—his life had just been threatened—because everyone wants/needs a vacation at some point (cf. the concept of Sabbath—whether day or year—in the Old Testament). Regardless, he came up to Antioch. And when Paul says, "I stood against his face," it is possible to understand the grammar of the introductory phrase—Cephas had come—as relaying the idea that "Peter may have already been there for some considerable time when the recorded incident took place."[3] In fact, as we will see, it really only makes sense to understand it this way.

But what was it that condemned Peter, that made Paul oppose him? Verses 12-13 explain:

> For prior to the arrival of certain men from James, he ate together with the nations, but when they came, he was withdrawing and separating himself, fearing those from [the] circumcision. And the rest of the Jews joined with him in hypocrisy so that even Barnabas was carried away by their hypocrisy.

Peter caused a rift in the Antioch church. The split was over race; the division was over religion; the schism was serious. And Peter influenced many others to follow him.

---

[3] R. Alan.Cole, *Galatians*, 114.

## Lesson 5: Galatians 2:11-21

In that day, meals were a form of fellowship. To show that someone got along with someone else, people would eat meals together. Jesus is a prime example; it's why the Pharisees had such a problem with him: "While He was reclining at the table in the house, many tax collectors and sinners came as guests to eat with Jesus and His disciples. When the Pharisees saw this, they asked His disciples, 'Why does your Teacher eat with tax collectors and sinners?'" (Matthew 9:10-11). Jesus accepted them; He got along with them. Peter, as well, had been eating with the Gentile believers in Antioch—showing that he fully accepted them as believers in Christ on equal footing as him—but then something happened that changed it.

Certain men from James. Cole writes:

> The words 'from James' are not as strong in Greek as in English, but they do express controlled indignation. Paul is not implying that James of necessity sent them (indeed, James denies this in Acts 15:24); but they were certainly men from James' circle, James' group, within the Jerusalem church. The implied criticism is that James should not have tolerated such views.[4]

Regardless of where specifically these men came from, they claimed to have been sent from James. They claimed his authority and his level of influence. This shook Peter to the core. MacArthur comments:

> The old Peter—weak, fearful, and vacillating—had come to the fore again. Here was the same Peter who under divine inspiration declared Jesus to be "the Christ, the Son of the living God" but who a short time later rebuked his Lord for saying that He must suffer and die (Matt. 16:16, 22). Here is the same Peter who boldly declared he would rather die than deny his Lord but who, before the night was out, had denied Him three times (Mark 14:29-31, 66-72). Here was the same Peter who was called to preach but who disobediently went back to fishing even after he had encountered the resurrected Christ (John 21:3).[5]

Peter was often afraid of people, and here it almost caused a disaster; in fact, it had already created a church split—Jew vs. Gentile. And this is where Paul

---

[4] R. Alan Cole, Galatians, 117.
[5] John MacArthur, *Galatians*, MacArthur New Testament Commentaries (Chicago: Moody, 1987), 51.

comes in with verse 14, in the spirit of Titus 3:9-10: "But avoid foolish debates, genealogies, quarrels, and disputes about the law, for they are unprofitable and worthless. Reject a divisive person after a first and second warning, knowing that such a person is perverted and sins, being self-condemned."[6] Thankfully, Peter was corrected on his first warning, because when we see him next—Acts 15—he's on Paul's side.

Galatians 2:14-21 contains Paul's speech to Peter, though, in the Greek, it is hard to tell exactly where the quotation ends. Some translations end it in verse 14; some end it in verse 16; some end it in verse 21. The HCSB, which I usually follow, ends it in verse 14.[7] However, I think it is best to understand it as going all the way through verse 21. It reads:

> But when I saw that they were not walking in line with the truth of the Gospel, I said to Cephas in front of everyone: "If you, being a Jew, live like a Gentile and not like a Jew, then how can you compel the Gentiles to Judaize? We are Jews by nature, and [we are] not sinners like [the] Gentiles, but having known that no person is made righteous by works of Law, but rather through [the] faithfulness of Jesus [the] Messiah, we have believed in [the] Messiah Jesus in order that we might be made righteous by [the] faithfulness of [the] Messiah and not by works of Law, because by works of Law no flesh [at] all will be made righteous. Now if, while seeking to be made righteous by [the] Messiah, we might also be found sinners, then is [the] Messiah a servant of sin? May it never be! For if I rebuild the very things I once destroyed, I show myself [to be] a transgressor. For through Law, I myself died to Law, in order that I might live for God. I have been crucified together with [the] Messiah, and I myself no longer live, but [the] Messiah lives in me, and the [life] which I now live in [the] flesh, I live by faith in the Son of God, the One who loved me and gave Himself up for me. I do not set aside the grace of God, for if righteousness results from Law, then [the] Messiah died in vain."

Paul's reason for publicly confronting Peter was to show him that, ultimately, his decision to separate from the Gentile Christians was basically to say that Christ's death didn't need to happen. Just as, if we told England that we wanted back under them after the Revolutionary War had ended, then

---

[6] Emphasis added.
[7] Cf. *Holman Christian Standard Bible* on Galatians 2:14-21.

## Lesson 5: Galatians 2:11-21

all the soldiers who had shed their blood for our freedom would have died in vain; so also, if we want to return to living under the Law, then Christ would have died in vain.

Peter was a Jew who lived like a Gentile for a while after his experience in Acts 10. People knew this. People also knew that he had stopped living like a Gentile and that instead, he was now expecting Gentiles to live like Jews. Paul called this hypocrisy in verse 13 and explained his meaning explicitly to Peter in verse 14.

In verses 15-16, Paul drops a theological bomb. He says:

> We are Jews by nature, and [we are] not sinners like [the] Gentiles, but having known that no person is made righteous by works of Law, but rather through [the] faithfulness of Jesus [the] Messiah, we have believed in [the] Messiah Jesus in order that we might be made righteous by [the] faithfulness of [the] Messiah and not by works of Law, because by works of Law no flesh [at] all will be made righteous.

In verse 16, Paul refers to the "faithfulness of [the] Messiah" two times, because his point is to prove that we, as a human race, are not faithful to keep the Law and that Jesus alone will ever fit that bill. Many translations want to take the phrase "faithfulness of Jesus [the] Messiah" and translate it "faith in Jesus Christ."[8] This emphasis on our faith detracts from Paul's point in this portion of his letter. Our faith is undoubtedly shown in the phrase, "we have believed in [the] Messiah Jesus," but we can't make ourselves righteous—even by believing. Justification (being made righteous) is a gift of God's grace alone.

Verse 17 solidifies this point.

> Now if, while seeking to be made righteous by [the] Messiah, we might also be found sinners, then is [the] Messiah a servant of sin? May it never be!

If seeking to be made righteous in Christ, as Paul teaches, really is just an excuse to break the Law, and thus leaves people guilty of sin, then Christ is leading people into sin. Cole explains it more clearly by paraphrasing Paul, "If, at the very moment when we say that we ourselves are justified by faith alone, we turn out to be preaching to others that 'faith alone' is inadequate,

---

[8] Cf. *Holman Christian Standard Bible* on Galatians 2:16. Note that the only difference is "faith" vs. "faithfulness." "Jesus Christ" is "Jesus [the] Messiah."

but that they must keep the law as well, does that not mean that trusting in Christ is only leading them into sin? for it is teaching them not to trust the law."[9] Paul exclaims, "That's blasphemous even to think!" Therefore, Christ's faithful Law-keeping is the only hope we have for salvation.

Paul explains what conversion means in verses 18-20.

> For if I rebuild the very things I once destroyed, I show myself [to be] a transgressor. For through Law, I myself died to Law, in order that I might live for God. I have been crucified together with [the] Messiah, and I myself no longer live, but [the] Messiah lives in me, and the [life] which I now live in [the] flesh, I live by faith in the Son of God, the One who loved me and gave Himself up for me.

Paul says that he tore down living a life under the Law, but that if he then decided—like Peter had done—to return to living under the Law, then he would be guilty of sin. Living under the Law had been Paul's sin of choice before being saved. Paul says that is him no more. He now lives to God. He was crucified with Christ—living under the Law was crucified with Christ—and he now lives by faith in Jesus Christ. It's the same with our sins of choice before salvation—and, in context, for Peter's as well.

Paul wants us to know that whatever thing holds us back from fully committed service to God was crucified with Christ and that since we no longer live, that thing was crucified when Christ was crucified, and Christ is now the one who lives through us. Now that Christ lives through us, we never have to return to cowering before people, we never have to return to yelling and fighting and anger at those we are supposed to be closest to, we never have to return to gazing at images on a screen. Christ died, and the old me died with Him. It's the same for you if you are in Him. Don't be found a transgressor because you are rebuilding the things you tore down!

I say, "If you are in Him," because someone may be reading this and not be in Him. Look at the end of Galatians 2:20: "the One who loved me and gave Himself up for me" The giving of Himself was the physical example of His love for you. He loved you so much that He didn't even consider His life worth keeping so long as He could have you for eternity. Think about that, believe that, and let thoughts of worthlessness, depression, and loneliness die.

---

[9] R. Alan Cole, *Galatians*, 123.

Jesus loved you. He gave Himself up for you to prove it.[10] Put your trust in Him today. Tear down the strongholds that are being rebuilt in your life. He is powerful.

Paul concludes his message to Peter by summing up his first argument (the one from experience). Experientially, he says:

> I do not set aside the grace of God, for if righteousness results from Law, then [the] Messiah died in vain.

Christ died for our freedom. Run to Him. Don't run to the Law. Don't run to sin. RUN TO HIM. Everything else is slavery. On this Independence Day, celebrate spiritual freedom!

# How HE Loves Us

The most beautiful truth in the world is written in many ways throughout the Scriptures, but one of the most beautiful presentations of it—especially in the book of Galatians—is this: "I have been crucified together with [the] Messiah, and I myself no longer live, but [the] Messiah lives in me, and the [life] which I now live in [the] flesh, I live by faith in the Son of God, the One who loved me and gave Himself up for me" (2:19b-20). This is the Gospel. Jesus, the Creator and sustainer of the universe, loved me enough to wrap Himself in a body of flesh and be tortured and executed like a common criminal.

I was a common criminal (spiritually) who deserved this death. I'd lied. I'd stolen. I'd lusted. I'd hated. I deserved this death. I had even cursed God. I *should have* died on that cross. But Jesus took my place.

Well, actually, if we read the verse carefully, "I have been crucified together with [the] Messiah." The old me was crucified with Jesus. I did die. The me who lives now is not the same me who cursed God.

However, we can't just leave it there. Paul writes verse 21 as well: "I do not set aside the grace of God, for if righteousness results from Law, then [the] Messiah died in vain."

---

[10] I've said this many times, but it bears repeating again here: Love is not a feeling. It is an action. And Jesus is our example. If you want to know how to love rightly, then study Jesus—both the facts of His life in the gospels and the implications of His life in the rest of the New Testament. Apart from knowing Him, you will not love rightly.

Christ died for a reason. He died to set me free from sin and death *and* Law. Now, this doesn't mean that I can keep sinning. This is impossible if the old me was crucified with Christ. But it does mean that my standing with God is not based on my works. It is based on Christ's actions. He lived perfectly. He perfectly loved God. He perfectly loved others. His love was shown in High Definition (4K) when He hung on the cross.

So, I ask you today, "Have you been crucified with Christ?" If so, your relationship with sin will look different. If so, your relationship with God will look different. If so, your relationship with the Word of God will look different. If so, your relationships with others will look different. You won't love sin. You will love God. And you will no longer stand in judgment over God's Word, but rather humbly hear and obey it, not to earn salvation, but in a desire to honor God in the way He will be most pleased. And you will relate to others as Paul describes in the last two chapters of this book (cf. Galatians 5-6).

So, have you been crucified with Christ?

If so, don't rebuild what you once destroyed.

If not, place your faith in Christ today! You will never find a better love anywhere!

# Reflection Questions

1. How does today's text show Paul's love for the church?
2. Was Paul wrong to publicly rebuke Peter?
3. Do you trust your belief in Jesus, or do you trust Jesus?
4. Are you rebuilding something from your previous life? If so, what?
5. Do you really believe that Jesus loves you?
6. Have you placed your faith in Jesus yet?

Lesson 5: Galatians 2:11-21

# Praying the Text

*Jesus,*

*Your love is amazing! Thank You for giving Yourself for me. Please help me to live a life that demonstrates to the world that You are worth it. Help me to never add any of my own works into my salvation equation. Please keep me from reverting back to old sins You freed me from. I need You desperately!*

# Lesson 6

## Galatians 3:1-5

¹Oh, mindless Galatians, what witch cursed you all, before whose eyes Jesus [the] Messiah was plainly set forward as being crucified? ²I only want to learn this from you all: Did you all receive the Spirit by works of Law or by faithful hearing? ³Thusly you all are mindless: After beginning by [the] Spirit, are you all now being completed by [the] flesh? ⁴Did you all suffer so many things for no benefit (if indeed [they were] for no benefit)? ⁵Therefore, [did] the One who ministered the Spirit to you all and who worked powerfully among you all, [do it] by works of Law or by faithful hearing?

# Testimony of the Galatians

So, I really like dubstep music, and I really like Star Wars, so when the two were combined, and my brother sent me a playlist he had compiled, I ate it up. One song contains the following quote from Darth Vader found in Episode V: "The force is with you, young Skywalker, but you are not a Jedi yet."[1] It got me thinking, "Can I say something similar as a Christian: 'The Spirit is with you, young Wingerd, but you are not a Christian yet'?" Absolutely not! The definition of a Christian is one who is indwelt by the Spirit. To say that something else must happen first is to cheapen everything about Christianity. The Spirit is with me, and I am a Christian. If the Spirit is with you, then you are a Christian. Because the Spirit was with the Galatians, they were Christians, and that is what Paul will prove in these five verses. They were foolish to say anything else was necessary!

This passage basically picks up where 1:9 left off. "As we have said before, I also now say again: If anyone evangelizes to you all different from what you all received, let [such a one] be cursed." He then spent almost two whole chapters explaining why he could be trusted as a reliable person to hear the Gospel from. And now, in 3:1, he jumps immediately back to where he left off in 1:9. He asks who was responsible for preaching a different Gospel to them. In fact, these five verses read like an interrogation. So, even though verse 1 talks about Jesus, verses 2-4 speak about the Spirit, and verse 5 talks about the Father, I'm going to work through it question by question.

Paul begins by making a conclusion. He calls the Galatians foolish.

Oh, mindless Galatians.

Now, lest we think he's insulting their intelligence, it's essential to see the difference between the word he uses here and another word that he could have used. The word he could have used is where we get our word "moron" from,

---

[1] *Star Wars: Episode V – The Empire Strikes Back*, directed by Irvin Kreshner (Beverly Hills, CA: Twentieth Century Fox, 2013), DVD.

which by necessity means foolish or stupid[2] and carries an almost abusive connotation (cf. Matthew 5:22). The word Paul uses more closely relates to "absence of mind" and insinuates "mental laziness and carelessness . . . The Galatians had foolishly fallen into Judaistic legalism because they had stopped believing and applying the basic truths of the Gospel Paul had taught them and by which they had been saved."[3]

When we start believing everything we're told, and when we cease practicing discernment, it is a sign of spiritual laziness. This is Paul's point in the introductory phrase. He says, "Look, I have proved that my Gospel was not from men and was not altered by man and that I have torn down (and refuse to rebuild) my life according to the Law. Now let me ask you some rhetorical questions to prove that you have become spiritually lazy."

Verse 1 concludes with the question:

> What witch cursed you all, before whose eyes Jesus [the] Messiah was plainly set forward as being crucified?

Paul's point in this question is not so much, "Who did this to you?" but more accurately, "How'd you let them hypnotize you, considering your experience?" (though the "Who?" aspect is certainly still present, and will come up again in 4:17, 5:7, 10, 12, 6:12). The word translated plainly set forward refers to a public notice being placed on a wall where people can see it and respond to it (think, "Wanted: Dead or Alive"). Another excellent example of a public notice would be in the book of Esther when Haman has the king write an edict for all his kingdom to see.

> Letters were sent by couriers to each of the royal provinces [telling the officials] to destroy, kill, and annihilate all the Jewish people—young and old, women and children—and plunder their possessions on a single day, the thirteenth day of Adar, the twelfth month. A copy of the text, issued as law throughout every province, was distributed to all the peoples so that they might get ready for that day. The couriers left, spurred on by royal command, and the law was issued in the fortress of Susa (3:13-15).

---

[2] J. H. Thayer, *Greek-English Lexicon of the New Testament*. "Equivalent to without learning or erudition . . . imprudent, without forethought or wisdom."

[3] John MacArthur, *Galatians*, 63.

## Lesson 6: Galatians 3:1-5

Paul wants the Galatians to remember just how convinced they were by Paul's preaching that Jesus Christ had been crucified. And he flat out tells them, "You're not thinking clearly. Snap out of this trance and tell me how you could let someone deceive you like this?" Interestingly, this verse comes right after 2:21, because Paul concluded that point by saying, "<u>If righteousness results from Law, then [the] Messiah died in vain.</u>" He wants them to remember the vivid reality of Christ's death of which they had been previously convinced so that they would remember that Christ's death really happened and was really necessary and that the legalism purported by the false teachers was undermining Christ's death.

I imagine their rhetorical answer being silence out of shame.

But Paul doesn't care. He writes in verse 2:

<u>I only want to learn this from you all: Did you all receive the Spirit by works of Law or by faithful hearing?</u>

Paul drops the bomb on them. He asks, "How did you get into this race? How'd you become a child of God? How'd you receive the Spirit? Did you have to keep Law to get the Spirit, or did you just hear my Gospel?"

And I imagine their rhetorical answer is, "Of course by faith."

Then Paul responds again:

<u>Thusly you all are mindless: After beginning by [the] Spirit, are you all now being completed by [the] flesh?</u>

Paul wants them to see that starting by faith—by grace alone (cf. Galatians 1:15-16)—only to revert back to the Law is the epitome of what it means to be lazy in the arena of spiritual discernment.

And far too often in modern Christianity, we do the same thing, even though our reverting back to the Law doesn't look like obeying Mosaic rituals. We come in by faith and accept the grace that washes us clean of all the junk in our past, but then act as if we have to perform now to stay in God's good graces. This is precisely what Paul is writing against here. All we've done in modern, American evangelicalism is westernize the Law to suit our tastes.

Here's a fictional (though too plausible) example: Let's say there's a homosexual man (since this is basically the "unforgivable sin" in our church world today) who is genuinely born again in Christ. For one, 1 Corinthians 6:9-11 would immediately say that he is no longer a homosexual—he used to be one. And let's say, by God's grace, he hates his sin. He hates that he is drawn toward men the way other men are drawn toward women. However, while he hates it, he still finds himself acting out on it (even if acting out on it goes no farther than thinking a guy looks attractive), but then feels absolutely convicted and crushed afterward. And our modern church world of "once in, keep yourself in by following the rules" would have absolutely nothing to offer this man except condemnation.

If you want to follow Law to stay saved, James says, "For whoever keeps the entire law, yet fails in one point, is guilty of [breaking it] all" (2:10), as if to say, "Once you've broken one part of God's Law, you've broken *His* Law, and you are guilty eternally because you've broken an eternal Law." Therefore, to trust the Law after trusting Christ is to tell Christ, "You're not good enough for me."

However, Jesus is better. He's better than sin, better than the Law, better than the best earthly blessing God has ever bestowed on you. And, it's not just trusting God's Law for salvation that is wrong. Paul condemns the whole world, even those who've never seen a Bible because they can't even perfectly keep the laws they place on themselves. Romans 2:14-16 says,

> So, when Gentiles, who do not have the law, instinctively do what the law demands, they are a law to themselves even though they do not have the law. They show that the work of the law is written on their hearts. Their consciences confirm this. Their competing thoughts will either accuse or excuse them on the day when God judges what people have kept secret, according to my Gospel through Christ Jesus.

So when we say, "I won't do this, so that I don't do that," and begin to trust "this" and "that" to keep us holy instead of trusting God and seeking Him, we are making laws for us to follow, laws that prove that we aren't righteous if we break them.

This is why Paul is incredulous that someone who starts the Christian life by faith would ever walk away from faith to be perfected by Law. It's why we must never place additional regulations on those we are trying to help break free from sin or addiction. The Spirit is our only hope, and to confound the Spirit's work by inserting legal codes instead will never sanctify. Romans 8:13 says, "For if you live according to the flesh, you are going to die. But if *by*

## Lesson 6: Galatians 3:1-5

<u>*the Spirit* you put to death the deeds of the body, you will live</u>."[4] The only way to have victory over the flesh is by the Spirit, and we're not very good at putting sin to death <u>by the Spirit</u> because it involves faith and not noticeable actions on our part. But I digress.

Regardless of that, I can see the Galatians responding to Paul's question by saying, "Yes. We can do it ourselves, and we will. The Law gives us power."

Then verse 4 gives Paul's next question based on that answer:

> <u>Did you all suffer so many things for no benefit (if indeed [they were] for no benefit)?</u>

Paul's point is that whatever they experienced was in vain if they decide to ignore his words and continue down the path of rejecting grace in favor of Law. However, he trusts that they have only been sidetracked for a short time and that they will be back on track again soon, because he adds, in a hopeful spirit: "<u>If indeed [they were] for no benefit</u>." He doesn't really believe that their Christianity is a sham. He trusts that the God who saved both him and them—who <u>chose them before the world's foundation</u> (Galatians 1:15-16; Ephesians 1:3-6; Romans 8:28-30)—would rescue them from the hypnotization they had experienced.

This tells us that we should always be hope-*full* in our dealings with other, weaker believers. We must tell them the truth—from the Scriptures—about the seriousness of their plight, but in so doing, we must be gracious and never harsh nor condescending. Our attitude must be the same that Peter recommended: "<u>With gentleness and respect</u>" (1 Peter 3:16).

And I imagine their answer to be, "No, no, no! We didn't receive God's Spirit in vain!"

Paul concludes his interrogation with verse 5, which looks an awful lot like verse 2.

> <u>Therefore, [did] the One who ministered the Spirit to you all and who worked powerfully among you all, [do it] by works of Law or by faithful hearing?</u>

---

[4] Emphasis added.

This tells us that God is the source of the Spirit. If a person has the Spirit, it is for no other reason than for the fact that God gave it to that person. No one has to do a single thing to get the Spirit, and no one has to do a single thing to keep the Spirit (cf. Ephesians 1:13; Romans 8:38-39). Paul points out and makes it clear that they didn't have to obey Law for God to display His power mightily amongst them. It was all by faith.

And I imagine the Galatians saying, "Of course it was by faith," pausing, and then adding, "Oh, I'm starting to understand."

But that's all for today. Paul will take his proofs for a Law-free Gospel (but not a Law-less Gospel) in a different direction next time. The point to be elaborated here is that the Gospel is believed by faith, Christian living starts by faith, and Christian sanctification continues by faith. At no point should a Christian ever revert to living under the Law. Once the Spirit has been given to a believer, she has all she needs for a life of godliness (cf. 2 Peter 1:3). Don't revert back to the Law. Run for refuge to Christ. He alone can save, and He is better!

## The Salve for Our Consciences

The Law (and our conscience) exists to prove to us that we are in desperate need of a Savior. The story of the Bible is the story of that Savior. History is rightly called (at least in English) His story. When we study history, we are studying God's sovereign plan in the world. And even though He rarely appears in High Definition in our history books, He most assuredly appeared 2,000 years ago during the peak of the Roman Empire. Even though our modern history books have changed BC (before Christ) to BCE (before common era), they can't escape the fact that the event that initiated the "common era" was the appearance of Christ on this earth.

You see, God knew that we were impotent to keep both His Law and the laws our consciences make for us. This is why He sent Christ to the earth. He lived the perfect life we could never live, and He died the gruesome death that we would never want. Three days later, He rose from the dead to prove that He is Lord even over death.

The Gospels—the first four books of our New Testaments—tell the story of Jesus' life since He is the subject of *the Gospel*. And the remainder of the New Testament pleads with its readers to believe in Christ, to see Him as He claimed Himself to be, and to love Him with all of our beings.

This is the One who commands you, through these words I've written, to believe. The fact of the matter is that the punishment for breaking God's Law is death. Either you will take that punishment yourself, or you will believe that Jesus died that death for you.

Believe in Him today!

# Reflection Questions

1. How does today's text show Paul's love for the church?
2. Can you sum up Paul's argument in Galatians so far?
3. Have you lost sight of Jesus in your Christian life? What replaced Him?
4. Have you perfectly kept the standards and rules you've made for yourself?
5. Have you placed your faith in Jesus yet?

# Praying the Text

*Jesus,*

*Thank You for being my only hope. Please help me to love and trust You more and more every day. I can't even perfectly keep the goals and rules I've made for myself. There's no possible way I could ever achieve eternal life by my own works. I need You. Please continue to reveal Yourself to me more and more every day. I love You.*

# Lesson 7

## Galatians 3:6-14

⁶Even so, Abraham believed God and it was registered to him as righteousness.
⁷You all need to know then that the ones of faith, these very ones, are sons of Abraham. ⁸And the Scriptures, after foreseeing that God justifies the nations by faith, evangelized before to Abraham, "In you, all the nations will be blessed." ⁹so that the ones of faith are being blessed with the faith of Abraham. ¹⁰For as many as are [seeking righteousness] by works of Law are under a curse; for it has been written, "A curse be upon everyone who does not continue to do every single thing that has been written in the Book of the Law." ¹¹Now, it is clear that no one is made righteous before God by [the] Law: "The righteous person will live by faith." ¹²but the Law is not by faith; rather, "The one who after doing them will live on account of them." ¹³[The] Messiah purchased us from the curse of the Law by becoming a curse for us, because it has been written, "A curse be upon everyone who is being hung upon a tree." ¹⁴in order that the blessing of Abraham might come to the nations through [the] Messiah Jesus, in order that we might receive the promise of the Spirit through faith.

# Basic Principles = Jesus Alone

I really like the movie *Hitch* with Will Smith, and it's not just because I can use it as an illustration of how men should view and treat women (don't be a Vance Munson; if you currently act like him, please stop [but I'll speak directly to that topic in my explanation of 3:28 and several times throughout Galatians 5]). Will Smith's character introduces the movie by giving a speech about "basic principles for a successful relationship," but then, by the end of the film, he says, "Basic principles? There are none." [1] The point being: If you are forced to follow a particular pattern for a relationship to be successful, then as soon as something breaks up that pattern, the relationship is doomed to failure. Smith's character learned quickly that his "rules for a successful first three dates" are not the only way in which a relationship could blossom. Every one of his rules was broken, and the relationship still bloomed (though I won't spoil the plot). In much the same way, in our passage today, Paul seeks to show through a contrast between Law and faith that if we are forced to follow our "basic principles," then we are still under a curse, and our relationship with God is doomed to failure.

So this passage seeks to answer more fully the rhetorical question Paul posed in 3:5: "Therefore, [did] the One who ministered the Spirit to you all and who worked powerfully among you all, [do it] by works of Law or by faithful hearing?" He then puts forward the first option: Faith like Abraham's, followed by the second: Stay cursed under the Law. He uses several Scriptures to prove his points, and it is interesting that the Scriptures he chooses all come from the Law of Moses (except for one). Paul saw the Law of Moses as authoritative, even if he didn't believe in following it in a ceremonial sense. This is very important to remember in these kinds of discussions. It's not that we become antinomian (anti-law) as Christians, but rather that we of all people can say, "So then, the law is holy, and the commandment is holy and just and good" (Romans 7:12). Paul clarifies in 1 Timothy 1:8, "But we know that the law is good, provided one uses it legitimately." So today's discussion

---

[1] *Hitch*, directed by Andy Tennant (Culver City, CA: Sony Pictures Home Entertainment, 2005), DVD.

is not about condemning the Law; instead, it's about how the Law is no longer allowed to condemn us. There's only one way in which this is possible, and Paul lays it out in verses 13-14.

But first, there was Abraham. Verses 6-9 say:

> Even so, Abraham believed God and it was registered to him as righteousness. You all need to know then that the ones of faith, these very ones, are sons of Abraham. And the Scriptures, after foreseeing that God justifies the nations by faith, evangelized before to Abraham, "In you, all the nations will be blessed," so that the ones of faith are being blessed with the faith of Abraham.

Paul's opponents were saying that Gentiles had to become Jews to be real followers of Jesus. Paul counters that by talking about Abraham, the father of Judaism.

Paul begins by relating Abraham's justification. It is originally told in Genesis 15:5-6. "He took him outside and said, 'Look at the sky and count the stars, if you are able to count them.' Then He said to him, 'Your offspring will be that [numerous].' Abram believed the LORD, and He credited it to him as righteousness." God made a promise to Abraham[2] about Abraham's offspring, and Abraham believed it. For the human today, it is no different: Believe the promise that God makes to you about Jesus as the source of eternal life (which is much more than just not going to hell when you die), and it will be counted to you as righteousness. The reason God made this promise to Abraham—that Abraham believed for righteousness—was because God had yet to give him a child. This was ten or so years after first being spoken to by God about becoming a great nation, so Abraham was naturally beginning to wonder when it would all start happening.

One commentator explains, "Engaging in something of a 'pity party,' Abram made seven references to himself (in the Hb) in the space of 22 Hebrew words [in verses 2-3] and twice utters the complaint that he was childless."[3]

God still showed grace to Abraham by making the promise that He does in verse 5, that He graciously allowed Abraham to believe in verse 6. So,

---

[2] Technically, at this point in the story, his name was still Abram, but for simplicity's sake I have referred to him as Abraham throughout, and I will only use his earlier name when quoting directly from the Old Testament.

[3] Jeremy Royal, Howard, ed, *HCSB Study Bible* (Nashville: Holman Bible Publishers, 2010), WORD*search*.

even though Abraham was probably acting contrary to a man who believed God (like we do much too often), God still made a promise that Abraham's small amount of faith believed, and it led to his salvation.

Verse 7 is an introduction to the next entry. It has to do with the fact that a person is not a Jew who is one outwardly, and [true] circumcision is not something visible in the flesh (Romans 2:28). It also has to do with what Paul writes in Galatians 3:15-18, specifically verse 16. I'll give a hint right now: The offspring mentioned in Genesis 15:5, though numerous, is a singular noun. Abraham will have one offspring that is numerous. We'll discuss that in-depth in Lesson 8, and even more in EXCURSUS: Seeking the Seed.

He hints at it at the beginning of verse 8. The Scripture predicted that God would justify the nations by faith and not by works, and it is shown both in the previously quoted passage (cf. 15:5) and in what follows. Genesis 12:1-3 is the call of Abraham: "The LORD said to Abram: Go out from your land, your relatives, and your father's house to the land that I will show you. I will make you into a great nation, I will bless you, I will make your name great, and you will be a blessing. I will bless those who bless you, I will curse those who treat you with contempt, and *all the peoples on earth will be blessed through you*."[4]

Paul explains Genesis 12:3 by writing verse 9:

The ones of faith are being blessed with the faith of Abraham.

The ones who are genuinely Abraham's descendants are those who were born of faith. It's almost as if Paul is saying, "When Abraham believed God, he became righteous and so did all his true descendants. Abraham's faith is what blesses us if we believe.[5] But basically, without letting it all get too complicated, Paul is telling us: Faith alone saves; nothing else. It worked for Abraham, and because it worked for Abraham, we don't need to do anything more than have faith to be justified.

And Paul proves this clearly in verses 10-12:

For as many as are [seeking righteousness] by works of Law are under a curse; for it has been written, "A curse be upon everyone who does

---

[4] Emphasis added.
[5] I discuss a similar concept in some depth on my blog. Joshua Wingerd, "Condemnation, Justification, and Federal Headship," *live in Love; find your true reward* (October 6, 2019) https://www.lilfytr.com/2019/10/06/federal-headship.

> not continue to do every single thing that has been written in the Book of the Law." Now, it is clear that no one is made righteous before God by [the] Law: "The righteous person will live by faith," but the Law is not by faith; rather, "The one who after doing them will live on account of them."

The Law presents a curse. Our own personal principles, even, present a curse. As soon as we fail to live up to them perfectly, we will never be able to live up to them perfectly.

Paul proves this in verse 10 by quoting Deuteronomy 27:26: "'Anyone who does not put the words of this law into practice is cursed.' And all the people will say, 'Amen!'" This verse comes at the end of a lengthy passage delineating what kinds of things would bring a curse on the people of Israel: Idolatry, dishonesty, perverted justice, or sexual immorality of various types—heterosexual and homosexual. And then verse 26 catches everything else in it: all 613 commands laid out from Exodus to the end of Deuteronomy must be followed perfectly. Basically, Paul here says, "Oh yeah. Guess what? If you try following the Law for salvation, you're already out of luck. If you've broken even one of them, you're under a curse, and the Law can't help you."

In verse 11, Paul explains that it is clear that the Law can't justify anyone, and he quotes Habakkuk 2:4 to prove it: "Look, his ego is inflated; he is without integrity. But the righteous one will live by his faith." In the original context, this is an answer from God to the prophet concerning the coming Babylonian invasion. Habakkuk was unsure about both the future of Israel and the character of God since God was allowing the evil Babylonians to attack and conquer Israel. Part of God's response is to say that Babylon will grow arrogant in its victory over Israel, and as such, God will eventually bring it down; in contrast, those who belong to God will prove it by humble faith and trust in God despite uncertain times. One commentator explains:

> This Babylonian self-righteousness, seeking their own ends, not only leads to pride and the sinful acts of the next verses, it can also lead to death (cf. Prov. 14:12, 16:25). This death is their implied though unstated end, in contrast to the life which awaits the righteous. This desired preservation of life will come to Judah if they show *faith*, waiting in patient assurance that Yahweh will act as he promised.[6]

---

[6] David W. Baker, *Nahum, Habakkuk, Zephaniah: An Introduction and Commentary*, Tyndale New Testament Commentaries (Nottingham, England: Inter-Varsity Press, 1988), 58.

## Lesson 7: Galatians 3:6-14

Attempts at keeping the Law, in the Galatians context, only lead to pride, and Paul wants to be clear that pride will be smashed because the truth is that faith is the only answer. A single misstep while trying to keep the Law brings a curse, so why subject yourself to that curse? Faith has always been what proves a person righteous—from Abraham to the exile to Babylon—and it's been no different since—whether in Paul's day or in ours.

And Paul makes clear in verse 12 that the Law is the opposite of faith. The righteous one lives by faith; the one who keeps the Law cannot live by faith, but instead lives by the Law. In fact, he essentially says, "the Law is the opposite of faith. You can see the Law and read the Law and obey the Law; it requires zero faith" (cf. 2 Corinthians 5:7). His quotation of Leviticus 18:5 helps prove just how much of a curse the Law keeps its hearers trapped under. "Keep My statutes and ordinances; a person will live if he does them. I am Yahweh." This is at the end of an introduction to a whole bunch of specific laws that the Gentiles were guilty of breaking. Leviticus 18:3 says, "Do not follow the practices of the land of Egypt, where you used to live, or follow the practices of the land of Canaan, where I am bringing you. You must not follow their customs." God is basically saying in this section that if you want to live, you have to follow all of these commands. For the Gentiles—remember that the Galatians were not Jews—it was basically hopeless for them to know God according to this standard. They were guilty of breaking these laws. Paul is telling the Galatians—though not explicitly—that following the Law will never allow them to live. He is telling them to stop listening to the deceivers that are telling them to return to the Law. "Why go back to being under a curse?" he asks in effect. Martin Luther concludes of trying to be justified by works,

> Men fast, pray, watch, suffer. They intend to appease the wrath of God and to deserve God's grace by their exertions. But there is no glory in it for God, because by their exertions these workers pronounce God an unmerciful slave driver, an unfaithful and angry Judge. They despise God, make a liar out of Him, snub Christ and all His benefits; in short they pull God from His throne and perch themselves on it.[7]

---

[7] Martin Luther, *A Commentary on St. Paul's Epistle to the Galatians*, 1538 (Grand Rapids: Christian Classics Ethereal Library, 1999), WORD*search*.

And then Paul writes verses 13-14. In them, he once again presents the Gospel in all its glorious beauty: Jesus Christ and Jesus Christ alone.

> [The] Messiah purchased us from the curse of the Law by becoming a curse for us, because it has been written, 'A curse be upon everyone who is being hung upon a tree,' in order that the blessing of Abraham might come to the nations through [the] Messiah Jesus, in order that we might receive the promise of the Spirit through faith.

And thus, he concludes the answer to his question from verse 5. Christians get the Spirit through faith, and we get the Spirit through faith because Christ became a curse in our stead. He was hung on a tree to symbolize publicly that He became a curse. Christ bought us out from under the curse of the Law by taking our place. This is what Paul means in 2:20 when he says, "The Son of God, the One who loved me and gave Himself up for me" That is crazy love right there!

And it wasn't just shown for Paul. There are things in my life and things in your life, even today, for which we deserve to be cursed. Maybe you have something you care about more than you care about God. Perhaps you don't honor your parents. Perhaps you aren't 100% honest in all your dealings with others. Perhaps you don't care for the poor and needy like you've been called to care for them. Or maybe in some way or another, you are sexually deviant.

Christ died to redeem us from the curse that our deeds earned. When He was crucified, the old you and I were also crucified! Let's never return to it again! Why rebuild what He destroyed (cf. Galatians 2:18)? That would be the epitome of foolishness!

So, Jesus is our hope. Jesus is our model. Jesus is our principle. Any other rules that we set above Him will only fail us. Let's keep our eyes on Jesus and refuse to fall prey to anything that seeks to take the glory from Him. Don't attempt to pull Him off His throne!

# Redemption Accomplished and Applied

In Galatians 3:13a, Paul writes:

## Lesson 7: Galatians 3:6-14

[The] Messiah purchased us from the curse of the Law by becoming a curse for us.

This is a humbling verse. We were all deserving of the curse of God. We were so worthy of the curse of God that Jesus chose to become a curse for us.

Now, I'm sure you're reading this thinking, "I don't deserve to be cursed."

Really?

God is holy. He is also perfect. If a judge failed to convict a felon who had broken into your home and murdered a loved one in the process, because that same person had never done anything else unlawful in his life, you would be outraged. And rightly so. Genesis 18:25 records the following: "You could not possibly do such a thing: to kill the righteous with the wicked, treating the righteous and the wicked alike. You could not possibly do that! Won't the Judge of all the earth do what is just?" And the rhetorical answer to this question is, "Of course He will!"

But now you probably want to protest, "Well, I'm a righteous person. I've never murdered or cheated on my spouse. Or, at the very least, at least I'm not as bad as Hitler."

And in a sense, you might be right. You might not be as bad as Hitler. But God isn't judging people based on whether or not they are worse than Hitler. In fact, it is God's grace alone that prevented Hitler from being worse than he was. It is God's grace alone that prevented you from becoming as evil as Hitler. We all have the potential to be the next Hitler.

God judges you according to Himself. It says in Numbers 23:19 that God doesn't even lie. So, if you've ever told a lie—even a little, white lie that "didn't hurt anyone"—you are guilty of breaking all of God's Law (cf. James 2:10). If a plate gets a crack in it, the whole plate is now broken, even though only one small portion of it is "flawed." Perfection means perfect. God is perfect.

Our sin leads us to be under His curse. But thankfully, He loved us enough to send Jesus to earth to take our curse for us (cf. John 3:16-18). And when Jesus was on the cross, and when He cried out, "My God, My God, why have You forsaken Me" (Mark 15:34), it was because God turned His back on Jesus, because Jesus had become a curse.

Paul Washer explained this well in his sermon from the *2016 Shepherd's Conference*. I have quoted him at length because it is essential to understand this truth:

> In the beatitudes, we have the blessings, don't we? Kingdom of Heaven. Seeing God. So, in a way, a curse would be the antonym of what we see in the beatitudes, wouldn't it? So, let's just rewrite those. Just listen. The blessed are granted the Kingdom of Heaven. The cursed are refused entrance. The blessed are recipients of divine comfort. The cursed are objects of divine wrath. The blessed inherit the land; the cursed are cut off from it. The blessed are satisfied; the cursed are miserable and wretched. The blessed receive mercy; the cursed are condemned without pity. The blessed shall see God; the cursed are cut off from His presence. The blessed are sons and daughters of God; the cursed are disowned and disgraced . . .
>
> When [Paul] talks about the curse, if we look in Deuteronomy 27-28, we find something unusual that happens with the camp of Israel . . . One part of the camp is sent to Mount Gerizim, and from Mount Gerizim, they are to cry out all the blessings that are to fall upon the covenant-keeper. But the other part of the camp is sent to Mount Ebal, where they are to scream out all the curses that are to fall upon the covenant-breaker. (I do not think I have to give you a dissertation on radical depravity to know which camp that you and I belong in.) But here's the thing that you need to understand: Jehovah has only ever had one Servant, one Witness, one Champion, one Son, one Covenant-keeper. And that Covenant-keeper took the place of His brethren—us. Nothing but vile, covenant-breakers, and rebels—the whole lot of us. But in love, and according to the eternal counsels of the Father, the Covenant-keeper took the place of the covenant-breakers, and suffered the curse that was theirs . . .
>
> When Christ cried out, "My God, My God, why have You forsaken Me" . . . the Father replied, "The Lord, the Lord Your God, damns you. The Lord sends upon You curses, confusion, and rebuke until You are destroyed, and You perish quickly. The Lord smite You with madness and with blindness and with bewilderment of heart, and You will grope at noon as the blind man gropes in darkness, with none to save You. The Lord delights over You to make You perish and destroy You, and You will be torn from the land. Cursed shall You be

in the city, and cursed shall ye be in the field. Cursed shall ye be when ye come in, and cursed shall You be when You go out. The heavens which is over Your head shall be bronze and the earth that is under You, iron. You shall be a horror and a proverb and a taunt among all the people. Let all these curses come upon You and pursue You and overtake You until You are destroyed. Because You would not obey the Lord Your God by keeping His commandments and His statutes which He commanded You."

Common grace is so overlooked. Every day of the sinner's life, heaven should be screaming this condemnation at him. Do you understand me? Every place you go, every step you take, every breath you draw in and let out, every beat of your heart, you would only hear resounding in your ears, over and over and over, "Cursed, cursed, cursed, cursed." And then God's cursing vindicated on the Day of Judgment, and then cast into hell, where you hear, "Cursed, cursed, cursed."

But our Elder-brother, the Covenant-keeper, the Messiah, the Son of God, the Victor, the Champion, He comes and takes our place, and He bears the curse in our place.[8]

This is the Gospel. This was the measure of Christ's love for you. It brings new meaning to what Paul said in Galatians 2:19b-21:

<u>I have been crucified together with [the] Messiah, and I myself no longer live, but [the] Messiah lives in me, and the [life] which I now live in [the] flesh, I live by faith in the Son of God, the One who loved me and gave Himself up for me. I do not set aside the grace of God, for if righteousness results from Law, then [the] Messiah died in vain.</u>

Believe this truth today, and refuse to ever return to the accursed Law!

And if you've already believed, keep believing it! And glory in the beautifully ugly truth that Jesus became a curse on your behalf.

There is no better news!

---

[8] Paul Washer, "General Session 9," *Shepherd's Conference 2016* (March 11, 2016), https://www.gracechurch.org/sermons/11837.

# Reflection Questions

1. How does today's text show Paul's love for the church?
2. How was Abraham justified (cf. Genesis 12-21; specifically, chapter 15)?
3. Is Paul saying that we should not follow a standard as Christians? Why do you say that?
4. How does the Law lead to a curse? And how does faith lead to "blessing"?
5. Have you placed your faith in Jesus yet?

# Praying the Text

*Jesus,*

*Increase my faith! It's sad that Abraham had faith 1600 years before Jesus was even born, but I still get too focused on making sure my life looks right. I have 66 books about how faith in Christ is the focus of salvation, but I still get derailed and start focusing on my works. I need to live by faith! Faith should be my lifestyle, not just something I confess in my creed. Increase my faith!*

# Lesson 8

## Galatians 3:15-18

<sup>15</sup>Brothers, I speak as a person: No one annuls or adds to a human covenant that had been previously ratified. <sup>16</sup>Now the promises were spoken to Abraham and to his seed. It does not say, "And to seeds," as [though] to many, but as to one, "<u>And to your seed</u>," which is [the] Messiah. <sup>17</sup>Now this I say: A covenant was previously ratified beforehand by God, [so] the Law having come—after four hundred and thirty years—does not cancel so as to destroy the promise. <sup>18</sup>For if the inheritance [is] by Law, then [it is] no longer by promise, but God has graced it to Abraham through a promise.

# Refocusing Our Attention

"If the plural of goose is geese, shouldn't the plural of moose be meese?" goes the popular grammar joke. And I believe it is a very logical question. When I use the word moose, you can't know whether it is being used of a single moose or of a whole herd of moose. This kind of thing doesn't just occur in English: the Greek word σπερμα (*sperma*) and the Hebrew word זרע (*zera'*) both mean "seed" and can be understood as a singular seed or as a whole group of seeds. This becomes very important in the book of Galatians.

So, at this point, Paul is deep into his proofs for dropping the Law and living by grace alone through faith alone. And in our passage today, he makes what I consider to be his most compelling points, even though some commentators believe that it contains "a highly compressed 'inset' which somewhat complicates the argument, [and] may be temporarily omitted without weakening it."[1] I wrote much more extensively on this passage elsewhere,[2] but the main thing we need to know from this passage is that Paul sees Jesus as central to everything, and we should too. In fact, he sees Jesus as so central to everything that he sees Jesus being promised as far back as Abraham.

And it's the concept of promise that he begins with. He draws a parallel to contemporary Greek and/or Jewish life (even American life if you will). Verse 15 says:

> Brothers, I speak as a person: No one annuls or adds to a human covenant that had been previously ratified.

We believe that covenants/promises/contracts/vows are important to keep and shouldn't be entered into lightly, because those involved will be held accountable (though sadly the marriage covenant falls through the cracks in our culture). Paul leaves his human illustration there, and then starts verse 16—where he spiritualizes it.

---

[1] R. Alan Cole, *Galatians*, 147.
[2] Cf. EXCURSUS: Seeking the Seed.

He explains in verse 16a:

> Now the promises were spoken to Abraham and to his seed.

There are at least four different occasions at which these promises are spoken to Abraham and his seed:

- "Then the LORD appeared to Abram and said, 'I will give this land to your offspring.' So he built an altar there to the LORD who had appeared to him" (Genesis 12:7).
- "I will give you and your offspring forever all the land that you see" (Genesis 13:15).
- "And to you and your future offspring I will give the land where you are residing—all the land of Canaan—as an eternal possession, and I will be their God" (Genesis 17:8).
- "The LORD, the God of heaven, who took me from my father's house and from my native land, who spoke to me and swore to me, 'I will give this land to your offspring'—He will send His angel before you, and you can take a wife for my son from there" (Genesis 24:7).

However, it's Genesis 15:18 that fits Paul's point here the best. "On that day the LORD made a covenant with Abram, saying, 'I give this land to your offspring, from the brook of Egypt to the Euphrates River'."[3] And we must pay attention to the fact that the covenant was one-sided. Abraham was asleep when God made it (cf. Genesis 15:12), to prove that God was making this promise regardless of anything Abraham would do in the future. It was a sure-to-happen thing; Abraham and his descendants would not be able to stop it.

But then Paul continues, and he points out something vital. Galatians 3:16b continues:

> It does not say, 'And to seeds,' as [though] to many, but as to one, "And to your seed."

Even though it can be used in the singular, though collective sense, Paul here—under the inspiration of the Holy Spirit—says that this word was kept singular for a purpose. The promise was not made to many people. The

---

[3] Emphasis added for all Genesis quotations on this page.

promise wasn't made to the people who follow the Law. The promise wasn't made to the Jews. The promise wasn't even made to the church. In its truest sense, the promise was made to Abraham and to his singular seed. Verse 16c concludes:

> <u>Which is [the] Messiah.</u>

There is a line of theological understanding that exists today that says that all of God's promises to Israel must still be fulfilled literally. There's another line that says those promises are symbolically fulfilled by the church. Paul claims here, and states it explicitly in 2 Corinthians 1:20 that "<u>every one of God's promises is 'Yes' in [Jesus]</u>." Jesus is the one who fulfills all of God's promises. We don't have to become Jewish to join this inheritance. We simply must be joined by faith to the One to whom the promises were made and in whom they were fulfilled.

It's a mistake to say the Jews still have some special place in God's plan—other than the fact that they, like us, are humans and need to hear the good news of the Gospel just like everyone, so they can be eternally saved. But it's also a mistake to say that the church is the greatest thing on the planet. Jesus deserves the glory—not man, not even an eternally saved, righteous through the blood of Christ group of people. Jesus alone is my focus. Jesus alone was Paul's focus. Is Jesus alone your focus? If you view anything else more highly than Him, you're guilty of idolatry; even very good things—the church, the Bible, theology, relationships, marriage, etc.—can become idols if we are not careful. But I'll step off my soapbox for now.

Paul then writes in verse 17:

> <u>Now this I say: A covenant was previously ratified beforehand by God, [so] the Law having come—after four hundred and thirty years—does not cancel so as to destroy the promise.</u>

This shows those who were deceiving the Galatians—and the deceived Galatians themselves—that the Law is not the answer. Something that God brought 430 years after He made an unbreakable (remember verse 15?) covenant cannot undo the covenant. (Paul will explain next time the actual purpose of the Law.)

Verse 18 concludes our passage for today:

> For if the inheritance [is] by Law, then [it is] no longer by promise, but God has graced it to Abraham through a promise.

If the way to the inheritance is through keeping the Law, then God fails to keep His promise to Abraham and to his seed—Jesus. God can't fail to keep His promises, because He doesn't lie (cf. Numbers 23:19). And then, as if saying, "I got you; what are you going to say to that?" Paul finishes the thought with 18b, "But God has graced it to Abraham through a promise." It's grace. No Law at all. Trust Jesus!

So that's all for today. Jesus is where our focus should be. He's the Seed that has been promised since Genesis 3:15. He's the one who was promised inheritance as Abraham's Seed. If we trust in Him, then we are in Him, and thus we are a recipient of the promises to Abraham and his Seed. But we must never move our focus off the original seed—Jesus. We don't think about Him enough! Let's think about Him more this week.

## A Tale of Two Seeds

The seed talk actually goes back farther than Abraham. In Genesis 3, we read about when Adam and Eve—our first parents—disobeyed God and ate from the tree of which they were commanded not to eat. They hid, after discovering that they were naked, and God called out to them. After a lot of blame-shifting, we read the following:

> Then the LORD God said to the serpent: Because you have done this, you are cursed more than any livestock and more than any wild animal. You will move on your belly and eat dust all the days of your life. I will put hostility between you and the woman, and between your seed and her seed. He will strike your head, and you will strike his heel.

God goes on and tells Adam and Eve the consequences for their sin as well, but the main focus in the passage is here in Genesis 3:14-15. God curses Satan in verse 14, and He proves how it will come to pass in verse 15.

God speaks of two seeds. The seed of the serpent and the seed of the woman.

Remember the Greek word for "seed" I mentioned at the beginning of this Lesson?

*Sperma*?

Sound familiar?

That's because women don't carry the seed. Men carry the seed. For this reason, this passage is clearly a reference—4,000 years ahead of time—to the virgin birth.

In the truest sense of the word, the Bible is a tale of two seeds. Satan knows he is doomed, so he does everything he can to try to prevent Jesus Christ from coming onto the scene. From Egypt to Babylon, from the Philistines to wicked kings of Israel, the serpent's seed throws everything they can at God's people to prevent Jesus from arriving in power.

But then, on a cold night 2000 years ago, Jesus was born of a virgin in a stable. Thirty years later, He was crucified on a Roman cross, and Satan thought he had won, but in fact, he had only bruised His heel. Jesus rose from the dead three days later, and now it is only a matter of time until Satan's head is fully and finally crushed.

This is the Jesus who demands your allegiance. He died to set you free from sin and death. If you've never placed your faith in Him, put it in Him today!

# Reflection Questions

1. How does today's text show Paul's love for the church?
2. Why does Paul spend so much time on the promise to Abraham?
3. Does Jesus being the focus of the Bible—even in the Old Testament—make you more eager to read the whole Bible?
4. Is there a sense in which Christians are also the seed of Abraham (cf. Galatians 3:29)? How does this work?
5. Have you placed your faith in Jesus yet?

# Praying the Text

*Jesus,*

*Thank You for being the fulfillment of promises made 4-6,000 years ago. Please help me never to get tired of hearing about You. Thank You for including me in Yourself. I want to live a life that makes You famous. Help me!*

# Lesson 9

## Galatians 3:19-29

[19]Therefore, why the Law? It was set down because of transgressions until the Seed to which it was promised might come, having been ordained through angels by [the] hand of a mediator. [20]Now the mediator is not [only] one, but God is one.

[21]Therefore, is the Law opposed to the promises of God? May it never be! For if a Law was given that was able to make [people] live, then righteousness would certainly be by Law, [22]but the Scripture shut up all things under sin in order that the promise might be given by [the] faithfulness of Jesus [the] Messiah to the ones who are believing.

[23]But before the coming of the faith, we were being kept, shut up together [with all things], under Law as to the faith about to be revealed, [24]so that the Law has been our tutor toward [the] Messiah, so that we might be made righteous by faith, [25]and since the faith came, we are [now] no longer under a tutor.

[26]For you are yourselves all sons of God through faith in [the] Messiah Jesus, [27]for as many of you all who were baptized into [the] Messiah have all been clothed with [the] Messiah. [28]There is not a Jew or a Greek, there is not a slave or a free [person], there is not male and female; for you all, yourselves, are one in [the] Messiah Jesus. [29]And if you all, yourselves, [belong to the] Messiah, then you all are Abraham's seed, heirs according to [the] promise.

# I Once was Trapped; Now I'm Free

There's a joke about kids in a daycare that helps us understand the next section of Galatians. It goes like this: A little boy decides he's had enough of sitting in the classroom, so he sneaks away from the group and eventually finds his way outside. Once outside, he goes up to the window to his class, and after spying a little girl who is coloring at the table next to the window, he says in his high-pitched, adorable kid voice, "I'm free!" She looks up from her coloring, turns around, and says, "Oh yeah, well I'm four!"[1]

The point is that the kid didn't want to be trapped anymore, so he found his way out of that situation, and when he proclaimed his newfound freedom, she totally misunderstood and didn't care.

Sin entraps, and it uses the Law to do so, but Paul writes in our passage today that it was all part of God's plan so that freedom in Christ would be rightly appreciated. Paul wants us to be the little boy in the joke and not the little girl. He wants us to be free!

Paul has been saying that the promise was given before the Law, that the promise was spoken to Abraham's singular Seed (Jesus), that the Law is not better than the promise, and finally that the Law does not change how the promise is inherited. So, by this point, it *seems* as though Paul has essentially said, "The Law is unnecessary and unimportant." And in essentially saying that, his opponents would jump on him and say, "How can you say that? You're a Jew. You were raised to love the Law of God as the very Word of God." So, in the remainder of Galatians 3, Paul sets out to answer the questions, "Why was the Law given? And what is the Law's function?" In verses 19-24, he answers the questions, and in 25-29, he explains how life is different for Christians on the other side of the Law.

Paul explains the reason for the Law in verses 19-20 by saying:

Therefore, why the Law? It was set down because of transgressions until the Seed to which it was promised might come, having been

---

[1] It probably works better vocally.

> ordained through angels by [the] hand of a mediator. Now the mediator is not [only] one, but God is one.

This explains the need for the Law. Cole points out, "The NEB, however, takes a stronger approach by paraphrasing 'to make wrongdoing a legal offence', which may well be correct."[2] Sin can be called "sin" because the Law that God gave to Moses proves that a failure to live up to its perfection is missing the mark that God established. That word until is critical. The Law was never meant to be an end in itself. It was to lead up to a point and then stop. Its purpose was to show things to be sin, both to prove guilt and to prevent further infractions. In the Law, God said, "This is the way: Walk in it. Don't touch that, don't taste that, don't do that; if you do, you're sinning against Me. And as Adam and Eve learned firsthand—sin has consequences."

Unfortunately for humanity, no one has ever lived up to all of these laws perfectly. Look at the fifth commandment in Exodus 20:12. "Honor your father and your mother so that you may have a long life in the land that the LORD your God is giving you." This is no one's natural inclination. Ask any parent if their child has perfectly treated them with the respect they deserve, and their answer—if honest—will be "No." We are all guilty of breaking God's Law, and even though most of the commands in Leviticus 18 are easy to follow, Leviticus 19 is what follows it, and Exodus 20:14 is also convicting.[3] This is why the Law was only given until the Seed to whom the promises were made arrived. He came—and He died—2,000 years ago. We don't need to subject ourselves to laws: "Don't handle, don't taste, don't touch" (cf. Colossians 2:20-23).

Paul then lays something out about just how inferior the Law is to the Gospel. The Law was mediated by angels. Paul says, in effect, "God didn't even give the Law directly to you like He gave the promise directly to Abraham. He gave it to angels who passed it on to Moses, who passed it on to you." This follows strict Jewish orthodoxy; Stephen said the same in Acts 7:53, "You received the law under the direction of angels and yet have not kept it." And then Paul adds the confession from Deuteronomy 6:4, "God is one," to show that God is not fighting against Himself in this whole Law/promise thing. It is all part of His perfect plan.

Paul explains the function of the Law in verses 21-24:

---

[2] R. Alan Cole, Galatians, 149. Commenting on the phrase I have translated, "Because of transgressions."

[3] Especially if we compare it to Jesus' words in Matthew 5:27-30.

## Lesson 9: Galatians 3:19-29

> Therefore, is the Law opposed to the promises of God? May it never be! For if a Law was given that was able to make [people] live, then righteousness would certainly be by Law, but the Scripture shut up all things under sin in order that the promise might be given by [the] faithfulness of Jesus [the] Messiah to the ones who are believing. But before the coming of the faith, we were being kept, shut up together [with all things], under Law as to the faith about to be revealed, so that the Law has been our tutor toward [the] Messiah, so that we might be made righteous by faith.

Since God is one, the Law cannot possibly be opposed to God's plan regarding faith in Christ, and thus it is also not contrary to God's promises to Abraham. Abraham's Seed will inherit precisely what God promised Him.

Paul starts by saying, much like Jesus does in John 5:39: "The Law cannot give life." The Law, in effect, proves that a person is in a state of death. He says that if it were able to give life, then righteousness would undoubtedly come from the Law. But Paul is adamant that righteousness cannot and will not come from attempting to keep the Law (more on this in future Lessons). So, it looks as though Paul has again hung himself on the nail that is labeled: "The Law is useless." But it is not to stay that way.

Paul then says in verse 22 that the Scripture has imprisoned everything under sin's power. Cole is again helpful here when he explains that the phrase translated "all things" is probably better understood as "all people."[4] And it's fascinating that Paul here changes from "Law" to "Scripture." The Scripture, specifically the portion known as the Law, imprisons all people under sin. It says, "You must die for your sin," and doesn't present the alternative (faith in Christ) clearly at all. Christ is certainly there, as Paul has shown throughout our time in Galatians 3, but it isn't clear like it is in the New Testament. The Law doesn't offer life or righteousness, it imprisons in sin. And if we're not careful, the whole Bible can do this to us (thus it's important that Paul says, "the Scripture").[5]

---

[4] R. Alan Cole, *Galatians*, 151.
[5] This is why it is necessary to read the Bible Christocentrically. We cannot turn our Bible reading time into a time where we try find a bunch of new things that God expects us to do. Christianity certainly leads to deeds (cf. Galatians 6:10; Ephesians 2:8-10; Titus 2:11-14, 3:14), but Christians find their life in Christ (cf. John 5:39, 15:5) and nowhere else.

The Bible is not a list of rules; it is not a playbook for life; it is not a list of prohibitions. The Bible is a love letter from the God of the universe, saying, "This is Who I Am. Get to know Me. Draw near to Me. Believe that I am who I claim to be. This is my Son, in whom I take delight. Put your faith in Him and be reconciled to Me. Apart from that, all your good deeds and rule-keeping (even out of this Book) are for naught."

We must study the Bible to know Jesus, not to try to become better people. If we study the Bible to become more moral, we make our morality an idol, and since we're being imprisoned in sin by the Scripture, we will never really become more righteous.

Trust the Word, read the Word, and study the Word to get to know the WORD—Jesus Christ!

Paul explains that the promise is given to those who believe. The promise comes to those who say, "I'm done working my way deeper and deeper into imprisonment and death." This is what every human does before being confronted and converted by the life-giving Gospel. The Law imprisoned us until faith came.

Paul then says, in verse 24, that the Law serves an instrumental and essential role. I say "serves," because it still does, even to this very day. The Greek verb was written in the perfect tense to show a past reality with present ramifications. It acts as our tutor. It served as a tutor for the Galatians and for you—if you've placed your faith in Christ—and it still works as a tutor for those that have yet to believe and are believing even as you read these words.

To understand what Paul means by referring to the Law as a tutor, I will quote Plato, who recorded a dialogue between a man (the first-person narrator) and a boy who lived under a tutor.

> "Someone controls you?"
> "Yes," he said, "my tutor here."
> "Is he a slave?"
> "Why certainly; he belongs to us," he said.
> "What a strange thing," I exclaimed; "a free man controlled by a slave! But how does this tutor actually exert his control over you?"
> "By taking me to school, I suppose," he replied.
> "And your schoolmasters, can it be that they also control you?"
> "I should think they do!"

## Lesson 9: Galatians 3:19-29

"Then quite a large number of masters and controllers are deliberately set over you by your father."[6]

God set the Law over us as a tutor to train us up and prepare us—even to beat us down at times[7]—for faith. God wanted us to come to faith, and He set up the necessary system to lead us there. The Law serves as a slave to discipline us and train us and beat us down. God stands as Father, saying, "Come to Me, all you who are weary and burdened.[8] Let me love you like a Father is supposed to!"

Verses 25-26 explain:

> And since the faith came, we are [now] no longer under a tutor. For you are yourselves all sons of God through faith in [the] Messiah Jesus.

If we are in Christ, then we have left that master of Law, and traded it for sonship to God. We are placed in Christ by faith. The Law prepares us for that, and then its job is done. Paul wants the Galatians, and us today, to move out from under the Law into the full blessing of sonship. Paul has now proven that the Law isn't worthless; we shouldn't throw it away. But, at the same time, we are no longer subject to it, to be enslaved and imprisoned and killed by it. We are sons of God by faith in Christ and by faith alone. If faith got us there, then faith alone will keep us there. Never give up on faith!

Paul explains how life is different for the believer in verses 25-29:

> And since the faith came, we are [now] no longer under a tutor. For you are yourselves all sons of God through faith in [the] Messiah Jesus, for as many of you all who were baptized into [the] Messiah have all been clothed with [the] Messiah. There is not a Jew or a Greek,

---

[6] Plato. "Plato, Lysis (English)." *Greek Texts & Translations*. http://perseus.uchicago.edu/perseus-cgi/citequery3.pl?dbname=GreekFeb2011&getid=1&query=Pl.%20Ly.%20208c. It is interesting to point out that there is a footnote next to the word "tutor" in the second line:

"The παιδαγωγός was a trusted slave who was appointed to attend on a boy out of school hours and to have a general control over his conduct and industry."

The Greek word in that quote is the exact Greek word Paul uses in 3:24.

[7] John MacArthur, *Galatians*, 96. "They were strict disciplinarians, scolding and whipping as they felt it necessary."

[8] Cf. Matthew 11:28.

> there is not a slave or a free [person], there is not male and female; for you all, yourselves, are one in [the] Messiah Jesus. And if you all, yourselves, [belong to the] Messiah, then you all are Abraham's seed, heirs according to [the] promise.

Five things are different about believers now: We aren't enslaved, we aren't alienated, we aren't naked, we aren't on different levels than other believers, and we aren't excluded from the promise.

As a child in Paul's culture was under a slave until he was old enough to be entrusted with the responsibilities of being a man, so also we—as children of God—have been freed from the Law. We aren't slaves to it anymore. We must live in this new way of freedom daily!

Instead of being the pupil of a potentially abusive tutor, we are the beloved children of God. We don't have to live in fear of the Law tearing us down and telling us we're worthless. Instead, we can hear our Father say, "I love you. The sacrifice of My Son is proof of that. You are no longer condemned. You are beloved. Look to Me!" Let's remember our status as sons and daughters of the King every single day!

The Law, since it imprisons in sin, strips us down and shows us that all we have to offer is rags and filth. Because of the promise, we have been clothed in Christ. God doesn't see our dirty rags; He sees the righteousness of His Son. Don't live condemned anymore. Live in joyful freedom!

The promise—since the Law imprisons all as equals—frees all people again as equals. In Christ, we are all united. We can't say, "because she's a woman, I'm better than her," or, "because he's a Greek (non-Jew) I'm better than him," or, "because his skin is a different color than mine, I'm better than him." Christ breaks down all barriers because, as sinners in God's eyes, we were all equal, but He loved all of us enough to free us and remake us equal in that improved status. Don't ever judge another believer[9] without saying to yourself first, "They're just as good as me—we've both been saved by Christ's perfect sacrifice. My treatment of them needs to demonstrate this fact."

---

[9] And yes, we are supposed to judge other believers. But it should not be for the purpose of condemnation, but rather for edification. If we read Matthew 7:1-5 carefully, then we see that the intention is to help another, and the only way to even realize that someone needs help is to pass a sort of judgment on them. But again, it is not a condemning judgment, but rather a hopeful, helpful judgment (an offer to help them improve in some aspect of their Christian walk).

Lesson 9: Galatians 3:19-29

If we are Christ's, then we will inherit the promises that God gave to Abraham. These promises clearly involve a future life on a new earth on which we will rule.[10] We will serve and worship God forever, having inherited the earth (cf. Matthew 5:5). When life looks bleak, remember that you are an heir of that fantastic promise! No matter what comes your way, know that God is preparing a place for you!

So, in conclusion, the promise is infinitely better than the Law! However, at the same time, the Law still serves an essential purpose. We must never forget that! Before we preach the cross, we must preach people into prison by allowing the Law to convince them that their sin has them in its grasp and that THE ONLY WAY for them to escape sin's grip is to place their faith in Christ. The five promises of newness of life are found in Christ alone.

# Law for Grace

Real quick. I have ten questions for you. Answer them honestly:

1. Have you ever worshipped another god?
2. Have you ever created an idol?
3. Have you ever misused God's name?
4. Have you ever worked on Saturday?
5. Have you ever disobeyed your parents?
6. Have you ever hated someone?
7. Have you ever lusted after someone?
8. Have you ever stolen something?
9. Have you ever lied?
10. Have you ever been jealous of your friend's success?

This is a summary of the Ten Commandments from Exodus 20:3-17. If your answer to any of them was, "Yes," then you are not righteous, and you can't stand before God. And, if you notice, these ten questions offer no hope in themselves.

It is only when we take it one step further and say, "Jesus answered every one of these questions with a 'No,' and then He died to take the curse

---

[10] Now when I say "rule," I don't mean like the Mormons mean. I said "earth," not different, varying planets.

we deserved for our failures in all ten of these areas. The Law proves our need for Jesus.

If you have never believed in Him, place your faith in Him today!

# Reflection Questions

1. How does today's text show Paul's love for the church?
2. What was the purpose of the Law?
3. Does this mean that we can live however we want now that we are Christians (cf. Galatians 5:19-23)?
4. What is Paul's point in Galatians 3:28?
5. Have you placed your faith in Jesus yet?

# Praying the Text

*Jesus,*

*Thank You for freeing me from the Law. Please help me to never revert to living under it. I need more of You every day. Help me never to treat the Law as though it is not important. It is the mirror that repeatedly shows me my desperate need for You. By showing me my imperfections, it should highlight your perfections to me. Help me to keep my focus on You! I need You desperately.*

# Lesson 10

## Galatians 4:1-7

¹Now I say, for as long as the heir is an infant, he is not at all different from a slave, [though] being lord of all, ²but he is under guardians and stewards until the time set beforehand by his father. ³Thusly also us: We were infants, having been enslaved under the fundamental principles of the world, ⁴but then the fullness of time came, [and] God sent forth His Son (born of a woman, born under the Law) ⁵in order that He might purchase those under Law so that we might receive the sonship. ⁶Now because you all are sons, God sent forth the Spirit of His Son into our hearts, who is crying out, "Abba, Father!" ⁷So that you are no longer a slave, but a son, and if a son, also an heir through [the authority of] God.

# Reigning, not Ruled

I remember a book I read as a child by Mark Twain. Sure, it was the condensed version, but it was called *The Prince and the Pauper*.[1] It is about two children who realize that they look almost identical, so they decide to switch places and learn about life through each other's eyes. One grew up in riches; the other grew up in poverty. The one who begins to experience life in more poverty than he is used to begins to understand what the poor have to go through daily; the one who moves up the social ladder is scared that he will be found out as a fraud.

Paul speaks to this in our passage today. However, he flips it. Believers are all royalty in God's eyes. We've already lived our lives of poverty in sin, and we don't need to go look back on those things with longing; at the same time, we don't need to fear being found out as frauds, because we truly are heirs of God and we can know it experientially through the Spirit.

So far in our study of this book, we have seen several things: Paul started by composing a letter to the Galatians in which the introduction holds up Jesus as the answer to the sin problem (cf. 1:1-5). From there, he showed shock at their current straying from that foundation (cf. 1:6-10). He continued by anticipating the objection, "Who are you to say this?" and answered by telling them, "Jesus revealed this to me" (cf. 1:11-24); then he said, "the Apostles at Jerusalem confirmed my message" (cf. 2:1-10). He continued by showing that he was not influenced by men in the proclamation of the Gospel, by relating the time he confronted Peter, and by arguing that the Gospel promotes freedom, not rules and regulations (cf. 2:11-21). Then he interrogated the Galatians about their straying from the truth (cf. 3:1-5). He explained that we need faith, which gives life, and not Law, which breeds death (cf. 3:6-14). He explained that the source of faith—promised 430 years before the Law to Abraham—is Jesus, the Seed of Abraham (cf. 3:15-18). And finally, lest people accuse Paul of being a blaspheming Jew who had turned

---

[1] It is currently on my to-read pile—the full version this time. The edition I plan to read is Mark Twain, *The Prince & the Pauper*, 1882 (Mineola, NY: Dover Publications, 2000).

his back on the Law, he explained that the Law does serve a purpose (cf. 3:19-29).

And it is there that we pick up today. Galatians 3:24 said, "The Law has been our tutor toward [the] Messiah, so that we might be made righteous by faith," and it is with that metaphor that Paul continues in 4:1-7. He seeks to show that while the Law is holy, and while it comes from God, it is not ultimate; it serves a purpose. He seeks to show that we should not submit ourselves to the Law as ultimate if we have been freed from it by Him Who is Ultimate. (Again, Paul is not teaching do-whatever-you-want theology; chapter 5, which follows chapter 4, is very ethically oriented; but we'll get there soon.)

Paul starts by relaying the tutor image again. However, this time, the focus is on the person under the tutor, not the tutor himself. Verses 1-2 say:

> Now I say, for as long as the heir is an infant, he is not at all different from a slave, [though] being lord of all, but he is under guardians and stewards until the time set beforehand by his father.

This is relatively simple to understand. Until a certain age, a child in ancient Greece had no privileges. He might have been from a wealthy family, and he might have been the heir of a large inheritance, but he couldn't take advantage of any of it. There were family slaves that watched, protected, and aided the child until he reached the appropriate age. He was treated as a slave by these slaves until the time came when he was old enough to inherit the rank of sonship from his father. Basically, the slaves prepared him for this day, treating him like a slave until he was old/mature enough to become an adult with responsibilities and privileges.

Paul continues by relating this analogy to our spiritual situation. Verses 3-5 say:

> Thusly also us: We were infants, having been enslaved under the fundamental principles of the world, but then the fullness of time came, [and] God sent forth His Son (born of a woman, born under the Law) in order that He might purchase those under Law so that we might receive the sonship.

He starts by saying we were in slavery. However, it is important to note that he doesn't say, "You were enslaved to the Law." This is important because the people he is writing to were Gentiles who had never had the Law of Moses. Acts 13-14 described the missionary journey of Paul when he ministered to the Galatians, and it was by way of checking in on them that he writes this letter. Instead of accusing them of being enslaved to the Law, he says, "We were infants, having been enslaved under the fundamental principles of the world." The fact that he includes himself would support the idea that the Law of Moses is part of the fundamental principles of the world. So, to what exactly were we enslaved?

The precise meaning of the Greek word translated "fundamental principles" is somewhat tricky to nail down. And while many scholars have debated, argued, and spilled much ink over the meaning of the phrase, one explanation screams for recognition.

> It denotes that whereon the existence of this world rests, that which constitutes man's being. Paul uses it in a transferred sense for that whereon man's existence rested before Christ even and precisely in pre-Christian religion, that which is weak and impotent, that which enslaves man instead of freeing him.[2]

The elemental things of this world are whatever building blocks upon which a person has built his identity. These things do nothing for us, except beat us up and show us our need for deliverance. For a Jew, it is clear that the Law of Moses functioned in this way. Paul's point to the Galatians is simple: "Don't put yourself back in slavery. You never experienced that kind. Don't go there now!"

However, some who are reading this are already returning to, or maybe have never even fled from the fundamental principles of this world.

Perhaps you find your identity in being able to drink more alcohol than the next guy; give it up, because it's enslaved you.

Perhaps you find your identity in a relationship with the opposite gender; you will never find true purpose or meaning there, so don't let it enslave you more.

Perhaps you find your identity in a homosexual relationship; again, it is enslaving, so turn away from it.

Perhaps your slavery of choice isn't so apparent to the world: Do you find your identity in being a good person, or in always being happy, or in

---

[2] Gerhard Kittel and Geoffrey William Bromiley, eds, *Theological Dictionary of the New Testament*, 10 vols (Grand Rapids, MI: Eerdmans, 1964-1976), VII:685.

helping other people? What's your motivation for these good things? If it is so people will think highly of you, you are in a heap of trouble. Our motivation for goodness should never be our reputation, but rather God's.

The second half of this list of six forms of slavery is the more dangerous side: Jesus said in Matthew 9:12, "<u>Those who are well don't need a doctor, but the sick do.</u>" Until a person can admit their need for a doctor, they will remain sick. Those who are enslaved to active sins—drunkenness, sexual deviance, murder, etc.—are more likely to see their need for help than those enslaved to passive sins—pride, self-idolatry, self-righteousness. Don't stay in slavery, regardless of which kind holds you in its clutches.

Paul continues by explaining how we can be released from slavery: It's through Jesus, the Son of God. I said in the previous paragraphs to turn from your preferred form of slavery, but I didn't say where to turn. This is where you need to turn. Jesus. Do it now! Admit your need for saving, admit your refusal to remain a slave any longer, and choose to believe that Jesus bore the curse meant for you on the cross, and choose to follow Him for the rest of your life.

Paul highlights two aspects of Jesus that are key to understanding our freedom from slavery: Jesus was born of a woman, and He was born under the Law. The fact that Jesus was born of a woman means that He was fully human. This means simply that He can relate to us. He understands our fears and our desires. He knows what it is like to be tempted and tried. He even knows what it's like to live under the Law: He was born under the Law, and the beginning of His life was marked by strict adherence to the Law (cf. Luke 2:21-24). In fact, this is what Paul means by the second phrase: born under the Law. However, the key here is how Paul words this section: "<u>God sent forth His Son.</u>" God didn't just send Jesus as a man. He sent Jesus as His own personal Heir. Jesus is the one who gave the Law, so the Law cannot hold Him down. In fact, He's above us and able to pull us out from under the Law and set us firmly on grace. He is amazing.

The purpose of Jesus' coming was so that we would receive adoption as sons. Just as Jesus was God's Heir, so also God wants us as His heirs. Jesus' death on the cross redeemed us from slavery to all sorts of various things and transformed us into sons and daughters of God. This is the Gospel. Believe it!

Paul concludes this section by explaining the significance of us as sons of God. Verses 6-7 say:

## Lesson 10: Galatians 4:1-7

> Now because you all are sons, God sent forth the Spirit of His Son into our hearts, who is crying out, "Abba, Father!" So that you are no longer a slave, but a son, and if a son, also an heir through [the authority of] God.

Paul says here that the proof of our sonship is the Spirit. And, interestingly, Paul doesn't say, "You cry out, 'Abba, Father,'" but rather, "the Spirit . . . is crying out, 'Abba, Father!'" The way it is worded, it is clear that the Spirit is actively crying out for God, and when we find ourselves crying out for God, it is a sign that we truly do belong to God.

The Spirit's crying out for God is proof that we are no longer slaves. In fact, it should be a powerful deterrent from anything in this world that would seek to re-enslave us. This is Paul's point here: "Galatians, you claim to have been redeemed by Christ, so why would you enslave yourselves to a new elemental thing when you have Jesus as your Savior, as the Ultimate Person?"

Paul is saying, if you are children of God, redeemed from a childhood of slavery, then don't return to your life as an infant. You did away with those things. John MacArthur relates how an ancient tradition in Rome at this time was burning one's toys to show that a person was no longer a child.[3] Galatians 2:18 says, "For if I rebuild the very things I once destroyed, I show myself [to be] a transgressor." Paul doesn't want this to be the case. He wants them to see that they have been remade anew and that the old no longer exists or exercises any authority, just like the tutor in a Roman household after the child under his charge comes to adulthood.

Paul takes another jab at the Judaizers (Paul's opponents who were trying to turn the Galatians to Jewish practices for salvation) by saying, "If a son, also an heir through [the authority of] God." It is not because the Law exercised power that someone became an heir of God; it is not because some other enslaving system of the world exercised power that someone becomes an heir of God; it is not even because a person did something that they become an heir of God. Instead, it is merely due to God's working that anyone becomes an heir of God. God is in control. Nothing else ultimately is. For this reason, we can trust God, and we should run to Jesus. He is our hope.

Let's live like the princes and princesses we are, and never return to the pauper life of sin.

---

[3] John MacArthur, *Galatians*, 104.

## "Let My People Go!"

Almost 1500 years before Paul penned this fantastic letter, his ancestors were slaves in Egypt. God called a man named Moses and sent him to Pharaoh to declare, "This is what Yahweh, the God of Israel, says: Let My people go, so that they may hold a festival for Me in the wilderness" (Exodus 5:1). Pharaoh said no, and God showed Himself powerful to Egypt, so much so that when all was said and done, even some Egyptians followed the Israelites out of Egypt (cf. Exodus 12:38). They knew that the gods of their homeland were nothing compared to the God of the Hebrews.

By the time of Jesus' ministry, the Jewish people had exchanged true worship of God for formalism and ritual centered around the Law that God had given to Moses. Jesus confronts the religious leaders about their slavery to both sin and Law. In their prideful attempt to say that they were not enslaved to either, they say, "We are descendants of Abraham, and we have never been enslaved to anyone" (John 8:33). This is a bold statement, especially since it was the descendants of Abraham who had been slaves in Egypt 1500 years prior.

The point is: Fallen man is so resistant to the grace of God that we make up the stupidest, most idiotic excuses as to why we cannot place our faith wholly in God. But as Jesus said, that spawned the Pharisees' lie, "You will know the truth, and the truth will set you free" (John 8:32). Jesus is the truth, and the words He speaks are the truth. He has the power to set you free.

I don't know who you are, and I don't know your life story. But I do know that you are human, and I know that as a human, you are not perfect. I also know that if you are honest with yourself, then there are things you are enslaved to. It might not be pornography or alcohol or marijuana, but that doesn't mean that an overwhelming desire to please people or to be liked by people or to talk about people behind their backs isn't enslaving.

The Gospel states that Jesus came to earth to set us free from whatever it is that enslaves us. We're all shackled to something, but the only thing we should be serving is Jesus. He is the only one worthy.

He proved His worth by dying on the cross for the very things that enslave us. And then to prove that He had dealt a death blow to our enslaving sins, He rose again from the dead. Death couldn't hold Him!

If you place your faith in Him, He will free you. It might not happen in the blink of an eye, but in God's sight, you will be a son/daughter and not a slave.

Lesson 10: Galatians 4:1-7

When Jesus declares, "Let My people go," sin and Satan cower in fright and submit to His Lordship.

Believe in Jesus today! Escape the tyranny of sin's slavery.

## Reflection Questions

1. How does today's text show Paul's love for the church?
2. Are you an heir of God? Or: Have you placed your faith in Jesus yet?
3. If you are an heir, do you act like it? Why or why not?
4. Do you believe you are an heir of God? Does this affect the answer to #3?
5. How should you live as an heir of God? What should the motivation be for this kind of living?

## Praying the Text

*Jesus,*

*Thank You for making me a child of the king. This is literally the most significant news in the history of the world. Help my lifestyle to evidence that I am a child of the king. I need more of You every day! Help me love You more each and every day.*

# Lesson 11

## Galatians 4:8-20

⁸But then indeed, having not [yet] known God, you all slaved for things being by nature not gods, ⁹and now, after knowing God—or rather having become known by God—how are you all again turning to the weak and bankrupt fundamental principles to which you all want to be enslaved again? ¹⁰You all are keeping for yourselves days, months, seasons, and years, ¹¹[and] I am afraid for you all that perhaps I have labored on you all's behalf in vain.

¹²Become like me, because I also became like you all, brothers. I beg of you all. You all did nothing to harm me. ¹³You all know that despite weakness of the flesh I evangelized to you the first [time], ¹⁴and (despite you all's temptation on account of my flesh) you all neither regarded [me] with contempt nor spat [at me], but you received me as a messenger of God, as [the] Messiah Jesus. ¹⁵Then where is your blessing? For I testify to you all that if able, you all, after scooping out you all's eyes, would have given [them] to me. ¹⁶So have I become you all's enemy by telling the truth to you all? ¹⁷They are zealous for you all, but not for good; instead they want to shut you all out in order that you all might be zealous for them. ¹⁸Now [it is] always good to be zealous for a good thing, and not only when we are together. ¹⁹My children for whom I am again suffering birth pains until [the] Messiah might be formed in you all, ²⁰I want to be present with you all now and to change my voice, because I am confused about you all.

# Loyalty Requires Perseverance

Since my last Galatians entry, I finished my first full television series.[1] It was originally aired a few years ago, but I started watching it on Netflix, and I had to purchase the complete series on DVD to finish it because it was removed from Netflix. While I can't recommend it as a perfectly clean, family-friendly show, it is definitely not evil. It is called *Chuck*,[2] and it is about a guy named Chuck Bartowski, who gets a supercomputer full of government secrets downloaded into his brain. As such, agents from two government agencies are sent to keep him safe. The camaraderie and loyalty exemplified, especially from Chuck, throughout the show's five seasons are my favorite thing about the show. He's not perfect—nowhere close—and in no way does he claim to have any ties to a particular religion, but for the most part, "loyalty," "faithfulness," and "perseverance when times get tough" describe him accurately. This is important because it ties very closely into what Paul is talking about in this section of his letter to the Galatians.

This section is closely connected to the previous. Especially at the beginning. However, the first word of verse 8 is but, and that is very important. It draws an important contrast between Paul urging the Galatians to realize their new position in Christ free from the "fundamental principles" to which they were enslaved, and his new strategy: "You've deserted me, the one you trusted so highly when I came to you." This section, especially verses 12-20, "[contains] the strongest words of personal affection Paul uses in any of his letters."[3]

Paul begins similarly to how he was speaking in the previous section. Verses 8-10 say:

> But then indeed, having not [yet] known God, you all slaved for things being by nature not gods, and now, after knowing God—or rather

---

[1] This Lesson was originally published as a blogpost on December 28, 2016. The previous Lesson had been originally published on December 10, 2016.

[2] *Chuck*, created by Josh Schwartz and Chris Fedak (Burbank, CA: Warner Home Video, 2008-2012), DVD.

[3] John MacArthur, *Galatians*, 114.

> having become known by God—how are you all again turning to the weak and bankrupt fundamental principles to which you all want to be enslaved again? You all are keeping for yourselves days, months, seasons, and years.

Paul wants to remind them that they were slaves to something before that ultimately had no power over them. Before they knew God, things enslaved them that didn't have any right to enslave them. He says that things are different now. He says that they know God now, and their knowledge of God should hinder them from returning to their former slavery because God really is God, and He truly has power. He explains in what way they've decided to return to slavery: The Jewish Law is full of special days, months, seasons, and years—Leviticus 23 and 25—that those under the Law were to follow. The Judaizers must have convinced the Galatians of their need to follow these calendar events for salvation, which in turn led them to remove themselves from the grace of the Gospel. The very Gospel Paul had brought to them.

Paul makes a curious statement in verse 9 that I can't merely gloss over. He says, "And now, after knowing God—or rather having become known by God." There is a theological point to be made here, but I would also emphasize that it is not Paul's primary point here. The theological point is that we are not the ones who seek to know God; God is the one who actively seeks to know us, and then our seeking of Him is simply our response to His initial seeking. Paul proved this theology through his own story in 1:15-16: "But when God (the One who set me apart from my mother's womb and called me through His grace) was pleased to reveal His Son in me (in order that I might evangelize Him to the nations)...." However, I don't believe for a minute that this was Paul's goal in using that phraseology in this section. Paul is seeking to make a transition from the Galatians' return to slavery to his love and concern for them. He is essentially saying in this phrase, "Galatians, God got to know you through my coming to you. He used me to get to know you. Don't turn your back on Him!" This transition is completed in verse 11 when Paul says, "I am afraid for you all that perhaps I have labored on you all's behalf in vain."

Verses 12-15 describe Paul's first experience with them:

> Become like me, because I also became like you all, brothers. I beg of you all. You all did nothing to harm me. You all know that despite weakness of the flesh I evangelized to you the first [time], and (despite

## Lesson 11: Galatians 4:8-20

you all's temptation on account of my flesh) you all neither regarded [me] with contempt nor spat [at me], but you received me as a messenger of God, as [the] Messiah Jesus. Then where is your blessing? For I testify to you all that if able, you all, after scooping out you all's eyes, would have given [them] to me.

This passage doesn't exactly make a lot of sense. All we know for sure is that Paul is describing his time with the Galatians. It is interesting that verse 13 does not say, "physical illness," but rather, "weakness of the flesh." Many have understood this as being a sickness, though literally "weakness of the flesh" often refers to temptation to sin. Martin Luther explains a third option, which I think is best, in the following lengthy quote:

> When Paul speaks of the infirmity of his flesh he does not mean some physical defect or carnal lust, but the sufferings and afflictions which he endured in his body. What these infirmities were he himself explains in 2 Corinthians 12:9-10: "Most gladly therefore will I rather glory in my infirmities, that the power of Christ may rest upon me. Therefore I take pleasure in infirmities, in reproaches, in necessities, in persecutions, in distresses for Christ's sake: for when I am weak, then am I strong." And in the eleventh chapter of the same Epistle the Apostle writes: "In labors more abundant, in stripes above measure, in prisons more frequent, in deaths oft. Of the Jews five times received I forty stripes save one. Thrice was I beaten with rods, once was I stoned, thrice I suffered shipwreck," etc. (2 Cor 11:23-25.) By the infirmity of his flesh Paul meant these afflictions and not some chronic disease. He reminds the Galatians how he was always in peril at the hands of the Jews, Gentiles, and false brethren, how he suffered hunger and want.
>
> Now, the afflictions of the believers always offend people. Paul knew it and therefore has high praise for the Galatians because they over looked his afflictions and received him like an angel. Christ forewarned the faithful against the offense of the Cross, saying: "Blessed is he, whosoever shall not be offended in me" (Matt 11:6). Surely it is no easy thing to confess Him Lord of all and Savior of the world who was a reproach of men, and despised of the people, and the laughing stock of the world (Ps 22:7). I say, to value this poor Christ, so spitefully scorned, spit upon, scourged, and crucified, more

than the riches of the richest, the strength of the strongest, the wisdom of the wisest, is something. It is worth being called blessed.[4]

They received Paul as Jesus Himself. In a very real sense, Paul is also saying that by heeding his message, they literally received Christ by believing in Him. They were not offended by Paul but rather drawn to the Savior.

Paul explains that they received him so eagerly, without being offended, that he could have asked them for anything, and they would have done it. The phrase, "If able, you all, after scooping out you all's eyes, would have given [them] to me," has often been understood as contributing to the view that Paul had a physical illness, perhaps an optical illness, and he required their eyes to see better. With the above understanding from Luther, this cannot be the case, and it is enough to say that they trusted Paul so highly that they would have done anything he asked. This is quite a contrast with the next verses.

Verses 16-20 describe Paul's current experience with them:

So have I become you all's enemy by telling the truth to you all? They are zealous for you all, but not for good; instead they want to shut you all out in order that you all might be zealous for them. Now [it is] always good to be zealous for a good thing, and not only when we are together. My children for whom I am again suffering birth pains until [the] Messiah might be formed in you all, I want to be present with you all now and to change my voice, because I am confused about you all.

This is where Paul's loyalty and perseverance for those he loves come into play explicitly. The simplest way to understand this section hinges on verse 16. He is anticipating their current response as they are reading the letter. "Are you upset with me for being honest?" Loyalty and faithfulness to people involve the difficult task of telling the truth. There's no more unloving thing to do than to actively withhold the truth from those who are erring off the path of life. Paul made it clear in 1:6 that the Galatians were standing over the pit of hell in their decision to follow the Judaizers instead of Jesus: "I am amazed that so soon you all are apostatizing yourselves away from the One who called

---

[4] Martin Luther, *A Commentary on St. Paul's Epistle to the Galatians*.

you all by grace to a different gospel." Paul has been telling the truth since the start of the letter, and here he asks them to be honest about their feelings: "Are you mad at me for loving you enough to tell you that you are wrong?" He then says, "Look, these Judaizers might try to tell you differently, but your eternal soul is at stake in this! Don't listen to them!"

Are we truth-tellers like Paul, or do we hope someone else is going to do the job God has given to us? I know that I am too often guilty of saying, "I'll raise spiritual issues later," when I'm not guaranteed a later time at which to raise those issues. The fact that Carrie Fisher died this week is proof that we don't know how much time we have on this planet.[5] This again ties back to *Chuck*.[6] As government agents, their lives were in danger every episode. As such, they had to be ready for the worst; how much more (in real life) must we be prepared for the end? If we know the truth, we must spread it to those we know. Especially if we, like Paul, are called to active ministry roles in a church, we must refuse to take the "I'll wait for someone more qualified to share the Gospel with my peers" attitude. We must do it ourselves.

Paul is fighting for them, and he compares his anguish for them to the pain of a woman in labor. They were his spiritual children, and he wanted to see them grow up into Christ. Cole explains,

> Paul says he is in labour all over again *until Christ be formed in you*, or 'until you take the shape of Christ' (NEB). No-one doubts his meaning: it is the agony of the pastor, watching for signs of Christian growth in his flock. Paul tells us in 2 Corinthians 11:28 that this was the heaviest burden which he had to bear. It is therefore inadequate to think of Paul merely as the prince of evangelists; he was also the prince of pastors, and nowhere is this more clearly seen than in passages like this.[7]

Second Corinthians 11:28 would prove that the weakness of the flesh Paul dealt with in front of the Galatians was the trials of ministry, and the fact that they were turning their backs on him made it even harder. Second Corinthians 11:28 says, "Not to mention other things, there is the daily pressure on me: my care for all the churches." This is why he concludes the Galatians section today by essentially saying, "I want to see you. I am at a loss about you."

---

[5] This Lesson was originally published as a blogpost on December 28, 2016.
[6] *Chuck*.
[7] R. Alan Cole, *Galatians*, 175.

Chuck Bartowski, from the television show *Chuck*, is loyal to all of his friends throughout that television series.[8] Similarly, Paul was faithful to his Galatian friends. Are we as loyal to our friends? Do we tell them the truth even at the risk of making them our enemies, as Paul did here? We should. The truth is that Jesus died on the cross to break down all enmity for those who believe in Him. And who knows, even if my sharing the Gospel with a coworker makes our friendship totally different, perhaps it will plant the seed that will eventually sprout elsewhere and destroy the enmity that I was worried about. I, for one, would rather risk enmity than know with certainty that a peer is headed to hell. Paul would agree with me on that. How about you?

## The Best of All News

The Gospel is the most crucial message in this world. It far outstrips the best news anyone can ever bring to you. It puts all news reports to shame—even the best ones. And it tells of One returning who is a better Ruler than the most celebrated president (or any other national leader) in history. All other news falls short compared to the message about Jesus Christ.

And the bad thing about this is that the statements I just made in the prior paragraph can often be met with hatred, anger, and stubbornness—sometimes even from church people. This should not be the case, but it goes to show what Paul means in Galatians 4:16: "So have I become you all's enemy by telling the truth to you all?"

We must proclaim the Gospel no matter what people think of us. We get too caught up in other, lesser news. We must proclaim the most excellent news of all time, even if we are made outcasts as a result.

Jesus came to earth 2,000 years ago. We were enslaved to various passions and pleasures. We didn't want to have anything to do with God. Jesus was crucified on a cross because of our sins. He died the death we deserve. But three days later, He rose again.

This is the Gospel. This is the message of salvation.

I beg you to place your faith in Christ today! If you haven't, you must. He only died for the sins of those found in Him by faith! If you refuse to believe, you must still serve the eternal punishment that your sins have earned you.

Believe in Jesus today! This is the greatest of all news!

---

[8] *Chuck*.

Lesson 11: Galatians 4:8-20

# Reflection Questions

1. How does today's text show Paul's love for the church?
2. Who do you need to reach out to this week with the truth and love of the Gospel?
3. What might keep you from reaching out to him/her?
4. Do you have someone in your life who loves you like Paul loved the Galatians?
5. Have you placed your faith in Jesus yet?

# Praying the Text

*Jesus,*

*Thank You for Paul, the model pastor and missionary. Please help me to develop a heart like his. I want to boldly preach You even to those who will not accept it. I need You. Keep me grounded in Your Gospel. I never want to depart from it.*

# Lesson 12

## Galatians 4:21-31

²¹Tell me, the ones who are wanting to be under Law, don't you all hear the Law? ²²For it has been written that Abraham had two sons: One from the servant-girl and one from the free-woman. ²³But whereas the one from the servant-girl had been born according to [the] flesh, the one from the free-woman [was born] as a result of [the] promise. ²⁴These things are allegorical, for these are two covenants: Indeed, the one from Mount Sinai bearing [children] into slavery is Hagar. ²⁵Hagar corresponds to Mount Sinai in Arabia—the present-day Jerusalem—for she is enslaved with her children. ²⁶But the Jerusalem above is free, who is our mother, ²⁷for it has been written,

"Rejoice, [O] barren woman, who is not giving birth,
Break forth and shout, the one who is not suffering birth pains;
Because the children of the desolate one will be many more than [those of]
the one who has a husband."

²⁸You all, yourselves—brothers—are children of [the] promise, like Isaac. ²⁹But even as then, the one who had been born according to [the] flesh persecuted the one [born] according to [the] Spirit, so also [it is] now. ³⁰But what does the Scripture say? "Throw out the servant-girl and her son; for the son of the servant-girl will not inherit with the son of the free-woman." ³¹Therefore, brothers, we are not children of [the] slave-girl, but of the free-woman.

# "It's a Trap"

As I've said before, I love *Star Wars*. And, as I may not have mentioned, the original trilogy is the best.[1] My favorite episode is 6: *The Return of the Jedi*. There is a line that has forever been immortalized by one rebel alien: "It's a trap."[2] When I think of Admiral Ackbar—the orange Mon Calamarian—I think of that line. In fact, when I saw his "cousin" in *Rogue One* a few weeks ago, I immediately thought of that line. And now, after studying this passage in Galatians, there is only one thing I can say: "It's a trap!"

Paul had concluded verse 20 by saying, "I am confused about you all," and Luther points out, "Here Paul would have closed his Epistle because he did not know what else to say. He wishes he could see the Galatians in person and straighten out their difficulties. But he is not sure whether the Galatians have fully understood the difference between the Gospel and the Law. To make sure, he introduces another illustration."[3] Paul had already gone through his personal encounter with Christ, and the agreement of the other apostles with Paul's status as an able teacher; he had already gone through all the theology about grace and Christ as opposed to the Law; he had even explained his own heart regarding his Galatian brothers, and he reminded them of their initial reception of him. With all that said, he says, "I don't know what to do about you," and then brings in an illustration that traps the Galatians if they want to continue in their current frame of thinking. Their only out is to admit, "Okay, Paul, we want to follow the way of promise."

Paul follows in the footsteps of Jesus, The Great Debater, when he totally turns his tone around in verse 21 by saying:

> Tell me, the ones who are wanting to be under Law, don't you all hear the Law?

---

[1] But I cannot tell a lie, so let's be real. We all know this to be the case, even though the prequels came out during my childhood.

[2] *Star Wars: Episode VI – Return of the Jedi*.

[3] Martin Luther, *A Commentary on St. Paul's Epistle to the Galatians*.

It harks back to Jesus, who often asked the Pharisees, "Haven't you read...?" (cf. Matthew 12:3, 5; 19:4; 22:31). In Jesus' case, the Pharisees were supposed to be top-notch scholars of the Word; Jesus repeatedly pointed out that they didn't know it even close to as well as He did, and as such, their indictments of Him could do nothing but fall flat. Paul here touches on the fact that the Galatians were wanting to follow the Law, so he brings up a passage where the Law itself says, "The Law leads to slavery."

Now before we go any farther, two potential objections must be put to rest. First, "The stories in Genesis are not the Law," and second, "This illustration has nothing to do with the original context in the Genesis story."

As far as the first, when Paul speaks of the Law, he is speaking of the תרה (Torah), the first five books of our Old Testament, often referred to as "the Law of Moses." Any Jew back then would have understood all of Genesis as being part of the Law.

As for the second objection, Paul indeed takes it farther than the original Mosaic intent. However, two things are true despite the fact that Paul took this illustration farther than Moses' original intention: First, the Jews had no problem with allegorical interpretations of their Scripture (cf. the writings of Philo);[4] second, this passage is in a text that is bound with other documents that fall under the description of 2 Timothy 3:16 (God-breathed, inspired Scripture). Even though allegory is not an accurate way for us to interpret Scripture today, God inspired that it should be used to accomplish His purpose in this specific passage.

To fully understand this passage of Scripture, I have adopted my outline from John MacArthur's commentary: Verses 22-23 are the historical background, verses 24-27 are the divine interpretation, and verses 28-31 are the personal application.[5]

Paul gives the historical background in verses 22-23.

> For it has been written that Abraham had two sons: One from the servant-girl and one from the free-woman. But whereas the one from the servant-girl had been born according to [the] flesh, the one from the free-woman [was born] as a result of [the] promise.

The story Paul is talking about is fleshed out by Moses in Genesis 15-16 and 21. In Genesis 15:1-6, God comes to Abraham and says, "You will inherit a

---

[4] R. Alan Cole, *Galatians*, 180.
[5] John MacArthur, *Galatians*, 123-127.

large reward." Abraham basically replies by saying, "How is that since it will leave my family after I die because my heir is a servant and not a true son?" God answers and says, "No. You will have a child. In fact, your descendants will be as numerous as the stars." Abraham believed that message. Chapter 16 picks up the story presumably when Sarah—Abraham's wife—hears the news. She says, "Abraham, I haven't been privileged to have a child. Sleep with my servant, and she will have your son for me." Abraham listens to her. Ishmael is born from the slave woman—Hagar. Then chapter 21 rolls around, and we read in verses 1-3, "<u>The LORD came to Sarah as He had said, and the LORD did for Sarah what He had promised. Sarah became pregnant and bore a son to Abraham in his old age, at the appointed time God had told him. Abraham named his son who was born to him—the one Sarah bore to him—Isaac.</u>" Thus, we see that Abraham had two sons, one by the flesh and the other according to the promise of God.

Paul explains the divine interpretation in verses 24-27:

<u>These things are allegorical, for these are two covenants: Indeed, the one from Mount Sinai bearing [children] into slavery is Hagar. Hagar corresponds to Mount Sinai in Arabia—the present-day Jerusalem—for she is enslaved with her children. But the Jerusalem above is free, who is our mother, for it has been written, "Rejoice, [O] barren woman, who is not giving birth. Break forth and shout, the one who is not suffering birth pains; Because the children of the desolate one will be many more than [those of] the one who has a husband."</u>

The Jews would have freaked out here. We can follow Paul's comparison easily, and so could they. The two women represent two covenants: Hagar's descendants were slaves, and Sarah's descendants were free. However, Paul switches it by saying that Hagar corresponds to present-day Jerusalem. Under the inspiration of the Holy Spirit, Paul understood Judaism, centered in Jerusalem, as being trapped in slavery.[6] The Jews—especially the Judaizers—would have declared Paul crazy. Paul's point, though, is that this is an interpretation of the Law, and the Law itself is here maintaining that the fleshly way—the one opposed to faith—is enslaving. While the Judaizers promised freedom, Paul says that they only enslave.

---

[6] I would go so far as to say that this is still the case <u>"present-day"</u> (cf. EXCURSUS: Seeking the Seed).

*Live Free or Die Lawfully*

He then says that while the Jerusalem on earth is enslaved, there is a free Jerusalem: The spiritual Jerusalem that bears children according to the promise. When Paul says, "<u>The Jerusalem above is free, who is our mother</u>" (verse 26), it is because he has just finished explaining that believers are now children of Abraham (cf. 3:10-29). God is our Father through the promise to Abraham. The main point is not that Sarah is our spiritual mother,[7] let alone that Abraham is our spiritual father (though Abraham truly is our spiritual father in the faith). The main point—the point that Paul has been aiming at since 3:1—is that God is a keeper of His promises, and there is absolutely nothing we can do to add to it or earn it. Paul then quotes a verse to encourage his readers: "Rejoice in this truth! Refuse to be deceived anymore and rejoice in your freedom and blessing."

Paul applies it to the Galatians personally in verses 28-31:

<u>You all, yourselves—brothers—are children of [the] promise, like Isaac. But even as then, the one who had been born according to [the] flesh persecuted the one [born] according to [the] Spirit, so also [it is] now. But what does the Scripture say? "Throw out the servant-girl and her son; for the son of the servant-girl will not inherit with the son of the free-woman." Therefore, brothers, we are not children of [the] slave-girl, but of the free-woman.</u>

And here Paul explicitly ties it all together, proving the point I made above. However, in the midst of it, he explains why the Judaizers have been troubling them. He refers back to Genesis 21:9, where Sarah sees Ishmael mocking Isaac. Paul says, "<u>But even as then, the one who had been born according to [the] flesh persecuted the one [born] according to [the] Spirit, so also [it is] now.</u>" The Judaizers were jealous of the Galatian's freedom, and they were trying to trouble them. Paul then quotes Genesis 21:10 to tell them what they should do with the Judaizers. "<u>Drive out this slave with her son, for the son of this slave will not be a coheir with my son Isaac!</u>" Paul wants them to kick out the deceivers. He wants them to not even feign fellowship with the fakes. He doesn't want them to be confused anymore about who they trace

---

[7] It is important that the free woman is never named as Sarah (or anyone else for that matter) in this allegorical interpretation that Paul gives.

their lineage from.[8] The Galatians are not from earthly Jerusalem, but spiritual Jerusalem. They are free; they are not slaves.

This is true of you today, too, if you are a believer in the Gospel of Jesus Christ. If you belong to Him, you are free; you are no longer a slave to sin, death, and the Law. It isn't about what you do or don't do; it is about who is your Father.

If you don't know Jesus, you are still a son or daughter of the slave woman. Here's the good news, though: God is in the adoption business. We all started out as children of Hagar, but through Jesus' death on the cross—believing that He was and is who He claims to be—we can be made children of God. If you don't yet believe, then I beg you to place your faith in Him today! If you do believe, never return to slavery! (More on that in Lesson 13.)

And just like that, Paul concludes the brunt of his theological section. Sure, there's more theology, but the focus of the rest of the book is application. Be prepared for challenges. And, now that you know that belief in Jesus is the way to escape the trap of slavery, warn everyone you meet—like Admiral Ackbar[9] did: "It's a trap to ignore the truth of Jesus and take any path but the way of God's promise."

# Free Indeed!

Since Paul spoke in a metaphor in this text, I want to give you another. Picture this:

> You are living in the tenth century. There is a power struggle between Saxons, Danes, Scots, and Norsemen for who will control what is now England. You are a simple peasant who works land belonging to a Saxon lord. (The Saxons fight for the Catholic Church in this metaphor, and thus represent civilized civilization.)
>
> Let's imagine, now, that you are out working in the fields when a row of horsemen appear on the horizon. They charge toward you, their swords glinting in the sunlight.
>
> You rush to your family and hurry them into the family hut, but you watch out your one window as the fields are set on fire, as

---

[8] How does Paul's seeming harshness fit into the "live in love" theology I have developed? Cf. EXCURSUS: Tough Love.

[9] *Star Wars: Episode VI – Return of the Jedi.*

neighboring houses are burned to the ground, as your neighbor's final screams echo in the distance.

For some reason, your house is spared, but in the end, you are separated from your wife and daughter, and all of you are sold into slavery.

For five years, you slave away for a crude, godless, angry, lustful Danish lord doing everything he tells you in fear of being whipped or worse. You cry at the thought of your wife and daughters' fate—knowing that for them, death would be a mercy.

One day you decide you've had enough, and you're going to let your master kill you because you want to be reunited with your family.

As your master orders you to do something, and as you are about to say, "No!" a trumpet sounds in the distance. You recognize it as the Saxon king. You realize that you are saved.

An hour later, your captors are dead, and you are looking in the eyes of your family who are miraculously alive and unharmed.

The end.

If you have been set free, as the character in our metaphor was, would you ever choose to return to your horrible life as a slave? Of course not.

Why do we return to our life of slavery to sin or Law after being set free by Jesus?

But perhaps you don't even know how incredible freedom is. Place your faith in Jesus! He died to make freedom a reality. Apart from faith in Him, you are cursed to remain a slave. Trust Him today!

# Reflection Questions

1. How does today's text show Paul's love for the church?
2. Can you summarize Paul's argument to this point in Galatians?
3. Why does Paul use an allegory in this passage?
4. Is there slavery in your life you need to throw out, whether doctrinal or practical?
5. Whose child are you? Have you placed your faith in Jesus yet?

Lesson 12: Galatians 4:21-31

# Praying the Text

*Jesus,*
*Thank You for freedom. Please help me to live in freedom. Help me to throw out of my life anything that might be holding me back from experiencing true freedom. I need Your grace. I cannot be set free on my own. Help me. I love You.*

# Lesson 13

## Galatians 5:1

[1][The] Messiah set us free for freedom; therefore you all must stand, and you all must not be again entangled in a yoke of slavery.

# The Main Thing

Have you ever received counsel that surprised you, but that later proved invaluable in a totally different situation? I have. It went like this: In the second half of 2012, I fell for a girl really hard, and it did not go at all according to plan. In reflecting on the results of that situation, I detected idolatry in my heart towards relationships. As such, my resolution for 2013 was, "I'm not going to date for a year."

But as it goes with the typical twenty-year-old male, another girl popped up on the radar less than 3 months into 2013. I told myself: "I have got to stick to my resolution, or else I'm not a man of my word." I talked to my pastor about it, and he told me something that I will never forget: "Stop it. You're a hard-wired legalist; you need to loosen up. Perhaps God brought this girl into your life to be your wife? If you stick to your self-made plan, you could seriously limit yourself. Go check out Galatians 5:1." (It wasn't those exact words of course, but the basic gist of his message was just that.) I read Galatians 5:1 — and maybe the whole book as well afterward — and since then, Galatians 5:1 has been etched in the back of my mind.

Fast forward two and a half years to the summer of 2015, and the girl from 2013 is no longer present in my life. However, I was receiving counsel from a pastor at another church — no longer in California, but rather in Missouri — and something seemed very off about the counsel I was receiving. The counsel was directly related to escaping the clutches of specific sin patterns, but looking back, I wouldn't call it counsel, I'd use a different word that starts with the letter "C." Condemnation.

Week in and week out it was the same: If I had not stood well, it would be a barrage of, "How can you know you are saved?" type statements; if I had stood well, the comments sounded as if he assumed I was a new believer as of that week. It got to the point where I was thoroughly surprised that I was even accepted as a member of the church (since membership is for believers only). Depression set in as a result of the counsel I was receiving — counsel that was devoid of hope, counsel that was devoid of Christ, counsel that was devoid of calling a sinner to both repentance and faith in the Gospel.

One day that summer, I sat down in the park with my Bible and a notebook, and I found myself in the book of Galatians. I started at the beginning and read the whole book, but the verse that stuck out to me more than any other was Galatians 5:1, and my pastor's counsel from 2013 reverberated back through my mind, "Don't submit to the yoke this current pastor is putting on you" (the application I discovered based on the situation and the previous counsel from my Gospel-saturated California pastor). As such, I left that church in August of 2015.

I share all of that to explain what Paul is saying in our passage today. It's only one verse today, but this one verse is where the whole letter hinges. Everything prior leads to it, and everything after flows out of it.

Paul writes in Galatians 5:1,

[The] Messiah set us free for freedom; therefore you all must stand, and you all must not be again entangled in a yoke of slavery.

Most commentators want to lump this verse in with 4:21-31, which is understandable: It ends by saying, "We are not children of [the] slave-girl, but of the free-woman," as if to say, "You have been set free." Paul concludes that section by essentially asking, "Why, then, do some of you want to go back to being like Ishmael, who was a slave, an outcast, and separated from God?"[1]

The subject of Galatians 5:1 is "[The] Messiah." Jesus is the one who is responsible for the Christian's freedom. This is very important in this day and age where it is too readily accepted—even in Christian circles—that you need to do your best and let Jesus do the rest.[2] That theology has no business at all in our churches. How much time did the thief on the cross have to do his best?

Paul hits the nail on the head in Galatians 5:1 by saying that it is Jesus—and Jesus alone—who is responsible for the Christian's freedom. Jesus said Himself, "You can do nothing without Me" (John 15:5), which means no thing; you cannot do anything apart from Jesus. He said in John 8:36, "Therefore, if the Son sets you free, you really will be free." Before Christ, we can't make ourselves free; after (with) Christ, we can't be more free. Jesus is the subject of Paul's sentence in Galatians 5:1. He is the One responsible for our freedom. And He is the One we must hold out to people regardless of the sin they struggle with.

---

[1] John MacArthur, *Galatians*, 128.

[2] One of my first mentors who came out of Mormonism once told me that one of the Mormon's beliefs is, "Do your best and let Jesus do the rest."

## Lesson 13: Galatians 5:1

What has Christ done for us according to this verse? "[The] Messiah set us free." Luther explains:

> There is also another kind of "liberty," when people obey neither the laws of God nor the laws of men, but do as they please. This carnal liberty the people want in our day. We are not now speaking of this liberty. Neither are we speaking of civil liberty.
>
> *Paul is speaking of a far better liberty*, the liberty "wherewith Christ hath made us free," not from material bonds, not from the Babylonian captivity, not from the tyranny of the Turks, but *from the eternal wrath of God*.[3]

When I argue for the utmost importance of the liberty that Christ has brought us, I cannot emphasize enough that this liberty does not mean that drunkenness, sexual deviance, or using filthy language are allowable for the believer. John Calvin said, "Our adversaries raise a prejudice against us among ignorant people, as if the whole object of our pursuit were licentiousness, which is the relaxation of all discipline. But wise and skillful persons are aware that this is one of the most important doctrines connected with salvation."[4] Paul will go on to say that this freedom cannot possibly excuse a Christian to live in sinfulness (cf. 5:13). In fact, given that the Galatians had never been under the Law before being converted, when Paul says, "You all must not be again entangled in a yoke of slavery" (emphasis added), he is actively calling their pagan practices an enslaving yoke that needs to be kept off.[5]

When I had voiced my concern to the judgmental pastor back in 2015, I was told that I was wrong, because putting more emphasis on my status as a believer in Christ would mean that I could justify my sin and would not take it seriously as a result. Paul would be incredulous at such a response because Paul is here teaching, "Christ set you free! Don't fear God as your enemy any longer! Cling to Him as your Father!"

---

[3] Martin Luther, *A Commentary on St. Paul's Epistle to the Galatians*. Emphasis added.

[4] John Calvin, *Commentaries on the Epistles of Paul to the Galatians and Ephesians*, 1548 (Grand Rapids: Christian Classics Ethereal Library, 2009), Kindle.

[5] J. B. Lightfoot, *The Epistle of St. Paul to the Galatians*, 185. Commenting on "again," he writes, "Having escaped from the slavery of Heathenism, they would fain bow to the slavery of Judaism."

Paul would emphasize freedom (not Law) because freedom proves Christ's victory, and Law only repeatedly shows us our failures. Knowing that Christ is victorious is a much better motivator to holiness than fearing that I will mess up again!

Paul writes, "for freedom," repeating the word "free" because he wants to engrain it in our minds. The Galatians are free. We are free. They didn't need Judaism to help them be free. We don't need lists of "thou shalt" and "thou shalt not" to be free. We are in Christ, and He won our freedom so that we would be free. The question is: Have we started truly living in this freedom? Spend some time reflecting on that today. What enslaves you? A sin? Maybe a good, spiritual thing done for the entirely wrong reason?

Christ is our hope! He set us free. Let's live in that freedom.

Paul brings in a "therefore," which proves that we needed the first four chapters to know what this is here for.[6] And, as such, it made my study of this book—verse by verse—absolutely vital to doing this passage justice today. One commentator said, "If Galatians is the Magna Carta of Christian liberty, then [Galatians 5:1] has reason to be considered one of the key verses of the epistle."[7] A short review will suffice to prove this point.[8]

The introduction demonstrates that Christ gave Himself so that we can be free—rescued "from the present evil age" (cf. 1:1-5). The next verses clearly show that the Judaizers' changing of the Gospel was opposed to standing firm in freedom (cf. 1:6-10). Then, in the first section of Paul's detailed chronology, we see that the faith Paul preached was agreed upon by the church, and is the Gospel that is presented throughout this book (cf. 1:11-24). Paul's second section of detailed chronology explains that he withstood all attempts to overthrow Christian freedom (cf. 2:1-5). Paul's third section of chronology proves that even the apostles agreed with Paul's Gospel of freedom (cf. 2:6-10). Paul's final section of chronology explains that Paul opposed anyone who undermined the Gospel's freedom and availability to all, regardless of their "status" (cf. 2:11-14). Paul then goes on to explicitly claim that freedom comes through justification, which is found in Christ and not in the Law (cf. 2:15-21). Paul asks a rhetorical question in 3:1 that proves

---

[6] Whenever you study Scripture, and you find a "Therefore," you need to think about what it is there for.

[7] Quoted in David Platt and Tony Merida, *Christ-Centered Exposition – Exalting Jesus in Galatians* (Nashville: Broadman & Holman, 2014), WORDsearch, 96.

[8] I will stick to sections, even though I could show almost verse by verse at points how everything in this letter screams, "5:1 is the thesis statement."

## Lesson 13: Galatians 5:1

someone was guilty of placing them in this yoke of slavery. Paul spends a lengthy amount of time differentiating between faith in the promise and works of the Law (cf. 3:2-14). Jesus is the promise about whom the Old Testament Law spoke (cf. 3:15-18). The Law enslaves, but Jesus frees (cf. 3:19-26). Slaves don't inherit, but free people do (cf. 3:27-4:7). Everyone is a slave of something, and for that reason, everyone needs Jesus to free them (cf. 4:8-11). Paul tells the Galatians they have to deal with God, not him, if they stay enslaved (cf. 4:12-20). Finally, Paul even quotes the Law to prove that it is better to be free (cf. 4:21-31). And thus, we arrive at 5:1.

Paul then gives a command, the first one that would have a visible result (cf. 4:12 and 4:21 for the only other two commands, but notice the difference between those and this one). I see this command being yelled by Paul: "Stand!" In understanding the force of this command, Martin Luther is again helpful. "'Be steadfast, not careless. Lie not down and sleep, but stand up. Be watchful. Hold fast the liberty wherewith Christ hath made you free.' Those who loll cannot keep this liberty. Satan hates the light of the Gospel. When it begins to shine a little he fights against it with might and main."[9]

Calvin adds, "It is an invaluable blessing, in defense of which it is our duty to fight, even to death; since not only the highest temporal considerations, but our eternal interests also, animate us to the contest."[10]

If we stop fighting for freedom in Christ, it is to our detriment. If we sit down in this fight, our flesh will overtake us and bind us down again. We must watch out for both legalistic pressure and licentious pressure, refusing both extremes, because both destroy our freedom.

Paul concludes the verse by telling the Galatians to not "be again entangled in a yoke of slavery." There are two things to say about this. The first is related to how a person gets in a yoke of slavery, and the second is about the yoke itself.

First, slavery is something that is done to a person, not something that a person chooses. However, as is apparent in this context, Paul is warning the Galatians that the only way to avoid being enslaved again is to stand. We must stand firm and not allow anyone to place a restrictive, condemning collar around us.

The "yoke of slavery" Paul is talking about avoiding at all costs is directly contrasted to another yoke mentioned in Scripture. Jesus tells of it in Matthew 11:28-30. "Come to Me, all of you who are weary and burdened, and

---

[9] Martin Luther, *A Commentary on St. Paul's Epistle to the Galatians*.
[10] John Calvin, *Commentaries on the Epistles of Paul to the Galatians and Ephesians*.

I will give you rest. All of you, take up My yoke and learn from Me, because I am gentle and humble in heart, and you will find rest for yourselves. For My yoke is easy and My burden is light." This is the yoke the believer in Jesus is called to wear. The burden Jesus speaks of is the burden of walking rightly as a light in this fallen world. But this burden is light because He is yoked with us, walking with us and enabling us to accomplish the task. If left to our own strength, we would fail. Paul says, "Don't submit to a yoke of slavery, because that yoke will kill you—fear, depression, hopelessness. Instead, submit to Christ's yoke, which is easy and freeing, especially in comparison to the yoke of slavery."

So with all that said: How do we stand? How do we prevent ourselves from being placed back in slavery?

We must preach the Gospel to ourselves every day.

But here's my question for you: Do you know the Gospel well enough to preach it?

It can be as simple as quoting Romans 5:8 and 10:9 and recommitting yourself each morning to an active lifestyle of saying, "The Gospel is true about me because Jesus is my Lord!" Or it can be as detailed as the answer another of my California pastors gave me when I conducted a survey this week.[11] He said the following:

> The Gospel is the good news of salvation in Jesus Christ. It is set against the bad news that all of humanity has sinned and has fallen short of God's glory. We all sin in various ways, and are therefore guilty before God and are at war with Him, even if we don't realize it. Jesus came to remedy this. He is the 2nd person of the Trinity, who came down as a man, born of a virgin (thus not inheriting the sin nature), and lived a perfectly obedient life to God. On the appointed day, He traded places with sinners by dying on the cross. There, the Father poured His wrath on the Son for our sins. After Jesus paid all the debt of everyone who would ever believe in Him, He died, thus completing the transaction. On the third day, He rose from the dead, was glorified, and later ascended to the right hand of the Father. Everyone who places their trust in Jesus and surrenders to Him as Lord will be saved. So the fornicator can get right with God by simply trusting Jesus for salvation, and believing that Christ truly paid His

---

[11] This Lesson was originally published as a blogpost on January 14, 2017.

debt and truly conquered death. If the fornicator gives his heart to the Lord, then his sins will be forgiven.[12]

The Reformation claimed that salvation was in Christ alone by grace alone through faith alone. The emphasis of our Gospel preaching must be on faith. It cannot be on the visible repentance that necessarily follows true faith. If we preach and teach about true belief, people will understand true repentance. If we have to repent before we can be saved, then we'd never be saved, because the Christian life is a life of continual repentance. Until my dying day, I'll be repenting, but it is my faith, placed squarely in the finished work of Jesus—who set me free—on July 1, 2010, that made me right with God. True faith leads to freedom, and true freedom is held onto by repentance, and true repentance is the other side of the coin that is faith.

The answer to the question, "How do I get right with God?" does not change if someone has two decades to live as opposed to two minutes. Belief in the finished work of Jesus is all that is required. Anyone who teaches otherwise needs to be thrown out of their pulpits, question their calling to ministry, and ask themselves, "Have I really placed my faith in Christ alone for salvation, or am I secretly also trusting myself?" This is why I left that church in 2015: They weren't encouraging me toward Christ's yoke, but rather toward a yoke of slavery. If you're in a similar church, find one that preaches the supremacy of Christ, that preaches the Gospel, and that pleads with people to believe. Only then can you stand safe against a possible lapse into a yoke of slavery.

I conclude with lyrics from Hillsong's song, "Christ is Enough." The bridge says,

*I have decided to follow Jesus,*
*no turning back, no turning back.*[13]

That's my anthem. Is it yours?

I pray it is, as I pray that it becomes such for every church in this nation that we call America.

---

[12] Pastor Stephen Feinstein, email to author, January 11, 2017.

[13] Hillsong Music, "Christ Is Enough," *Glorious Ruins* (Sydney, Australia: Hillsong Music, 2013), Spotify.

# No Turning Back!

Slavery is a terrible thing. By now, you're probably tired of hearing about slavery. But Paul brought it up again in this verse, so I must discuss it.

> [The] Messiah set us free for freedom; therefore you all must stand, and you all must not be again entangled in a yoke of slavery.

Up to this point in the letter, he has been focusing on legalistic tendencies as enslaving. But in the following sections, he will discuss other forms of slavery.

Some people are enslaved to sex. Some people are enslaved to alcohol. Some people are enslaved to drugs. Some people are enslaved to attention. Some people are enslaved to lying. Some people are enslaved to cursing.

And some people try to say, "Well, if Jesus has set me free, then it doesn't matter what I do now."

Paul would flip his lid if he heard this. Romans 6:1-2 proves this to be a fact. "What should we say then? Should we continue in sin so that grace may multiply? Absolutely not! How can we who died to sin still live in it?"

Sin is enslaving. Jesus said it Himself. "I assure you: Everyone who commits sin is a slave of sin" (John 8:34). So, if you excuse sin in the name of "Jesus will forgive me," you need to remember that Paul said, "You all must stand, and you all must not be again entangled in a yoke of slavery" (Galatians 5:1). If you are excusing your sin, then you need to remember the Gospel. Here it is: Jesus goes on to say, "Therefore, if the Son sets you free, you really will be free" (John 8:36).

Jesus died on the cross to put sin to death. He rose again to prove that sin and death have been defeated. If you look longingly on sin, then you do not know Jesus.

Renew your faith in Jesus today. Beg Him to help you stand firm against all forms of slavery. You don't need sin. You don't need rules. You need Jesus!

Trust Him today!

# Reflection Questions

1. How does today's text show Paul's love for the church?

2. Can you explain how this verse is the hinge to understanding the whole letter?
3. Is your preferred slavery more law-based or sin-based?
4. What does it look like in your life to stand firm?
5. Have you placed your faith in Jesus yet?

# Praying the Text

*Jesus,*

*Thank You for the freedom of the Gospel! Please help me never to use that freedom as a cover-up for sin. I need to stand firm in You every day! I need to know You better, and I need to better love You for this to be a reality. Help me to stand. Be more lovely to me than both sin and Law. You are glorious!*

# Lesson 14

## Galatians 5:2-12

²Behold, I, myself—Paul—say to you all that if you might get circumcised then [the] Messiah is of no benefit for you all. ³Now I testify again that every man who is getting circumcised is obligated to keep the whole Law. ⁴You all were cut off from [the] Messiah, the ones of you all who are trying to be made righteous by Law; you all fell away from grace. ⁵For we ourselves are eagerly awaiting faith, hope, and righteousness by [the] Spirit. ⁶For in [the] Messiah Jesus neither circumcision nor uncircumcision is any influencer, instead faith working itself out through love.

⁷You all were running well, [so] who cut in on you all to persuade you all to disobey the truth? ⁸The persuasion [is] not from the One who called you all. ⁹"A little yeast spreads throughout the whole lump [of dough]." ¹⁰I myself have confidence in [the] Lord that you all will think nothing different, but the one who is troubling you all will bear the judgment, whoever he might be. ¹¹But if I myself, brothers, still preach circumcision, then why am I still being persecuted? Then the scandal of the cross has been abolished. ¹²I wish that the ones who are troubling you all might also emasculate themselves.

# Turning Up the Heat

There once was a man carrying a massive burden upon his back. He had just set out on a lengthy journey. The burden was doing nothing but slowing him down, tripping him up, and making him lose his footing. The man's name was Christian. So it delighted him greatly when a stranger approached him and asked, "How now, good fellow, whither away after this burdened manner?" When Christian explained that he would love to get some counsel, the man replied, "I would advise thee, then, that thou with all speed get thyself rid of thy burden; for thou wilt never be settled in thy mind till then; nor canst thou enjoy the benefits of the blessing which God hath bestowed upon thee till then." Christian then explains that he had already been sent toward a solution by one named Evangelist. The stranger cautioned him against his advice by saying, "Thou art like to meet with in the way which thou goest, wearisomeness, painfulness, hunger, perils, nakedness, sword, lions, dragons, darkness, and, in a word, death, and what not." He continues:

> "Why wilt thou seek for ease this way, seeing so many dangers attend it? Especially, since (hadst thou but patience to hear me) I could direct thee to the obtaining of what thou desirest, without the dangers that thou in this way wilt run thyself into; yea, and the remedy is at hand. Besides, I will add, that instead of those dangers, thou shalt meet with much safety, friendship, and content."
>
> Christian: "Pray sir, open this secret to me."
>
> "Why, in yonder village (the village is named Morality) there dwells a gentleman, whose name is Legality, a very judicious man, and a man of a very good name, that has skill to help men off with such burdens as thine are from their shoulders; yea to my knowledge, he hath done a great deal of good this way; aye, and besides, he hath skill to cure those that are somewhat crazed in their wits with their burdens. To him, as I said, thou mayest go, and be helped presently. His house is not quite a mile from this place; and if he should not be at home himself, he hath a pretty young man to his son, whose name is Civility, that can do it (to speak on) as well as the old gentleman

> himself: there, I say, thou mayest be eased of thy burden; and if thou art not minded to go back to thy former habitation, (as indeed I would not wish thee,) thou mayest send for thy wife and children to thee to this village, where there are houses now standing empty, one of which thou mayest have at reasonable rates: provision is there also cheap and good; and that which will make thy life the more happy is, to be sure there thou shalt live by honest neighbors, in credit and good fashion."
>
> . . .
>
> So Christian turned out of his way to go to Mr. Legality's house for help: but, behold, when he was got now hard by the hill, it seemed so high, and also that side of it that was next the wayside did hang so much over, that Christian was afraid to venture further, lest the hill should fall on his head; wherefore there he stood still, and he wot not what to do. Also his burden now seemed heavier to him than while he was in his way. There came also flashes of fire, out of the hill, that made Christian afraid that he should be burnt. Here therefore he did sweat and quake for fear.

Just then, Evangelist returned, and he rebuked Christian for listening to the stranger:

> The man that met thee is one Worldly Wiseman, and rightly is he so called; partly because he savoreth only the doctrine of this world (therefore he always goes to the town of Morality to church); and partly because he loveth that doctrine best, for it saveth him from the cross. And because he is of this carnal temper, therefore he seeketh to pervert my ways, though right.
>
> . . .
>
> He to whom thou wast sent for ease, being by name Legality, is the son of the bond-woman which now is, and is in bondage with her children, and is, in a mystery, this Mount Sinai, which thou hast feared will fall on thy head. Now if she with her children are in bondage, how canst thou expect by them to be made free? This Legality, therefore, is not able to set thee free from thy burden. No man was as yet ever rid of his burden by him; no, nor ever is like to be: ye cannot be justified by the works of the law; for by the deeds of the law no man living can be rid of his burden: Therefore Mr. Worldly Wiseman

## Lesson 14: Galatians 5:2-12

is an alien, and Mr. Legality is a cheat; and for his son Civility, notwithstanding his simpering looks, he is but a hypocrite, and cannot help thee. Believe me, there is nothing in all this noise that thou hast heard of these sottish men, but a design to beguile thee of thy salvation, by turning thee from the way in which I had set thee.

And thus, John Bunyan describes the book of Galatians in allegorical form in the opening chapter of his famous novel, *The Pilgrim's Progress*.[1]

I share this excerpt from Bunyan's famous novel because it clearly describes what Paul is seeking to prove in the eleven verses of today's text. To leave the way of grace and promise, and to enter into the way of works and Law is to desert the way of Christ. It accomplishes nothing, it leads to fear—not peace—and it removes a person from the path of life.

Last time, we saw that we have been set free because of Christ, and as such, we should refuse to submit again to slavery. This time, Paul elaborates by showing what it looks like if we ignore his advice in 5:1.

Verses 2-4 discuss the futility of trying to achieve righteousness by the Law:

> Behold, I, myself—Paul—say to you all that if you might get circumcised then [the] Messiah is of no benefit for you all. Now I testify again that every man who is getting circumcised is obligated to keep the whole Law. You all were cut off from [the] Messiah, the ones of you all who are trying to be made righteous by Law; you all fell away from grace.

Before diving into the above verses, it is necessary to explain why "circumcision" pops up five times in these eleven verses, while it has only occurred six times to this point in the first four chapters of Galatians. The earlier grouping of the circumcision discussion was when Paul was describing his time with the Jerusalem church (cf. 2:1-14). He brought it up there because this was the issue that spawned the book of Galatians. It is the issue described in Acts 15:1, when Luke writes, "Some men came down from Judea and began to teach the brothers: 'Unless you are circumcised according to the custom prescribed by Moses, you cannot be saved!'" Paul started in chapters 1-2 by

---

[1] John Bunyan, *The Pilgrim's Progress*, 1678 (New Kensington, PA: Whitaker House, 1973), 15-24.

explaining his story—from persecutor to passionate preacher—and he explained that the Gospel that Christ gave to him had nothing to do with circumcision. Then, in chapters 3-4, he described the theological proof that works of Law have never contributed anything to salvation. And now, he returns to the initial discussion of circumcision, before diving into a whole slew of application.

It boils down to the question: "What are you trusting in for your righteousness?"

While God had given circumcision to the Jews as a symbol of His faithfulness to His covenant, "most Jews looked on it as having spiritual value in itself." MacArthur continues, "The symbolism of cutting off the male foreskin was to be a constant reminder to all generations of Jews, for whom God desired to cut away the evil from their hearts."[2]

So, circumcision in itself is not legalism, just like refraining from alcohol, tobacco, filthy language, or dating is not legalism. However, if you look at your life and say, "I am circumcised, so now God will accept me," or "I have never smoked, drank, or cussed; God has to accept me," or "I haven't dated in six years so God must think I'm extra spiritual," you are being legalistic. And if your refraining from those things causes you to heap judgment on another brother or sister, who may be struggling in one of those areas (recovering alcoholic, smoking quitter, or ex-sailor mouth) or who maybe doesn't view those things as sinful, then you are definitely being legalistic and wrong.

Paul here says that if you look to these things for your righteous standing before God, then you really have no need for Christ. Paul is saying that Christ can't add anything to you. Paul is not saying that you don't need Christ in this situation, but rather that "a supplemented Christ is a supplanted Christ. To trust in human effort is to trust in law, which is totally incompatible with grace . . . Whether before or after conversion, trust in human works of any kind is a barrier between a person and Christ and results in unacceptable legalism."[3]

The reason why Christ is of no benefit to this kind of person is because if you want to be a Law-follower in *part*, Paul essentially says, "then you have to be a Law-follower in *all*."

---

[2] John MacArthur, *Galatians*, 132.
[3] John MacArthur, *Galatians*, 134.

## Lesson 14: Galatians 5:2-12

Martin Luther said, "If we permit Moses to rule over us in one thing, we must obey him in all things."[4]

If you want to follow circumcision for salvation, then you must also follow all the sacrifices of Leviticus for salvation—in addition to the rest of Genesis to Deuteronomy. The only way to be saved is to realize that you can't perfectly keep the Law. So, if you can't do a part, then you've broken all of it (cf. James 2:10), and you need Christ and Christ alone. If, after trusting Christ alone, you then revert back to trusting yourself, then you are essentially saying, "Jesus, I don't really need You; I got this," which then returns you to the bondage of keeping the whole Law, under which you can do nothing but fail.

Paul essentially says, "You are no longer associating yourselves with Jesus if you are relying on the Law."

To try to be sanctified by works of the Law apart from active, real faith in Christ is to say, "I got this on my own, Jesus. Don't bother me. I don't want to associate with You anymore."

Paul says that if someone has this attitude—proven because they are not standing in freedom (cf. 5:1)—then they "fell away from grace." This is a harsh word that sounds like Paul is saying someone can lose their salvation. However, that is not the right way to understand it. Paul wants the Galatians and us to be sure we have the salvation that we think we have.

I love Bunyan's book for this very reason. I love the metaphor of the Christian life as a journey. Salvation is a lifelong thing. It is founded on a past event, worked out in the present, and finally received ultimately in the future. The fact that Christian was led off the path does not mean that he lost his salvation; the fact that he is pointed back to the path proves that everyone strays at times. However, it is in the times of straying that we are forced to ask ourselves, "Is this salvation that I claim to possess real?"

If Christian would have stayed off the path and continued down Worldly Wiseman's road, then he would have never arrived at the Celestial City, and it would have proven that he never had salvation. For this reason, we must always ask ourselves when we stumble on tough verses like this, "Am I on the right path, or have I erred somewhere?"[5] Paul wants the Galatians to know they are in a precarious place if they go ahead and listen to

---

[4] Martin Luther, *A Commentary on St. Paul's Epistle to the Galatians*.

[5] Hebrews 6 comes to mind clearly on this point, along with several other passages as well.

the Judaizers; however, the next verse shows the alternative to justification (or sanctification) by works.

Paul says in verse 5:

> For we ourselves are eagerly awaiting faith, hope, and righteousness by [the] Spirit.

This righteousness is both justifying righteousness and sanctifying righteousness. Both justification (positional righteousness before God) and sanctification (practical righteousness in daily life) must be by Christ alone and not by works of Law (the Greek word is simply "righteousness"). Paul trusted the Spirit to make him righteous. Who are we trusting? If we aren't trusting the Spirit, we are in a heap of trouble according to these verses (if we don't repent and turn back to Christ).

Take some time now to ask the Lord to reveal to you the source of your motivation for righteousness.

Verse 6 is the primary application from this letter that Paul will expound throughout the rest of Galatians:

> For in [the] Messiah Jesus neither circumcision nor uncircumcision is any influencer, instead faith working itself out through love.

Now, I know what you're thinking: "I thought you said 5:1 was the main point?"

It is. Paul's statement in 5:1 is the main point of Galatians. However, the way that main point is applied in daily life is described clearly in 5:6-6:15. Paul could have simply written:

> [The] Messiah set us free for freedom; therefore you all must stand, and you all must not be again entangled in a yoke of slavery . . . For in [the] Messiah Jesus neither circumcision nor uncircumcision is any influencer, instead faith working itself out through love . . . For you all, yourselves, were called to freedom, brothers; only not the freedom of an occasion for the flesh, instead, [the freedom] to serve one another through love.
> (5:1, 6, 13.)

## Lesson 14: Galatians 5:2-12

However, he first wanted to reiterate the foolishness of trusting in works (cf. 5:2-5), and then the folly of false teaching (cf. 5:7-12), before laying out the application (cf. 5:13-6:10).

Interestingly, 6:15 says, "For neither circumcision nor uncircumcision is anything, instead a new creation." It is almost identical to 5:6. This is called an inclusio, and it means that the main point is the same for everything inside of this section: "Faith working itself out through love."

Paul essentially says, "If you're circumcised already, so what! If you're not circumcised already, so what!" To parse it into modern parlance, "If you've kept yourself totally sexually pure, so what! If you've come from a shady past sexually, so what!" Paul then explains what does matter: "Faith working itself out through love." This means that whatever you used to find identity in—circumcision, uncircumcision, purity of body, total promiscuousness—no longer matters. Your identity is now Christ. You live as He lives in this world (cf. 1 John 4:17). For the formerly promiscuous person, this means that promiscuity is at an end: promiscuity is not love! Verses 13-15 (Lesson 15) will elaborate greatly on this love concept.[6]

With Paul's discussion set up to lay out a ton of application, he pauses in verses 7-12 to speak to the Judaizers. He does this in a backhanded way by questioning the Galatians, but his emphasis is on the Judaizers.

> You all were running well, [so] who cut in on you all to persuade you all to disobey the truth? The persuasion [is] not from the One who called you all. 'A little yeast spreads throughout the whole lump [of dough].' I myself have confidence in [the] Lord that you all will think nothing different, but the one who is troubling you all will bear the judgment, whoever he might be. But if I myself, brothers, still preach circumcision, then why am I still being persecuted? Then the scandal of the cross has been abolished. I wish that the ones who are troubling you all might also emasculate themselves.

This section immediately brings 3:1 back to mind. Paul there asked, "What witch cursed you all?" Here he essentially asks, "Who cut in on your race and tripped you up? You were doing well." The rhetorical answer is the same in both instances: The false teachers known as the Judaizers. Paul answers this question himself by saying, "The persuasion [is] not from the One

---

[6] Cf. Joshua Wingerd, "Love Wins: Paul and the Content of the Earliest Christian Gospel," *Academia* (November 8, 2015), https://www.academia.edu/25063760/Love_Wins.

who called you all." He says, "You didn't learn this from me, the one God used to call you vocally, and you certainly didn't learn this from God, the One who called you spiritually behind my audible vocals." Paul points out that the hindrance the Galatians are now dealing with was dangerous, and the metaphor he uses in verse 9 proves this. It is a favorite metaphor that Paul uses to describe the subtlety and danger and pervasiveness of sin (cf. 1 Corinthians 5:6-8). It doesn't just stay in one person; it spreads to all until it rises and becomes visible. Paul is here trying to nip it in the bud before it gets worse for these believers.

Paul makes an interesting statement at the end of verse 10: "The one who is troubling you all will bear the judgment, whoever he might be." This is a warning to anyone who teaches the Scripture. It is a specific warning to anyone who pushes for legalism instead of Jesus Christ. If we are not pointing people to Christ, but instead telling them to try harder, do better, hold out longer, then we are in danger of judgment. It may not be eternal damnation in hell, but it might be; we don't know (cf. discussion on verse 4 above).

James wrote, "Not many should become teachers, my brothers, knowing that we will receive a stricter judgment" (3:1), and Jesus said, "But whoever causes the downfall of one of these little ones who believe in Me—it would be better for him if a heavy millstone were hung around his neck and he were thrown into the sea" (Mark 9:42).

Paul concludes the section by asking rhetorically why he's persecuted if his ministry is a ministry of circumcision? He explains that he is persecuted for the very reason that he does not promote a circumcision Gospel. He clings wholeheartedly to the scandal of the cross—a scandal because it totally undermines everything a legalistic Jew would hold dear. Again, MacArthur is helpful: "The Jews were scandalized by the cross because it nullified not only the Mosaic law but also their highly revered rabbinic traditions."[7] And Paul concludes his underhanded comments to the Judaizers by showing just how opposed he is to their "gospel" of circumcision: "They'd be quieter if the knife would slip while they are circumcising themselves!"

Paul's gotten pretty fired up in this letter, and verse 12 probably marks the high point of his heat. He has said that submission to the Law is to deny Christ's power, so if you submit to the Law in one place, then you have to submit to the Law in every place.

---

[7] John Macarthur, *Galatians*, 142.

However, before we all say, "Hurray! The Christian doesn't have to follow any Law," let's reflect on Galatians 5:14 until we get to Lesson 15: "For all of the Law has been summed up in one word, in this one, 'You all must love your neighbor as yourself.'"

Paul says that our faith should be "working itself out through love." How loving will you be this week?

# Living in the Future

Everybody has a past. There is no escaping this truth. We all have things that we have clung to our whole lives. These might be sins (especially if you didn't grow up in the church), or it might be your perceived goodness (especially if you did grow up in the church). But even if you did grow up in the church, you might hold onto sin, and even if you didn't grow up in the church, you might hold onto your perceived goodness.

No matter which way you happen to lean, the simple fact of the matter is that while Christianity is rooted in a past event (the crucifixion and resurrection of Jesus), we are to look toward the future. We are to fix our eyes on Jesus, the author and perfecter of our faith (cf. Hebrews 12:2). He is in heaven, and He is going to come back again (in the future, cf. Revelation 22:20-21).

We cannot allow our pasts to hold us back. And we cannot live in the past. I know it's hard to move past it, but just because you always coped with anger and frustration by drinking a fifth of liquor doesn't mean that you still need to respond that way. That was the past. Jesus offers a new alternative. He told the woman caught in adultery, "Neither do I condemn you. Go, and from now on do not sin anymore" (John 8:11). In Jesus, there is no condemnation for the past, but there is an expectation for the future.

You cannot stop sinning on your own. Just like you cannot stop legalistically clinging to rules and regulations on your own. You need the Spirit.

But the crazy thing is that Paul has already told us how you can receive the Spirit: "In order that the blessing of Abraham might come to the nations through [the] Messiah Jesus, in order that we might *receive the promise of the Spirit through faith*." (Galatians 3:14).[8]

---

[8] Emphasis added.

You need the Spirit. Believe in Christ by faith today! His life, death, and resurrection! If you refuse to believe by faith, then you will have to bear the judgment of eternal separation from God! I don't want this for you. Come to Jesus today!

# Reflection Questions

1. How does today's text show Paul's love for the church?
2. What do you look at in your life to prove to yourself that you are a Christian? Would Paul say that you are right to do this?
3. How loving are you? How do you define love?
4. If you're a teacher of the Bible, does your teaching hint at receiving a good judgment or a negative one? If you're a listener, do your teachers preach faithfully, or are they in danger of a negative judgment?
5. Have you placed your faith in Jesus yet?

# Praying the Text

*Jesus,*

*Thank You for the Gospel. Please help me to live out of it every day. I need Your grace for this task. Please don't let me revert back to my old, past habits any longer. I need to live free every day! I trust You for this.*

# Lesson 15

## Galatians 5:13-15

[13]For you all, yourselves, were called to freedom, brothers; only not the freedom of an occasion for the flesh, instead, [the freedom] to serve one another through love. [14]For all of the Law has been summed up in one word, in this one, "You all must love your neighbor as yourself." [15]But if you all are biting and devouring one another, you all must watch out lest you all are destroyed by one another.

# Live in Love!

As you may know, liL fytr is my rapper moniker. I released a single discussing the biblical view of sexuality in 2017. One of the central lines in the song says:

> *The goal of the Christian life is love to all*
> *From the bedroom to the mall to the Islamic radical*[1]

And that line, by putting "bedroom" with "Islamic radical," forces one to ask, "How do you define 'love'?"

And my answer, hopefully made clear throughout the song, is that it is the same in both cases. It's a matter of thinking of others before yourself. And, if your curiosity has been piqued, search for the song wherever you find your music and give it a listen or two. The point for today is that Paul hits on the exact same theme in our Galatians passage.

Paul has thus far explained that the Law is not necessary for the believer. He's said that the Law exists to point us to Christ—showing us our need. He's demonstrated that all the Law is capable of is enacting slavery on those who are under it. Finally, in 5:1, he said that Christ set us free for the purpose of freedom. We are not to ever return to slavery. In 5:2-12, he showed one side of the slavery that we are not to return to, and he hinted at the path of real freedom (cf. 5:6). Here, in 5:13-15, Paul shows us the opposite side of slavery that we are not to return to (cf. 5:13a), and he elaborates on the path of real freedom (cf. 5:13b-15).

Paul begins by describing the other form of slavery that we are not to return to in 13a:

> For you all, yourselves, were called to freedom, brothers; only not the freedom of an occasion for the flesh.

---

[1] liL fytr, "Teach Me Some Respect (feat. Pastor Stephen Feinstein)," *Teach Me Some Respect* (Victorville, CA: FYTR records, 2017), Spotify.

He has now snuffed out any argument that would claim, "If there's no Law, then we can do whatever we want!"

Paul holds that living by the flesh is just as enslaving as the Law is enslaving, and Jesus agrees with him. Jesus said, "I assure you: Everyone who commits sin is a slave of sin" (John 8:34).

And I would point out that Jesus is not talking about the occasional slip into sin. He literally says, "Everyone who is doing sin." He explains in verse 36 that there's a difference between a lapse into sin and being a sin's slave: "Therefore, if the Son sets you free, you really will be free." The epistle of 1 John is helpful on this point. In 3:9, John writes what can be literally translated, "Everyone who has been born of God is not continually doing sin, because His seed abides in him; and he is not able, as a result continually to sin, because he has been born of God." Thus, the one who is not born of God *is* continually doing sin.[2] A literal translation of 1 John 2:1 highlights the difference and explains what a believer's sin looks like: "If anyone might sin, we have an Advocate with the Father, Jesus Christ the righteous."

While unbelievers are only able to sin—due to them being slaves of sin—believers do not have to sin. While unbelievers *do* sin—sin being the thing that is practiced—believers merely occasionally sin. While unbelievers are not born of God—not set free from slavery—believers are free, because they have been born of God. The word translated "sin" in 2:1 is in the subjunctive mood, which means it is not a necessary thing, which is why I translated it with the word "might."

The point being: If you're a believer, you're not a slave to sin. You don't have to continue in sin. If you do, and if you enjoy it—often thinking about it—then you should question whether or not you really have been born of God and set free. Just as much as it is slavery to submit to rules of Law, it is slavery to feed your selfish passions and desires. One commentator explains, "Later, the rabbis used various metaphors to describe the insidious enslavement of sin: 'At the beginning it is like a spider's thread, but finally it will be like a ship's rope' (R. Akiba), 'at the beginning it is like a guest, later it will become the ruler of the household' (R. Jicchaq)."[3]

Paul wants believers to have complete freedom. Flirting with sin and/or following Law is incompatible with freedom.

---

[2] The discussion comes down to this: Is sin an occasional action, or the thing that you do daily?

[3] Colin F. Kruse, *John: An Introduction and Commentary*, Tyndale New Testament Commentaries (Downers Grove, IL: InterVarsity Press, 2003), WORD*search*, 208.

## Lesson 15: Galatians 5:13-15

As such, Paul lays out the path to true freedom in 5:13b-14:

> Instead, [the freedom] to serve one another through love. For all of the Law has been summed up in one word, in this one, "You all must love your neighbor as yourself."

Right out of the gate, Paul defines love. He says, "Serve one another." This is the kind of love that Jesus describes in John 13:35: "By this all people will know that you are My disciples, if you have love for one another."[4]

And, as a side note, all sin is a lack of love—whether to God or to man. Fleshly living is loveless living. Paul says that freedom doesn't give an excuse to live by the flesh, and then says that freedom does allow us to serve (love) others. A practical application of what he's saying is that for any sin you are trying to defeat, you need to preach the lovelessness of the sin to yourself and look for the loving alternative to it.[5]

Paul sums up the Law of Moses by saying that it is fulfilled in one statement: Leviticus 19:18. "Love your neighbor as yourself; I am Yahweh." Now before explaining what this means, allow me to let John Calvin explain what it does not mean. He explains that most teachers in his day held that: "The love of ourselves must always hold the first rank." He then continues:

> This is not to interpret, but to subvert our Lord's words. They are asses, and have not even a spark of the love of their neighhour; for if the love of ourselves were the rule, it would follow that it is proper and holy, and is the object of the divine approbation. But we shall never love our neighbors with sincerity, according to our Lord's intention, till we have *corrected* the love of ourselves. The two affections are opposite and contradictory; for the love of ourselves leads us to neglect and despise others, — produces cruelty, covetousness, violence, deceit, and all kindred vices, — drives us to impatience, and arms us with the desire of revenge. *Our Lord therefore enjoins that it be changed into the love of our neighbor.*[6]

---

[4] Proof of this is found in the fact that if we look at this verse's wider context, it is found in a passage where Jesus serves His disciples by washing their feet. (Feet washing was cultural, and I firmly believe that it has zero business in our churches today, but that's a whole exegesis of John 13:3-15 in itself; it'll be a while before I get to it, but it is on my list.)

[5] I give examples of this strategy in the song I referenced at the beginning of this post.

[6] John Calvin, *Commentaries on the Epistles of Paul to the Galatians and Ephesians*. Emphasis added.

It is not a matter of loving ourselves more so we can love others better, but instead of asking ourselves, "How do I want to be loved?" This is further explained by Jesus Himself, in the Sermon on the Mount, when He says, "Therefore, whatever you want others to do for you, do also the same for them—this is the Law and the Prophets" (Matthew 7:12). Martin Luther explains,

> But what more needs to be said? You cannot find a better or nearer example than your own. If you want to know how you ought to love your neighbor, ask yourself how much you love yourself. If you were to get into trouble or danger, you would be glad to have the love and help of all men. You do not need any book of instructions to teach you how to love your neighbor. All you have to do is to look into your own heart, and it will tell you how you ought to love your neighbor as yourself.
>
> My neighbor is every person, especially those who need my help, as Christ explained in the tenth chapter of Luke. Even if a person has done me some wrong, or has hurt me in any way, he is still a human being with flesh and blood. As long as a person remains a human being, so long is he to be an object of our love.[7]

The whole Law is fulfilled in this statement. If we assume, for the sake of keeping this concise, that the entirety of the Law is Exodus 20:2-17, then the reason for the Ten Commandments is to protect our neighbors (and us by extension). Paul explains in Romans 13:9-10, "The commandments: Do not commit adultery; do not murder; do not steal; do not covet; and whatever other commandment—all are summed up by this: Love your neighbor as yourself. Love does no wrong to a neighbor. Love, therefore, is the fulfillment of the law." How much easier is it to say, "Love your neighbor," than, "Thou shalt not do $x$, $y$, $z$"? The burden of worrying about all the things you need to do or not do are condensed down to the following question: What is the most loving thing to do in this situation?

MacArthur explains, "When a Christian genuinely loves others, he fulfills all the moral elements of the Mosaic law."[8]

Paul then concludes today's passage with a warning:

---

[7] Martin Luther, *A Commentary on St. Paul's Epistle to the Galatians*.
[8] John MacArthur, *Galatians*, 148.

## Lesson 15: Galatians 5:13-15

> But if you all are biting and devouring one another, you all must watch out lest you all are destroyed by one another.

When love is lacking, this is the picture that emerges. The word translated "bite" is often used of snakes. "Paul is . . . referring to conduct more fitting to wild animals than to brothers and sisters in Christ."[9]

Unfortunately, this verse too accurately describes a lot of churches today. Sometimes, it's due to theological disagreements, but other times it's due to people not thinking of others ahead of themselves. And here's the thing: People are too good at preaching, "Love others selflessly," but not good at all at practicing what they preach.

We can allow others to be bitten and devoured if we aren't serving them through love, if we reason, "I'll let someone else care for that person; it's not my responsibility." This is passive biting and devouring, which is still just as sinful. Galatians 6:1 proves this: If we aren't carrying others' burdens, we're allowing them to drown, and we're not acting like Christ to them (cf. Matthew 11:28-30).

If every member of Christ's church loved biblically—thinking of others first, as Paul has described in this section—just imagine how beautiful the church would be. It might actually be attractive to the culture, and it might grow without requiring the aid of gimmick advertising and meatless preaching (cf. Hebrews 5:12-14).

Paul, through these three verses, would equate not loving others—allowing them to be bitten and devoured either actively or passively—with being fleshly. The very last thing that freedom in Christ can possibly mean is the freedom to neglect actively loving others by serving them. Love is not a noun; it is a verb! We have to practice it! To fail to exercise selfless, sacrificial love actively is to practice sin passively.

In conclusion, allow more lyrics from my upcoming song to sum up this post:

> *Trust Him today, say you're done with your sin*
> *If you truly do this, I promise you that He'll come in*
> *He'll shovel out your filth, He'll make you brand new*
> *It won't be immediate change, but He'll be living through you*[10]

---

[9] R. Alan Cole, *Galatians*, 209.
[10] liL fytr, "Teach Me Some Respect."

We'll never love perfectly. That's why the lyrics fit perfectly here. Martin Luther explains, "Let nobody think that he knows all about this commandment, 'Thou shalt love thy neighbour as thyself.' It sounds short and easy, but show me the man who can teach, learn, and do this commandment perfectly. None of us heed, or urge, or practice this commandment properly."[11]

Pray this week that God would help you be more loving than you were last week. I know I will be praying for this.

## True Love

There are hopefully only two possible things you are thinking right now. First, "I'm terrible at this whole love thing," or second, "I want to experience this kind of love for the first time."

And regardless of which one of these things you're currently thinking, the answer for you is a name: Jesus.

If you're terrible at loving people, and if you really want to put the command of today's passage into practice, but you fear you fall too far short every day, then look to Jesus. He lived a perfect life, including loving others perfectly, and then He died on the cross, selflessly giving up His life for you in love. This is why there is hope for you when you fail to love perfectly. Jesus already did. This is why He couldn't come to earth as a 33-year-old man and die on the cross the next day. He had to live a perfectly loving life—each and every day of His life—so that He could fulfill the righteousness that you never could.

When you fall short, you can trust that He never did. When you fall short, look to Him and say, "I do believe; help my unbelief; help me cling to You better next time." He is ready and willing to forgive you. Recommit yourself to trusting Him!

If you want to experience true love for the first time, I beg you to believe in Jesus! He is love incarnate. He didn't have to come to earth, but He did because He wanted a relationship with you. He wanted you to be able to spend eternity with Him. He died so that if you believe in Him, you would never perish even though you will likely die one day. Jesus said, "<u>I am the resurrection and the life. The one who believes in Me, even if he dies, will live</u>" (John 11:25).

---

[11] Martin Luther, *A Commentary on St. Paul's Epistle to the Galatians*.

Lesson 15: Galatians 5:13-15

Believe in Him today. He will never turn you away! But please, don't wait too long to believe; you never know when death might strike. Place your faith in Him right now!

## Reflection Questions

1. How does today's text show Paul's love for the church?
2. Why would love be the fulfillment of the Law?
3. What does it mean to "love your neighbor *as yourself*"?
4. What sins do you struggle with, and how can true love help overcome them (practically)?
5. Have you placed your faith in Jesus yet?

## Praying the Text

*Jesus,*

*Thank You for love. Help me to know You better so that I can better model You to a watching world. You are love. You are not angry and vindictive. Help me to fulfill the Law by loving as You love. I need You daily!*

# Lesson 16

## Galatians 5:16-18

¹⁶Now I say: You all must walk by [the] Spirit, and you all will not at all fulfill fleshly lust. ¹⁷For the flesh desires [what is] opposed to the Spirit, and the Spirit [desires what is] opposed to the flesh, because these things are opposing one another so that you all might not do the very things you all might want [to do]. ¹⁸But if you all are being led by [the] Spirit, [then] you all are not under Law.

# The Struggle is Real!

Have you ever thought, "Well, that's easy for you to say"?

If so, you're like most of us. When someone gives excellent advice that seems impossible actually to carry out, we are likely to say, "That's easy for you to say; however, I'd like to see you actually do it."

Paul was no stranger to this kind of response. In fact, He anticipates it in our passage today. It is easy to say, and it is simple to do also; the problem is that it is not easy to do, and Paul here explains why.[1]

Paul is continuing to describe the path of true freedom. The complete thought of this lengthy passage continues past the struggle to give hope to the struggling Christian that there is an end to the battle—that Christ has already won the victory—and to keep our eyes on the goal—not only to stop sinning, but even more than that: To practice active righteousness. As Andy Mineo rapped,

> *Putting on new, taking off old*
> *If you only take off, you'll be waking up cold.*[2]

Paul has already stated that we are free, and our freedom is not to sin but to serve through love. He has also stated that we are not to submit to another yoke of slavery. Here's a bold statement this post will seek to prove: If you say, "That's sin—I can't do it," then you are submitting to Law and another yoke of slavery, and ultimately—rather than resisting the sin—it will only cause you to commit the sin.

Paul begins in 5:16 by saying:

Walk by [the] Spirit.

---

[1] In fact, Paul shares his own experience with this very concept in Romans 7:7-8:17. More on this concept later in this post.

[2] Andy Mineo, "Every Word (feat. Co Campbell)," *Formerly Known* (Atlanta: Reach Records, 2013), Spotify.

This is a command. We cannot get out of this command. We are not to walk by the Law, but we're not to walk in sin either. We are to walk by the Spirit. (Lesson 17 will specifically describe the opposite of walking by the Spirit—5:19-21—and Lesson 18 will describe walking by the Spirit—5:22-24.) To put it simply now—walking by the Spirit means walking in "<u>love, joy, peace, patience, kindness, goodness, faith, gentleness, [and] self-control.</u>" Keep in mind that as these are commanded in 5:16, it isn't a natural occurrence—just like it isn't natural to avoid the things listed in 5:19-21. We must actively put on love, joy, peace, etc.

It is important to note that this injunction comes directly after a caution about biting and devouring one another. Martin Luther explains, "No flesh, not even that of the true believer, is so completely under the influence of the Spirit that it will not bite or devour, or at least neglect, the commandment of love. At the slightest provocation it flares up, demands to be revenged, and hates a neighbor like an enemy, or at least does not love him as much as he ought to be loved."[3]

Paul wanted the Galatians then—and us now—to know that if we find ourselves in a place where we are biting and devouring one another, then it proves that we are not walking in the Spirit. However, at the same time, Paul wants us to know that repentance is possible. The word translated "<u>Walk</u>" often carries the idea of "way of life."[4] And it is helpful to use the term "<u>walk</u>" because even the most sophisticated person—while walking—may occasionally slip or stumble. It does not mean that they are unable to walk, it just means they aren't infallible.

In the same way, even the most dedicated, Spirit-filled believer will not successfully walk by the Spirit 100% of the time. If they could, they would have no need for Jesus. (This should never become an excuse for sin, but it is a comfort for the troubled believer, cf. Romans 6:1-2.)

If you're walking and you trip, then you get up, and you keep going. It must be the same way in the Christian life. Hebrews 12:1 would urge us to remove whatever causes us to stumble so that we can run more victoriously in the future.

It's why Paul concludes verse 16 by saying:

<u>And you all will not at all fulfill fleshly lust.</u>

---

[3] Martin Luther, *A Commentary on St. Paul's Epistle to the Galatians*.
[4] John MacArthur, *Galatians*, 152.

## Lesson 16: Galatians 5:16-18

There are two meanings within this, and I believe Paul is aware of and intending both.

First, if we emphasize the words "will not," then we see that if we walk by the Spirit perfectly we will never do anything fleshly. Additionally, with this viewpoint, it is clear that if we as believers fail to walk by the Spirit, it is not at all the Spirit's fault, but rather ours alone.

Second, if we emphasize the words "fulfill fleshly lust," we see that even when we fail to walk by the Spirit, we are unable to carry out fleshly desires to their ultimate end—death (cf. 5:21). John Calvin helpfully explains, "We ought to mark the word fulfill; by which he means, that, though the sons of God, so long as they groan under the burden of the flesh, are liable to commit sin, they are not its subjects or slaves, but make habitual opposition to its power."[5]

The point is that the believer is free, and she will never again be enslaved, and as a result, even when she sins, she did not do it out of slavery, but rather freely chose to do so. It's why Paul commands in Romans 6:13, "And do not offer any parts of it to sin as weapons for unrighteousness. But as those who are alive from the dead, offer yourselves to God, and all the parts of yourselves to God as weapons for righteousness." When we sin, we essentially say, "I want to serve you," and it paints a confusing picture because we are no longer slaves of sin and can never be such again.

And then Paul says in verse 17:

> For the flesh desires [what is] opposed to the Spirit, and the Spirit [desires what is] opposed to the flesh, because these things are opposing one another so that you all might not do the very things you all might want [to do].

This helps to explain the previous discussion further. If the believer cannot fulfill the desires of the flesh, and if the desires of the flesh are against the Spirit, then it stands to say that the believer can't thwart the Spirit. We may make jabs at the Spirit by our sin, but ultimately the Spirit will win in the end (cf. Genesis 3:15).

Many people want to compare this verse to Romans 7:7-25. I don't believe that that is a valid interpretation of Paul's point in that chapter of Romans. If we look closely at Romans 7:7-25, we will notice that the Spirit is

---

[5] John Calvin, *Commentaries on the Epistles of Paul to the Galatians and Ephesians*.

nowhere to be found, but it is clearly shown here. The Spirit is opposed to the flesh. Romans 8:12-15 are more relevant to this discussion:

> So then, brothers, we are not obligated to the flesh to live according to the flesh, for if you live according to the flesh, you are going to die. But if by the Spirit you put to death the deeds of the body, you will live. All those led by God's Spirit are God's sons. For you did not receive a spirit of slavery to fall back into fear, but you received the Spirit of adoption, by whom we cry out, "Abba, Father!"

Again, we will come back to Romans 7 before the end, but for now, it's enough to know that the struggle of holy living is real. In fact, Calvin explains,

> Carnal men have no battle with depraved lusts, no proper desire to attain to the righteousness of God. Paul is addressing believers . . . Paul therefore declares, that believers, so long as they are in this life, whatever may be the earnestness of their endeavors, do not obtain such a measure of success as to serve God in a perfect manner.[6]

As such, I would posit that the true believer is capable of becoming more distressed, more discouraged, and more depressed than a non-believer. It is why Paul starts chapter 6 by saying, "Carry one another's burdens" (cf. 6:2). If a believer is isolated, and if he has no one to carry his burdens, then he can end up in a worse place than even a non-believer because he sees his sin as being directly against God, he sees his sin as active and present, and he sees the holy standard that he is failing to live up to, and these things grieve him to the core.

And then Paul concludes his introduction to the Spirit/Flesh dichotomy. And, as he does so, he throws us a curveball:

> Verse 16: Spirit vs. flesh
> Verse 17: Spirit vs. flesh
> Verse 18: Spirit vs. ~~flesh~~ Law

Where we would expect Paul to say, "But if you all are being led by [the] Spirit, [then] you all are not under the flesh," he says instead:

---

[6] John Calvin, *Commentaries on the Epistles of Paul to the Galatians and Ephesians*.

Lesson 16: Galatians 5:16-18

<u>But if you all are being led by [the] Spirit, [then] you all are not under Law.</u>

As such, he returns to his discussion of Law that has been the primary focus throughout Galatians. For all practical purposes, this is the last time the Law comes up in this letter. And this occurrence is monumental! Paul essentially places flesh and Law on the same level. Here's where Romans 7, specifically verses 7-12, comes in:

> <u>What should we say then? Is the law sin? Absolutely not! On the contrary, I would not have known sin if it were not for the law. For example, I would not have known what it is to covet if the law had not said, Do not covet.</u> And *sin, seizing an opportunity through the commandment,* produced in me coveting of every kind. For *apart from the law sin is dead.* Once I was alive apart from the law, but *when the commandment came, sin sprang to life* and I died. The commandment that was meant for life resulted in death for me. For sin, seizing an opportunity through the commandment, deceived me, and through it killed me. So then, the law is holy, and the commandment is holy and just and good.[7]

Paul has already explained in 3:24 that the Law was created to lead us to Christ. In Romans 7, Paul explains that the Law does this because sin commandeered it and uses the Law to incite sinful desires. The Law shows us what we are supposed to be living like, but because of sin, we are unable to live that way. The Law has no power to help us live rightly, and it, therefore, shows us our need for Jesus—leading us to Him.

*Pilgrim's Progress,* by John Bunyan, is again helpful. Bunyan relates the following parable that Christian is shown in the house of Interpreter:

> Then he took him by the hand, and led him into a very large parlor that was full of dust, because never swept; the which after he had reviewed a little while, the Interpreter called for a man to sweep. Now, when he began to sweep, the dust began so abundantly to fly about, that Christian had almost therewith been choked. Then said the

---

[7] Emphases added.

Interpreter to a damsel that stood by, "Bring hither water, and sprinkle the room;" the which when she had done, it was swept and cleansed with pleasure.

Christian: "What means this?"

Interpreter: "This parlor is the heart of a man that was never sanctified by the sweet grace of the Gospel. The dust is his original sin, and inward corruptions, that have defiled the whole man. He that began to sweep at first, is the law; but she that brought water, and did sprinkle it, is the Gospel. Now whereas thou sawest, that so soon as the first began to sweep, the dust did so fly about that the room by him could not be cleansed, but that thou wast almost choked therewith; this is to show thee, that the Law, instead of cleansing the heart (by its working) from sin, doth revive, put strength into, and increase it in the soul, even as it doth discover and forbid it; but doth not give power to subdue.

"Again, as thou sawest the damsel sprinkle the room with water, upon which it was cleansed with pleasure, this is to show thee, that when the Gospel comes in the sweet and precious influences thereof to the heart, then, I say, even as thou sawest the damsel lay the dust by sprinkling the floor with water, so is sin vanquished and subdued, and the soul made clean, through the faith of it, and consequently fit for the King of Glory to inhabit."[8]

In much the same way, someone who is trying to use the Law to be sanctified will only succeed in stirring up dust and choking himself on more sin. Paul illustrates this principle well in Romans 7:13-25—proving that even he wasn't able to perfectly walk by the Spirit. Romans 7 is not describing sanctification, but rather anti-sanctification. Romans 7 is followed by Romans 8, which talks extensively of the Spirit's power in sanctification.

Paul has questioned in Galatians 3:2-3, "Did you all receive the Spirit by the works of Law or by faithful hearing? Thusly you all are mindless: After beginning by [the] Spirit, are you all now being completed by [the] flesh?"[9] He equated Law and flesh there, and he does so again in 5:18 because he wants us to know that the more we rely on Law instead of Christ, the more fleshly and sinful we will end up being.

---

[8] John Bunyan, *The Pilgrim's Progress*, 31.
[9] Emphases added.

This is why I said at the beginning: If you say, "That's sin—I can't do it," then you are submitting to Law and another yoke of slavery, and ultimately—rather than resisting the sin—it will only cause you to commit the sin.

Saying, "I can't do that," is putting a law on yourself in a certain way of thinking. The better method is to say, "Jesus, this action would be unloving. Help me to act lovingly instead." We have to put on—not simply take off—because if we only take off, then something is going to be put on, and it will be sin if we are not actively putting on righteousness.[10]

If you're an unbeliever, the truth is that your life is Romans 7. The things you want to do you cannot do, and the things you do not want to do, you keep on doing. Even if your only goal is to live by your own standards of good, you fall short of it. Jesus is here saying, "Believe in me—that I died for you—and be saved from your fruitless efforts that only frustrate you." If you are not a believer, then you are actively opposing the Spirit every day, and the fact is that you will ultimately lose. The Spirit wins (cf. Genesis 3:15), and those who are not in Christ will be crushed like the snake. Please trust Him today and let the Spirit enable you to live for Him truly.

With that, Paul has introduced us to the Spirit/flesh dichotomy. This dichotomy continues through Galatians 6:10, though the emphasis after 5:21 is on the Spirit.

The struggle is real for the believer who is trying to obey the Lord by walking in the Spirit. But we are guaranteed ultimate victory if we get up and keep walking after we stumble.

## Stop Fighting Fruitlessly

There is only one hope in this world. If you try to do it on your own, then you will be unable to do anything but sin. There are several reasons for this. First, you are weak. I don't care if you go to the gym seven days a week. You are weak. You don't have the spiritual strength to withstand the allures of sin.

And even a believer who's believed for fifty years is weak. On his own, he will always hone in to sin's shouts, like the Siren's in Homer's *Odyssey*. The call is inescapable.

---

[10] Read that sentence again slowly and digest it; I don't know how to say it more clearly.

Second, even if you are above addiction and currently keep the Ten Commandments perfectly (though you might want to consider studying the ninth one a little more closely), I would still say that all you're doing is sin. Why? Because you're patting yourself on the back. You should be giving God credit. Romans 3:23 says "All have sinned and fall short of the glory of God." This essentially means that the primary sin is not glorifying God. If you're proud of yourself for your goodness, then you are stealing glory from God. This is a sin.

This is why you need Jesus. Even if by some miracle you could have lived a "perfect" life your whole life, if you fail to give glory to God, you are no better than Adolf Hitler.

I know it hurts. But Romans 3:23 says, "All have sinned." It doesn't say, "All have sinned, but Hitler sinned more." It doesn't even say, "Some sin more than others." It merely says, "All have sinned."

But the Gospel is that Jesus did not sin. He lived a perfect life, and He gave God all the credit for it. Then He died on the cross for our sins. He took the punishment we deserved.

Because we fail to glorify the eternal God properly, we deserve the eternal wrath of God in hell. But He loves us enough to send His Son to take our place.

All you have to do is believe in Him. Place your faith in Jesus today! To place your faith in Him and to lean wholly on Him is to give God glory. And there is no greater glory you can give God than believing in the name of His Son.

And from now on, know that He has given you His Spirit. When you live, the Spirit lives. When you do good things, the Spirit of Christ is acting through you. When you sin, you are resisting the Spirit's leading.

Trust Christ today, and forever submit to His Spirit's leading. And when you find yourself failing to follow the Spirit, turn back in faith and repentance.

Have you placed your faith in Him yet?

# Reflection Questions

1. How does today's text show Paul's love for the church?
2. Have you experienced the struggle Paul described in these verses?

Lesson 16: Galatians 5:16-18

3. Does knowledge of this struggle encourage you or make you upset?
4. What wins more often: Spirit or flesh?
5. Have you placed your faith in Jesus yet?

# Praying the Text

*Jesus,*

*Thank You for encouraging me in this struggle. It is incredibly disheartening at times. I know what I'm called to, and I know how badly and often I fall short. But the fact that I do struggle means that You are dwelling inside me, and that is beyond encouraging. Please give me the grace to be more often successful in resisting the allures of the flesh. I love You, and I want to love You more.*

# Lesson 17

## Galatians 5:19-21

[19]Now the works of the flesh are manifest, which are: Fornications, immoralities, sensualities, [20]idolatries, sorceries, hostilities, discords, jealousies, rages, strifes, dissensions, heresies, [21]envies, drunkennesses, carousings, and the things similar to these, about which I say to you all, as I said before, that the ones who are practicing these things will not inherit [the] Kingdom of God.

# Only 7 Deadly Sins?

In a faraway land, many, many years ago, a small hero was thrust into the middle of a struggle much, much bigger than himself. However, despite his size, and despite the magnitude of the situation, the fate of his whole world hung around his neck. At one of the darkest points in his journey, he is hiding behind a rocky ledge as the leader of a dark army stares in his direction.

> There was a pause, a dead silence. Maybe it was the Ring that called to the Wraith-lord, and for a moment he was troubled, sensing some other power within his valley. This way and that turned the dark head helmed and crowned with fear, sweeping the shadows with its unseen eyes. Frodo waited, like a bird at the approach of a snake, unable to move. And as he waited, he felt, more urgent than ever before, the command that he should put on the Ring. But great as the pressure was, he felt no inclination now to yield to it. He knew that the Ring would only betray him, and that he had not, even if he put it on, the power to face the Morgul-king—not yet. There was no longer any answer to that command in his own will, dismayed by terror though it was, and he felt only the beating upon him of a great power from outside. It took his hand, and as Frodo watched with his mind, not willing it but in suspense (as if he looked on some old story far away), it moved the hand inch by inch towards the chain upon his neck. Then his own will stirred; slowly it forced the hand back and set it to find another thing, a thing lying hidden near his breast. Cold and hard it seemed as his grip closed on it: the phial of Galadriel, so long treasured, and almost forgotten till that hour. As he touched it, for a while all thought of the Ring was banished from his mind. He sighed and bent his head.[1]

And I find that to be a handy analogy to describe what Paul has been talking about in Galatians recently: "For the flesh desires [what is] opposed to the

---

[1] J. R. R. Tolkien, *The Two Towers*, 1954 (New York: Del Rey, 2012), 356-357.

Spirit, and the Spirit [desires what is] opposed to the flesh, because these things are opposing one another so that you all might not do the very things you all might want [to do]" (5:17). Frodo was in the midst of this struggle here, but he came out on top because of a gift from a higher power. Paul is very clear that we don't have to give in to the flesh because we have the Spirit—a gift from the Highest Power.

And today, we are going to look at a partial list of vices that daily wage war against the Spirit. These are vices that we are all prone to fall prey to, but that we are to fight against by the Spirit. Calvin writes, "The apostle therefore now points out to us those sins against which we must fight, in order that we may not live according to the flesh."[2]

Because we have the Spirit, we have no excuse to fall prey to these vices, but the fact that they are fighting against us, along with the fact that we are not yet glorified, means that we will fall at times. But let's get into it: First, we'll look at the main point of the passage, and then we'll break down each individual vice.

Paul says in 5:19 and 21:

> Now the works of the flesh are manifest . . . about which I say to you all, as I said before, that the ones who are practicing these things will not inherit [the] Kingdom of God.

He has two points in this section: First, the obvious nature of the works of the flesh, and second, a warning about the result for those who practice these things.

Paul says (literal word order of verse 19), "manifest now is the works of the flesh." In Greek, the word order reflects the emphasis. The first word carries the most emphasis. Paul here wants us to know that the works of the flesh are *manifest*.

In my study, I wrote a question: "Does 'manifest' mean 'shown' as in he's laying them out, or 'obvious,' as in he doesn't even have to name them?"

And if I'm forced to work with those two options, I would opt for the second. However, Jesus said in Mark 7:20-23:

> What comes out of a person—that defiles him. For from within, out of people's hearts, come evil thoughts, sexual immoralities, thefts,

---

[2] John Calvin, *Commentaries on the Epistles of Paul to the Galatians and Ephesians*.

## Lesson 17: Galatians 5:19-21

murders, adulteries, greed, evil actions, deceit, promiscuity, stinginess, blasphemy, pride, and foolishness. All these evil things come from within and defile a person.

The opposition between flesh and Spirit begins in the mind/heart, but fleshly thoughts are manifested/shown to be fleshly thoughts when they come out as an action, like the things Paul lists in Galatians 5:19b-21a. I don't believe Paul has the "They're so obvious I don't even have to mention them" thought in his head.

Paul concludes our passage today by saying that those who practice the things I will describe in detail will not inherit the kingdom of God. This is a warning along the lines of Revelation 22:14-15, "Blessed are those who wash their robes, so that they may have the right to the tree of life and may enter by the gates. Outside are the dogs, the sorcerers, the sexually immoral, the murderers, the idolaters, and everyone who loves and practices lying."

What makes the kingdom of God good is that God is there. Those who inherit the kingdom inherit God as a benevolent Father. What makes being outside so bad—forgetting the fire and brimstone for now—is that God is not a benevolent Father to those outside. However, as omnipresent God, He is still outside (cf. Psalm 139:7-8), and that is what makes being outside so bad. For a sinner's whole life, she tries to avoid the presence of God because it convicts her of her sin, but God's presence will be unescapable in eternity, repentance will be impossible, and that's primarily what will make hell what it is—hell. Paul doesn't want anyone to end up outside the kingdom, and I don't either, so he gives this warning, and I repeat it now: Those who practice the following things will not inherit the Kingdom of God. And Paul's list of vices can be divided into three categories: Sex, religion, and (inter)personal.[3]

The first item on the list can be translated simply as "fornications." It is from the Greek word that transliterates to *porneia*, whose root is the word *pornos*, which literally means "harlot for hire."[4] *Porneia* covers all forms of sexual immorality, including adultery and homosexuality.[5] In the Apocryphal work Ecclesiasticus, the author writes, "Two kinds of individuals multiply sins, and a third incurs wrath. Hot passion that blazes like a fire will not be quenched until it burns itself out; *one who commits fornication with his near of kin will never cease until the fire burns him up*. To a fornicator all bread is sweet; he

---

[3] Cf. John MacArthur, *Galatians*, 161.
[4] Kittel, *TDNT*, VI:580.
[5] Kittel, *TDNT*, VI:581.

will never weary until he dies" (Ecclesiasticus 23:16-17)[6]. One scholar translates the phrase, "fornication with his near of kin" more literally as "fornication with his own flesh," which likely suggests masturbation as a form of *porneia*.[7] Since the word for fornication comes from the root that refers to prostitutes, it is possible to understand any kind of sexual activity outside the bounds of a marriage covenant (one man and one woman) as prostituting oneself—selling yourself. Prostitution arose in Greek culture with increased prosperity. "The main cause of prostitution is the Greek view of life which regards sexual intercourse as just as natural, necessary and justifiable as eating and drinking." The same writer notes in a footnote, "Sexual abstinence was regarded as more harmful than moderate free intercourse." And he cites one ancient writer as saying that it is hubris to resist love.[8] By the time between the Old and New Testaments, the word *porneia* had assuredly come to mean (at least for the Jews) "'sexual intercourse' in general without more precise definition."[9] So when Paul comes around in Galatians 5, and throughout the New Testament,[10] and puts *porneia* on lists of fleshly sins, it comes as a shock to his Gentile hearers. The culture did not see it as a problem. But any form of sexual activity outside of heterosexual marriage is *porneia*—a manifestation of the flesh—and must be fought against.

The second sexually related vice can be translated as "immoralities." While *porneia* refers to the actual sexual acts, this word, transliterated as *akatharsia*, refers to the uncleanness that results from *porneia*. "Gentile [uncleanness] is the direct opposite of the righteousness of Christian sanctification."[11] When people commit *porneia*, they are left unclean in the sight of God. It has a reference back to the discussion of ceremonial cleanness in Leviticus: "You must distinguish between the holy and the common, and the clean and the unclean" (Leviticus 10:10). One commentator explains further, "The two following words (*akatharsia* and *aselgeia*) probably describe

---

[6] NRSV, emphasis added.
[7] Kittel, *TDNT*, VI:588. "Suggests self-pollution" is the language the author uses.
[8] Kittel, *TDNT*, VI:582.
[9] Kittel, *TDNT*, VI:587. Italics added.
[10] "The New Testament is characterized by an unconditional repudiation of all extra-marital and unnatural intercourse" (Kittel, *TDNT*, VI:590.) Almost every vice list in the New Testament contains a form of *porneia* in it (Matthew 15:19, Mark 7:21-22, 1 Corinthians 6:9-10, our passage today, Ephesians 5:3-5, Colossians 3:5, 1 Thessalonians 4:3, 1 Timothy 1:9-10, Revelation 22:15). It is telling that out of all words that occur first in these vice lists, *porneia* is the one that fronts the lists more than any other.
[11] Kittel, *TDNT*, III:428.

## Lesson 17: Galatians 5:19-21

some of the sexual perversions (such as the practice of homosexuality and lesbianism) which, as Paul reminds us in Romans 1:26-27, were common in the pagan world, and indeed often characterize the world of today."[12] Regardless, "Young Christianity regards the sexual immorality of the Hellenistic world as ungodly [uncleanness]."[13] Paul is here calling for Christians to remain pure in every way in a perverted world. "Do everything without grumbling and arguing, so that you may be blameless and pure, children of God who are faultless in a crooked and perverted generation, among whom you shine like stars in the world" (Philippians 2:14-15).[14]

The third sexual vice that Paul mentions can be translated as "sensualities." Calvin summarizes the first three by saying that they are sins that are forbidden by the seventh commandment. "[Sensuality] . . . is applied to those who lead wanton and dissolute lives."[15] John MacArthur says, "It is unrestrained sexual indulgence, such as has become so common in the modern Western world. It refers to uninhibited sexual indulgence without shame and without concern for what others think or how they may be affected (or infected)."[16] Promiscuity would be the attitude that leads to acting out in *porneia*, which would then cause *akatharsia*. Paul says that if this attitude is present in a person's mind, they will not inherit the Kingdom of God.

And then we get to idolatry, which introduces the religious vices. The Apostle John concludes his first epistle by saying, "Guard yourselves from idols," essentially saying, "Beyond all else, if you keep away from idols, everything else will work well for you." But when I explain his words that way, hear what I'm saying: Everybody is naturally an idolater. Maybe you worship sex, or your job, or your family, or a wooden idol. Regardless of what it is—even biblical theology can be an idol[17]—anything that keeps your mind occupied more than Jesus Christ keeps your mind occupied is idolatry. Anything that motivates you in life more than Jesus Christ motivates you is idolatry. Paul says, and no one in his context would have disagreed with him, that idolatry is a work of the flesh that will keep you out of God's kingdom. MacArthur comments, "All human religion is based on self-effort, on man's

---

[12] R. Alan Cole, *Galatians*, 215.
[13] Kittel, *TDNT*, III:429.
[14] Emphasis added.
[15] John Calvin, *Commentaries on the Epistles of Paul to the Galatians and Ephesians*.
[16] John MacArthur, *Galatians*, 160.
[17] Cf. Tim Conway, "Is Theology Your Idol?" *I'll Be Honest* (August 20, 2009), https://www.illbehonest.com/is-theology-your-idol-tim-conway.

sinful insistence that he can make himself acceptable to his humanly conceived God by his own merits. Consequently, human religion is the implacable enemy of divine grace and therefore of the Gospel."[18] We must root all idolatry out of our lives!

The other religious vice can be translated as "sorceries," which comes from a Greek word that transliterates to *pharmakeia*. This is the word from which we get our modern word "pharmacy." It only occurs three times in the New Testament (cf. Galatians 5:20 and Revelation 9:21, 18:23), and is translated as "sorcery" by the HCSB in all 3 occurrences.[19] MacArthur is helpful: "It was originally used of medicines in general but came to be used primarily of mood- and mind-altering drugs similar to those that cause so much havoc in our own day."[20] This is my new anti-medical-(and especially recreational)-marijuana verse since 1 Corinthians 6:19 is actually talking about sex—not drug use. I have nothing against pharmacies helping people get over illnesses. However, I think that people being dependent on pharmacies to keep them functioning is where *pharmakeia* becomes very real in our Western world.[21] Also, when we use *pharmakeia* to rectify other works of the flesh—e.g. the morning after pill—we are being included in Paul's description of those who will not inherit the Kingdom of God. In fact, I would claim that birth control is *pharmakeia*, mainly because its primary use is to allow for fewer consequences while practicing other works of the flesh, but also because if you're using it for its other purposes, 1) you're not thanking God for the body He gave you, or 2) you're not fighting your corruption by the Spirit, but instead by pills. Now, let me clarify: If your hormones are a wreck, then use medication to help, but the goal should be to get off the medication. God will help you by His Spirit. As Flame raps in his song, "Read 'Em and Weep,"

> *There ain't no habit we can't shake*
> *No addiction we can't kick*
> *No personality trait*
> *That can keep us in them chains*

---

[18] John MacArthur, *Galatians*, 161.

[19] Cf. *Holman Christian Standard Bible* on Galatians 5:20, Revelation 9:21, and Revelation 18:23.

[20] John MacArthur, *Galatians*, 161.

[21] Paul is not here dissing Harry Potter. If he was, he'd also be dissing Lord of the Rings and Star Wars, because all contain occultic, magical elements. Hogwarts School of Witchcraft and Wizardry is simply the river that carries the story, the same way in which the Dark and Light sides of the Force carry the Star Wars storyline.

## Lesson 17: Galatians 5:19-21

*Boy I'm breaking out of mine*
*Sayonara to the world*
*Gotta leave it all behind*
*We really dead to the flesh*
*when it's knocking at the door*
*We ain't gotta say yes*
*got the power to say no*
*So we do not lose heart*
*though our bodies waste away*
*Our inner man has been renewed*
*day by day*[22]

By the Spirit, we have all that we need to defeat all the negative aspects of our personality, all the sins of our flesh, and all the temptations that come from elsewhere. If a medication helps for a while to get you glued into Jesus Christ, that is awesome! However, Jesus Christ needs to be your focus; medication is a cheap substitute that can quickly become an idol.

Paul then moves into (inter)personal works of the flesh. These all bring Galatians 5:15 back to mind: "But if you all are biting and devouring one another, you all must watch out lest you all are destroyed by one another."

There are a lot of these, and the first on the list is "hostilities." The word refers to enmity between men, and it described Herod and Pilate's relationship before Jesus' crucifixion (cf. Luke 23:12). One scholar explains that it does not refer to "God's enmity against us . . . but ours against God as in Romans 8:7."[23] If we are hostile towards God, then we will never be anything but hostile to people. Paul says here that this keeps someone out of the Kingdom of God.

The next work of the flesh can be translated "discords." One commentator explains that it is "something like 'a contentious temper'."[24] MacArthur understands it as the outward manifestation of a hostile attitude.[25] Strong's dictionary offers these possible meanings: "Contention, debate, strife, variance,"[26] for the four occurrences throughout the New Testament.

---

[22] Flame, "Read 'Em and Weep," *Royal Flush* (St. Louis, MO: Clear Sight Music, 2013), Spotify.

[23] Kittel, *TDNT*, II:815.

[24] R. Alan Cole, *Galatians*, 216.

[25] John MacArthur, *Galatians*, 162.

[26] James Strong, *Strong's Talking Greek & Hebrew Dictionary* (Austin, TX: WORDsearch Corp., 2007), WORDsearch.

Regardless of the specific sense, it refers to a lack of unity and peace, and Paul warns that this is enough to keep someone out of God's kingdom.

The word translated "jealousies" comes from a word that can also be translated "zealous." And the best way to understand it is as zeal to promote self, due to being jealous of someone else's position.[27] This attitude keeps someone out of God's kingdom.

The next work of the flesh can be translated as "rages," and it comes from a root that originally referred to violent movements of world elements. "Everywhere in the New Testament it means 'wrath'."[28] It is an uncontrollable anger that causes destruction. Paul says that this will keep someone out of the Kingdom of God.

"Strifes" comes from a word that means, "to work as a day-labourer." It was used in the ancient world to describe "those who procure office by illegal manipulation, and therefore [strife] is their attitude." In fact, it is used "of the harlot who offers herself to a man or who entices him. [Strife] is thus the attitude of self-seekers, harlots, etc., i.e., those who demeaning themselves and their cause, are busy and active in their own interests, seeking their own gain or advantage."[29] Later, the same article tells us how best to understand this word, "It's best to understand as 'base self-seeking,' ... the nature of those who can't lift their gaze to higher things."[30] People who are overly concerned with petty things would be described by this vice. Paul says it exempts people from God's kingdom.

The word translated "dissensions" is explained best as signifying "objective disunity in the community."[31] If people know that believers are believers by their love and unity, then that helps to prove why this word and the related ideas in this third section are sins that keep people from God's kingdom.

The word I translated as "heresies" is usually translated "factions,"[32] but since "heresies" is a simple transliteration of the Greek word, I left it in the original language. It is important to note the context in which this word occurs. It is in a list of fleshly works. And it's in a specific section that is describing interpersonal relationships. Because the word literally means "faction" or

---

[27] Kittel, *TDNT*, II:881-882.
[28] Kittel, *TDNT*, III:167.
[29] Kittel, *TDNT*, II:660.
[30] Kittel, *TDNT*, II:661.
[31] Kittel, *TDNT*, I:514.
[32] Cf. *Holman Christian Standard Bible* on Galatians 5:20.

## Lesson 17: Galatians 5:19-21

"party," it has come to describe different branches of theology, specifically ones that are not conservatively, biblically accurate. One scholar writes and explains the connection: "[Church] and [faction] are material opposites."[33] This is accurate because the church is supposed to signify unity, and factions prove the existence of disunity. I once made the case that, "The fact that Paul uses ['heresy'] in 1 Corinthians 11:19, with the fact that it is the only defined use of the word apart from 'the *sect* of the Pharisees' or similar usages in the New Testament, would argue that the only true heresy in Christianity is a lack of love."[34] In 1 Corinthians 11:19-21, Paul says:

> There must, indeed, be [heresies] among you, so that those who are approved may be recognized among you. Therefore, when you come together, it is not really to eat the Lord's Supper. For at the meal, each one eats his own supper ahead of others. So one person is hungry while another gets drunk!

Self-seeking while partaking of the Lord's supper is the only explicitly defined use of heresy in the New Testament. However, after reflecting on this passage in Galatians this week, I'd posit that it contains another defined use, based solely on the placement of it within other specific lacks of love/unity. Don't corrupt unity/love within the body, or you are a true heretic, and God will not allow you into His Kingdom.

The final interpersonal vice can be translated "envies." There is no need here to try to dig deeper for a fuller meaning. If you have "ill-will (as detraction), i.e., jealousy (spite) - envy"[35] towards someone, Paul is here warning that you cannot enter the kingdom of God.

"Drunkennesses" refers to abusing alcohol to the point of intoxication. It only occurs in lists of vices in the New Testament,[36] as we find it here. Luther explains, "Paul does not say that eating and drinking are works of the flesh, but intemperance in eating and drinking, which is a common vice nowadays, is a work of the flesh."[37] Paul wants us to be moderate and careful if we partake of strong drink, and he expects us not to let it lead to debauchery and other

---

[33] Kittel, *TDNT*, I:183.
[34] Joshua Wingerd, "Love Wins."
[35] James Strong, *Strong's Talking Greek & Hebrew Dictionary*.
[36] Kittel, *TDNT*, IV:547.
[37] Martin Luther, *A Commentary on St. Paul's Epistle to the Galatians*.

sins of the flesh. If we are uncontrollable in this area, we are exempt from God's kingdom.

The last-named item in the vice list can be translated "carousings," and would be well understood as resulting from drunkenness.[38] One lexicon helps us understand the word by contextualizing it in ancient Greece:

> A nocturnal and riotous procession of half-drunken and frolicsome fellows who after supper parade through the streets with torches and music in honor of Bacchus or some other deity, and sing and play before the houses of their male and female friends; hence, used generally, of feasts and drinking-parties that are protracted till late at night and indulge in revelry."[39]

Paul says that this kind of activity is unfit for those entering into the Kingdom of God.

And then Paul adds this phrase:

And the things like these.

The list just described does not include everything that exempts a person from the kingdom of God, but it does include a lot. Paul's point is that if you understand that these things keep a person out of the kingdom, then you can also recognize other things that disqualify people as well. It is important to note that if you read the KJV, verse 19 reads, "Now the works of the flesh are manifest, which are *these*; Adultery, fornication, uncleanness, lasciviousness."[40] You'll notice that the very first one was not mentioned in my discussion. This is because "adultery" does not occur in the best manuscripts that we possess. Since 1611, when the KJV was published, we have discovered many more manuscripts that have greatly helped us figure out the most likely original text. One rule is that the shortest reading is likely correct. Thus, "adultery" was probably a later scribal addition. But, if we understand *porneia* as describing all sexual activity outside of the marriage covenant, then adultery is included within *porneia*.[41]

---

[38] Cf. John MacArthur, *Galatians*, 162.

[39] J. H. Thayer, *Greek-English Lexicon of the New Testament*.

[40] Cf. *King James Version* of Galatians 5:19.

[41] I'm planning on writing a lengthy paper on the trustworthiness of the Bible despite manuscript variants at a future time. For now, you can find my thoughts on the subject on my

## Lesson 17: Galatians 5:19-21

And perhaps you say, "Uh, oh. I'm described by this list."

My first question would be, "Do you claim Christ as Lord and Savior?"

If not, you must, or you will be excluded from the Kingdom of God for these and other sins. If so, I want to show you an important word. Paul says, "<u>The ones who are practicing these things</u>" are the ones exempt from the Kingdom. Practice is different from struggle. Martin Luther helpfully explains,

> Christians also fall and perform the lusts of the flesh. David fell horribly into adultery. Peter also fell grievously when he denied Christ. However great these sins were, they were not committed to spite God, but from weakness. When their sins were brought to their attention these men did not obstinately continue in their sin, but repented. Those who sin through weakness are not denied pardon as long as they rise again and cease to sin. There is nothing worse than to continue in sin. If they do not repent, but obstinately continue to fulfill the desires of the flesh, it is a sure sign that they are not sincere.[42]

"<u>The Spirit is willing, but the flesh is weak</u>," Jesus said, and this is why we have to "<u>stay awake and pray</u>" and walk by the Spirit (Matthew 26:41). If we find that we are in a path leading to (or that just led to) the manifestation of a work of the flesh, we must get up, repent, and fight harder by the Spirit.

In conclusion, the struggle is real, but we have the Spirit. In Lesson 18, I will explain how the fruits of the Spirit need to be focused on and practiced in order to avoid the works of the flesh, but for now, let's just remember that even when everything seems dark, and even when temptation to sin is hard at your heels and weighing you down, God has given you the power to resist, just like Frodo Baggins had an alternate course given to him by Galadriel for that fateful moment.

God is good! We must trust Him more daily and repent of our fleshly works!

# Convicted and Concerned?

---

blog. Joshua Wingerd, "'God-Breathed Scripture' Necessitates It Be Inerrant," *live in Love; find your true reward* (September 24, 2018), https://lilfytr.com/2018/09/24/mark1_2-3-and-inerrancy.

[42] Martin Luther, *A Commentary on St. Paul's Epistle to the Galatians*.

Which sin on this list do you most struggle with? I'm sure if you're honest with yourself, you struggle with at least one of them:

- Fornication
- Immorality
- Sensuality
- Idolatry
- Sorcery
- Hostility
- Discord
- Jealousy
- Rage
- Strife
- Dissension
- Heresy
- Envy
- Drunkenness
- Carousing
- Things like these

At the very least, the last one describes you. Essentially, the question is: Do you look just like the culture around you? If you do, if you are "*practicing these things,*" then the bad news is that "the ones who are practicing these things will not inherit [the] Kingdom of God" (Galatians 5:21).

But the good news is that Christ died on the cross for your sins. He suffered on the cross as a fornicating, immoral, sensual, idolator, who practiced sorcery, who harbored hostility, discord, jealousy, rage, strife, dissension, heresy, and envy in his heart; and who was often drunk and carousing. He died for people like this so that by His power and Spirit they could escape this enslaving life.

He rose from the dead three days later to prove that those sins stayed in the grave, but He was eternally untouched by them. For everyone who places their faith in Him, their sins will be buried as well, never to rise again.

So I beg you today: "Believe in Him."

If you do, then He will tell you, "Neither do I condemn you. Go, and from now on do not sin anymore" (John 8:11).

This is the Gospel!

I pray that you believe it.

# Reflection Questions

1. How does today's text show Paul's love for the church?
2. Why does Paul say "the works of the flesh are manifest"?
3. Which sins from this list do you most struggle with?
4. Are there any sins you would add to this list? Why?

Lesson 17: Galatians 5:19-21

5. Have you placed your faith in Jesus yet?

# Praying the Text

*Jesus,*

*Thank You for showing me the path to avoid as I live this Christian life. I pray that You would help me to avoid these destructive sins. I need Your grace each and every day. Help me to believe! I want to be a part of Your Kingdom, both today and for eternity.*

# Lesson 18

## Galatians 5:22-24

²²But the fruit of the Spirit is love, joy, peace, patience, kindness, goodness, faithfulness, ²³gentleness, [and] self-control; there is no Law opposed to such things. ²⁴But the ones belonging to [the] Messiah Jesus crucified the flesh with [its] passions and desires.

# Proofs Called Fruits

If you're anything like me, you hate contradictions. Maybe it's just the suppressed mathematical side of my psyche that comes out in these instances, or the fact that the English sentence, "I don't have no fruit," really means (though most don't realize this) "I actually do have fruit." The literally translated Greek sentence, "Walk by [the] Spirit, and you will not never fulfill fleshly lust" (Galatians 5:16) doesn't contain a double negative for them; it contains an accentuated negative; "not never" means "not at all." I bring this up because, to properly understand our passage today, we need to realize that Paul is not contradicting himself.

In Galatians 5:22-24, Paul is describing—not commanding—the free life under the yoke of Christ. Paul is not saying, "Thou shalt be loving, joyous, peaceful, etc." He is holding up a mirror and saying, "If you have the Spirit, then your life will demonstrate these characteristics."

That's why it is essential to translate the first word of verse 22 as "but," instead of another potential option, "now." Paul is contrasting this description with the previous. Previously he said, "Your old slavery to sin looked like this," and now he is saying, "This is what life with the Spirit looks like." If Paul were commanding these traits, then he would be commanding we follow Law, and that's what he's spent the whole book arguing against.[1] However, despite this clarification, it is important to note, as MacArthur does, "All of the nine manifestations of the fruit of the Spirit are also *commanded* of believers in the New Testament."[2] I will try to show, in Lesson 19, that all nine are manifested (and thus commanded) through one illustration (cf. 5:25-6:5).

---

[1] I guess that if we are going to be consistent, Paul was not *commanding* abstinence from the vices last time either. He was describing the unconverted person's life. Application flows out of both lists regardless, but it's not Paul's primary point. And as far as this passage is concerned: While Paul is not commanding that love, joy, peace, etc... be practiced, he has already commanded that we walk by the Spirit (cf. Galatians 5:16), and if today's passage is a description of the life that is ordered according to the Spirit, then these traits are a sign that we *are* obeying the command to "Walk by the Spirit." It is not enough to just be a "nice," "kind," "loving" person. We must possess the Spirit, or our niceness is just a morally acceptable path to hell.

[2] John MacArthur, *Galatians*, 164-165. Emphasis in original.

Right now, though, we have some fruit to digest. First, we will discuss the importance of the fruit concept; second, we will break down each individual fruit and find biblical examples of them being put into action (apart from next week's text); and finally, we will discuss why Paul writes what he does at the end of 23-24.

Fruit. Apples. Oranges. Pineapples. Some are good, some are bad. Biblically, the word makes fifty-nine occurrences in the New Testament alone.[3] And, Jesus agrees that this list is more for demonstration than it is for obeying. In Matthew 7:15-20, He said:

> Beware of false prophets who come to you in sheep's clothing but inwardly are ravaging wolves. You'll recognize them by their fruit. Are grapes gathered from thornbushes or figs from thistles? In the same way, every good tree produces good fruit, but a bad tree produces bad fruit. A good tree can't produce bad fruit; neither can a bad tree produce good fruit. Every tree that doesn't produce good fruit is cut down and thrown into the fire. So you'll recognize them by their fruit.

Paul wants us to know that we are discerned for what we are by what we do. And, while Jesus literally says that they'll be recognized by their fruits—plural (cf. NASB of Matthew 7:20)—Paul today describes the fruit—singular—of the Spirit, and then he proceeds to name off nine different virtues. While there have been many attempted explanations at why this is, and while I primarily lean toward one option—namely that all the fruits are proofs of the first (love)—I will allow John MacArthur to talk:

> The first contrast between the deeds of the flesh and the fruit of the Spirit is that the products of the flesh are plural, whereas the product of the Spirit is singular ... there is also a contrast between the degrees to which the deeds and the fruit are produced. A given person may habitually practice only one or two, or perhaps a half dozen, of the sins Paul mentions here. But it would be practically impossible for one person to be habitually active in all of them. The fruit of the Spirit, on the other hand, is always produced completely in every believer, no matter how faintly evidenced its various manifestations may be."[4]

---

[3] Cf. *Holman Christian Standard Bible*.
[4] John MacArthur, *Galatians*, 164.

## Lesson 18: Galatians 5:22-24

The first manifestation of the Spirit is <u>love</u>. The Greek word is *agape*, and it is of uncertain etymology before biblical usage. That is not to say it was not used prior to the New Testament era, but rather that it meant something more akin to "I prefer" than the "Others first" emphasis that the New Testament clearly gives it, and most of the time was overpowered by *eros* (sexual, powerful love) and *phileo* (warm affectionate love) in ancient writings.[5] One thing is clear about the word from ancient sources: It means "love or the demonstration of love."[6] One scholar explains that this type of love "in the Greek sense is respect and sympathy between equals. *Agape* derives from a consciousness of equal unworthiness before God and His mercy." While *eros* love is all about getting, the church "knows of a love that does not desire, but gives."[7] This is the love of which Jesus said, "<u>By this all people will know that you are My disciples, if you have love for one another</u>" (John 13:35). And, just so we're clear out of the gate on what this love looks like in action, John writes in 1 John 3:16: "<u>This is how we have come to know love: He laid down His life for us. We should also lay down our lives for our brothers.</u>" This love that flows from the Spirit is—simply put—the opposite of a vast majority of the vices Paul put forward last time. If this kind of love is manifest in your life, you are likely not committing those sins.

The second manifestation of the Spirit is <u>joy</u>. In ancient Greek, the word referred simply to merriment.[8] When this concept appears in the Greek translation of the Old Testament, it is understood that joy is not just something inward, but that it arises from a cause and finds an outward expression.[9] David understood the concept of joy when he prayed in Psalm 51:12, "<u>Restore the joy of Your salvation to me.</u>" The primary evidence of salvation is a joy that comes from the Spirit. In a psalm he wrote at about the same time, reflecting upon God's forgiveness of his sin, David said, "<u>How joyful is the one whose transgression is forgiven, whose sin is covered! How joyful is the man the LORD does not charge with sin and in whose spirit is no deceit! . . . Be glad in the LORD and rejoice, you righteous ones; shout for joy, all you upright in heart</u>" (Psalm 32:1-2, 11). By the time of the New Testament, and specifically for Paul, the most important aspect of joy is maintaining joy in

---

[5] Kittel, *TDNT*, I:36.
[6] Kittel, *TDNT*, I:38.
[7] Kittel, *TDNT*, I:55. Italics added.
[8] Kittel, *TDNT*, IX:360.
[9] Kittel, *TDNT*, IX:363.

suffering.[10] If we look carefully at the book of Philippians, we will see an obvious example of joy in action: Paul is in prison, but his emphasis in the letter is joy, and while reading the letter it is just about impossible (at least for the Christian) to not be rejuvenated to joy.

This manifestation of the Spirit—as David explains in Psalm 51—can be quickly extinguished by sin. So the existence of this fruit in a person's life is a good sign that there isn't any unconfessed sin in a person's life. So, again, this fruit is the opposite of everything on the prior list. You can't be joyful and a fornicator or heretic at the same time.

The third manifestation of the Spirit is peace.[11] In classical Greek usage, this word typically meant nothing more than the opposite of war.[12] By the time the Greek Old Testament was completed, it referred to well-being or salvation.[13] In the New Testament it is frequently used to speak of peace between men.[14] One clear example of what this peace looks like is seen in Romans 5:1: "Therefore, since we have been declared righteous by faith, we have peace with God through our Lord Jesus Christ." Faith in Christ leads to peace with God, where prior there was nothing but enmity (cf. the vice list of 5:19-21). Romans 5:10 explains, "For if, while we were *enemies*, we were reconciled to God through the death of His Son, [then how] much more, having been reconciled, will we be saved by His life!"[15] As such, this manifestation of the Spirit is also the exact opposite of a vast majority of the items found in the vice list from Lesson 17. The reason this is possible for people from all different walks of life was explained in Galatians 3:28, "There is not a Jew or a Greek, there is not a slave or a free [person], there is not male and female; for you all, yourselves, are one in [the] Messiah Jesus." The Spirit accomplishes this.

The fourth manifestation of the Spirit is patience. It is extremely rare in non-biblical Greek. When it is used of humans, it speaks of forced acceptance of occurrences in life.[16] This word is used repeatedly of God in the New Testament. It is used as a verb in 2 Peter 3:9, and says, "The Lord does not delay His promise, as some understand delay, but is patient with you, not

---

[10] Kittel, *TDNT*, IX:370.

[11] The study of this Greek word completely changes how we think of the angels' news in Luke 2!

[12] Kittel, *TDNT*, II:401.

[13] Kittel, *TDNT*, II:406.

[14] Kittel, *TDNT*, II:411.

[15] Emphasis added.

[16] Kittel, *TDNT*, IV:375.

## Lesson 18: Galatians 5:22-24

wanting any to perish but all to come to repentance." Literally, the word has the same root as the word translated "rage" or "outbursts of anger" from the vice list, but has a prefix on the front that makes it really mean, "slow to rage." God is slow to rage with us, wanting all of us to come to repentance. In Romans 9:22, it says that God is even slow to rage towards those who are not elect. How good He is! He could strike them down the moment they're conceived (cf. Psalm 51:5), or the moment they're born (cf. Ephesians 2:1), or the moment they commit their first conscious sin, but He is slow to rage and does not do this. For this reason, all creation—elect and non-elect—must praise Him one day (cf. Philippians 2:10-11). In Romans 2:4, God's slowness to rage defines the next manifestation of the Spirit and is said to exist to let people reach repentance. For believers, it is pretty clear what this one should look like in our lives. We shouldn't be quick to blow up at people in anger (or to blow up in anger at God for things that we are still waiting for from Him). If we are habitually slow to anger, then we have good evidence that we belong to God and are walking by the Spirit.

The fifth manifestation of the Spirit is kindness. In non-religious Greek contexts, it referred to honesty, respectability, and worthiness.[17] As mentioned above, God displays His kindness through His slowness to rage (cf. Romans 2:4). The kindness of God was also demonstrated through Jesus (cf. Ephesians 2:7). According to John, we received grace and truth from God through Jesus (cf. John 1:17). These are two things that we desperately need, but we do not at all deserve either of them. God kindly gave them to us in the person of Jesus. In fact, the fact that Jesus is Christ and kindness translates from *chrestotes* is noteworthy. One commentator says,

> The common slave-name *Chrēstos* comes from this root, so that the word must suggest some quality that was desired in the ideal servant, as indeed do all the other qualities listed here: it has been well said that they are a list of 'slave virtues'. If these are the qualities of the 'servant Messiah', on whom Christians are called to pattern themselves, this is not surprising.[18]

If you treat people better than they deserve—which is absolutely vital for successful life within the church—then you are showcasing this fruit of the

---

[17] Kittel, *TDNT*, IX:489.
[18] R. Alan Cole, *Galatians*, 221.

Spirit; thus, it is clear how opposed to the works of the flesh this manifestation of the Spirit is.

The sixth manifestation of the Spirit is goodness. This word simply "indicates the quality a man has who is good."[19] That's a super simple explanation, but that's because it's a straightforward word to understand. Jesus used it in all three synoptic gospels when talking to the rich, young ruler. Jesus essentially says, "No one is good but God" (cf. Matthew 19:17; Mark 10:18; Luke 18:19). The same author who gave us our simple definition also explains that the "natural existence of man is incapable of reaching [goodness]."[20] Thus, to be able actually to achieve this manifestation, one must be empowered by the Spirit. If a person is not empowered by the Spirit, the following is certainly true of him: "There is no one who does what is good, not even one" (Romans 3:12).

The seventh manifestation of the Spirit is faithfulness. In classical Greek, it typically referred to confidence or trust.[21] In the Greek Old Testament, this word almost always replaces the Hebrew for faith, which—in Hebrew—carries a strong element of obedience.[22] If we look at Hebrews 11 closely, we will see faith being used in the aspect of faithfulness. All the saints who are held up as examples are said to have faith, and as such, they are said to have done something to prove that faith. For the believer wondering about the fruits of the Spirit, faithfulness is what results from faith, and it is shown by obedience to God—fighting the fleshly vices that want to come out in our lives.

The eighth manifestation of the Spirit is gentleness. This word refers to "mild and gentle friendliness in secular Greek." It also refers to "remaining calm even amidst abuse.[23] This word is exactly the same as the word that appears in the Sermon on the Mount in the third beatitude. Jesus said, "The gentle are blessed, for they will inherit the earth" (Matthew 5:5). Jesus exemplifies this manifestation of the Spirit perfectly. Philippians 2:5-8 says:

> Make your own attitude that of Christ Jesus, who, existing in the form of God, did not consider equality with God as something to be used for His own advantage. Instead He emptied Himself by assuming the

---

[19] Kittel, *TDNT*, I:18.
[20] Kittel, *TDNT*, I:16.
[21] Kittel, *TDNT*, VI:176.
[22] Kittel, *TDNT*, VI:197.
[23] Kittel, *TDNT*, VI:646.

## Lesson 18: Galatians 5:22-24

<u>form of a slave, taking on the likeness of men. And when He had come as a man in His external form, He humbled Himself by becoming obedient to the point of death—even to death on a cross</u>.

Paul also references Christ's gentleness in another book he wrote, "<u>Now I, Paul, make a personal appeal to you by the gentleness and graciousness of Christ</u>." (2 Corinthians 10:1). Jesus had all the power in the universe, but He exhibited gentleness and humility in not using it for His advantage. This is what the fruit of the Spirit looks like. This is why it is the opposite of many of the fleshly works Paul described in 5:19-21.

The final manifestation of the Spirit (that Paul gives in this list) is <u>self-control</u>. This word comes from a stem that "denotes power or lordship, and which expresses the power or lordship which one has either over oneself or over something."[24] Many of the ancient Greek philosophers highly valued this quality, and by way of contrast, "it plays a strikingly small role in biblical religion."[25] The same author explains, "The reason for this is that biblical man regarded his life as determined and directed by the command of God. There was thus no place for the self-mastery which had a place in autonomous ethics."[26] Again, I emphasize, Paul is not saying, "Be self-controlled!" but rather, he is saying, "As a follower of the Spirit, self-control will naturally start to exist in your life." And, by way of contrast to the emphasis of secular philosophers, John Calvin points out:

> There have often appeared in unrenewed men remarkable instances of gentleness, integrity, temperance, and generosity; but it is certain that all were but specious disguises. Curius and Fabrieius were distinguished for courage, Cato for temperance, Scipio for kindness and generosity, Fabius for patience; but it was only in the sight of men, and as members of civil society, that they were so distinguished. In the sight of God nothing is pure but what proceeds from the fountain of all purity.[27]

---

[24] Kittel, *TDNT*, II:339.
[25] Kittel, *TDNT*, II:340-341.
[26] Kittel, *TDNT*, II:341.
[27] John Calvin, *Commentaries on the Epistles of Paul to the Galatians and Ephesians*. The "fountain of all purity" is the Holy Spirit of God.

Most noticeably, this manifestation of the Spirit is directly opposed to sexual immorality, moral impurity, promiscuity, drunkenness, and carousing of the items from the vice list. If you consistently resist these vices, it is good evidence that you are being controlled by the Spirit and bearing good fruit.

We have looked at all nine manifestations of the fruit of the Spirit. We've seen how they all differ from the works of the flesh by looking at how they are manifested in a person's life. But then Paul concludes verse 23 by saying:

There is no Law opposed to such things.

One commentator explains that it can be more literally understood:

> As 'such things as these', and the sense would be excellent. No law forbids qualities like these; such virtues are in fact the 'keeping', or 'fulfilling', of the law. But, in view of the personal nature of the reference in verse 21 . . . 'those who habitually behave thus', it is better to translate personally here too, as 'such people', not 'such things'. The phrase will then become 'The law was never meant for (or "was never directed against") people like this'."[28]

In explaining it this way, it is also necessary to see that just as the list of fleshly works in 5:19-21 was not complete, this list also is not complete. If we look at 2 Peter 1:5-7, we will see a list with similar qualities, but also with different ones. No list of sins or virtues in the New Testament is an exhaustive list.

Paul says that there is no Law against people who live like this (because of the Spirit's power producing this kind of life). MacArthur explains one option for what this means,

> Even unbelievers do not make laws against such things as those which the fruit of the Spirit produces . . . There is certainly no law of God against such things . . . The believer who walks in the Spirit and manifests His fruit does not need a system of law to produce the right attitudes and behavior—they rise from within him."[29]

---

[28] R. Alan Cole, *Galatians*, 222.
[29] John MacArthur, *Galatians*, 170.

## Lesson 18: Galatians 5:22-24

Martin Luther takes it even farther. "A true Christian conducts himself in such a way that he does not need any law to warn or to restrain him. He obeys the Law without compulsion. The Law does not concern him. As far as he is concerned, there would not have to be any Law."[30] Thus, through the Spirit bearing fruit in the believer's life, the Law is fulfilled. And, since Galatians 5:14 said, "<u>For all of the Law has been summed up in one word, in this one, 'You all must love your neighbor as yourself.</u>'" I believe that every manifestation of the Spirit is actually a manifestation of the first in the list—*agape* love.

In addition, every work of the flesh is a breaking of the Law and is opposed to agape love. Thus, we see that if one is in the flesh, they must, by necessity, be under the Law, because only in those controlled by the Spirit is there no Law. Also, committing deeds of the flesh is breaking God's Law. And finally, striving to keep the Law (by your own strength) will only produce more fleshly works, because the Spirit is taken out of the equation.

Paul proves as much in verse 24 when he writes, "<u>But the ones belonging to [the] Messiah Jesus crucified the flesh with [its] passions and desires.</u>" He says they crucified the flesh, but in the previous verse, he said there is no Law. The two are closely united.

And maybe we get to this point, and you say, "But my flesh isn't dead! How do I know I'm saved and following the Spirit?"

Crucifixion doesn't necessarily mean death has occurred, but it does mean that death is inevitable. Crucifixion was an extremely lengthy process, and it is worth pointing out that Jesus' was probably one of the shortest in history. (Remember that He was already dead when they broke the legs of the criminals.) So, if you question your standing, I would ask you, "Do you believe in the life, death, and resurrection of Jesus? Does your life exhibit an increasing pattern of Spirit manifestations and a decreasing pattern of serious fleshly failures?" (I say serious, because every single day for all of our life we will give in to the flesh in "small" ways, but the big sins—think David and Bathsheba failures—will be few and far between.) If you have believed in Jesus' death, then you can know that when He was crucified, your flesh was put on the cross too. His death promises your flesh's eventual death, and His resurrection is the assurance of your future glorification. The day you believed in Jesus, your flesh was officially pinned to the cross, and you can rest in the assurance that it will finally bleed out and expire the day you enter into glory—through the door known as death. While the passions and desires still exist here, and

---

[30] Martin Luther, *A Commentary on St. Paul's Epistle to the Galatians*.

while we struggle against them—and often fail—the Spirit is our down payment (cf. Ephesians 1:14), and His fruit is for our assurance (cf. Galatians 5:22-23). How much fruit are you producing?

In conclusion, I'm not going to say, "Go love, have joy, make peace, be patient, show kindness, exhibit goodness, stay faithful, be gentle, and control yourself." Instead, I will simply ask, "Do these qualities appear in your life on a good day? Can you honestly say, 'This is not my doing. If it were up to me, I'd be totally described in 5:19-21'?"

If so, Paul's point in this passage has been accomplished. Thank God for His Spirit and trust Him now for the power to live differently. No contradictions here. The fruit of the Spirit is not another set of rules for people to be placed under!

# Failing to Find Fruit?

Do you look at your life and stress out because you don't see any fruit in your life?

If so, you're in a better place than you might think. The desire to produce fruit is a sign that you are a good tree. But, allow me to encourage you.

A tree doesn't stand outside, day after day, *striving* to produce fruit. It is merely a tree, and as such, it will produce fruit in keeping with its kind. If you are a believer, you will undoubtedly produce good fruit in season.

Also, if you're anything like me, then you are your own worst critic. You think you should be producing more fruit than you are. You think every day should be a plentiful harvest of fruit, even though it takes months for a tree to produce even one good piece of fruit. Give yourself a break. Look to Jesus!

If you're striving for fruit, but don't see any, don't beat yourself up. If you make a list of good deeds to do each and every day and you fail to accomplish them, don't beat yourself up. Look to Jesus! The simple truth of the matter is that we can't even live up to our own expectations for ourselves. And our expectations are weak compared to God's expectations for us. He demands that we be perfect.

But we can't be perfect. Because even if we controlled ourselves negatively—perfectly—and we never sinned, we wouldn't do all the good deeds we need to do to be perfectly righteous as well. There's a difference between not being sinful and actually possessing righteousness. We need both. We need to be free of sin and full of righteousness.

This is where Jesus comes in. He died on the cross because that was the punishment that our sins deserved. But before that, He walked on earth for thirty-three years, not only refraining from sinning, but also taking care of practical needs. He loved God perfectly; He also loved His neighbors perfectly. His life was marked by love, joy, peace, patience, kindness, goodness, faith, gentleness, and self-control. This is where we can find hope.

If you believe in Jesus (or if you've already believed in Him), He did more than just banish your sins to the grave. His perfect righteousness was credited to you as well. When you fail to respond patiently to your spouse, God doesn't see that sin. He sees Jesus' perfect patience. When you lash out in anger instead of practicing self-control, God doesn't see your sin. He sees Jesus' perfect self-control.

So when you look at your life, and you feel like you should be living more righteously, you are right. But it shouldn't lead you to beat yourself up and try harder. It should lead you to take a more extended look at Jesus, the only one who could ever perfectly fulfill both God's Law and His own expectations for Himself.

If you turn inward and try to work harder at producing the fruit of the Spirit, then you are missing the whole point of Galatians. Remember Galatians 5:1, "[The] Messiah set us free for freedom; therefore, you all must stand, and you all must not be again entangled in a yoke of slavery." Don't turn the fruit of the Spirit into a yoke of slavery!

Trust Christ today! He is your only hope!

# Reflection Questions

1. How does today's text show Paul's love for the church?
2. Why does Paul say there is no law against these actions?
3. Which of these fruits is most apparent in your life?
4. Which of these fruits do you most need more of in your life?
5. Have you placed your faith in Jesus yet?

## Praying the Text

*Jesus,*

*Thank You for the Spirit. Please help me to live each day by His power and grace. I cannot do it on my own. I want to produce good fruit. I want to live in the Spirit's freedom. I want to no longer be under either the flesh or the Law. Help me!*

# Lesson 19

## Galatians 5:25-6:5

[25]If we live by [the] Spirit, we should also order [our lives] by [the] Spirit. [26]We must not become conceited, provoking one another, envying one another.

[1]Brothers, if indeed a person might be caught in any transgression, you all who are spiritual must yourselves restore such a one in a gentle spirit, watching yourselves lest you also might be tempted. [2]You all must carry one another's burdens, and thusly you all will fulfill the Law of the Messiah. [3]For if someone might consider [himself] to be something, being nothing, [then] he deceives himself. [4]But let each man's work show for himself, and then for his [work] alone he will have reason for boasting, and not for another's [work], [5]for each one will have to carry his own burden.

# Lessons in Love (with Legos)

I like Legos. I really like Legos. And while modern building kits expect you to separate the pieces into like colors before beginning to build, I prefer to dump all 800+ pieces into one pile and dig through it until I find the piece I need. For me, it's part of the experience that makes Legos so much fun. And I took a few pictures to demonstrate what I mean. Legos are meant to interact with each other. They are not intended to be segregated by color, or even by type. So here we see characters interacting and segregated by their roles: Pilots in a group, droids in a group, and mechanics in a group:

Here we see them how they should be: All interspersed and interacting with each other:

And I bring all that up because that is a straightforward way to illustrate the point of what Paul is saying in Galatians 5:25-6:5. Based on everything he's said up to this point, this passage screams, "Put it into practice!"

Let's get back into the context.

So at this point, Paul has theologically proven that we don't need the Law any longer as believers. He's shown that if you return to the Law, then you are returning to slavery. He's shown at the same time that as believers, we are to fulfill the Law, but we do it not by obeying rules, but rather by loving others. And then Paul said that the Spirit—which wants to express love—is harassed and assaulted by the flesh. Paul later described what life in the flesh is characterized by, and he contrasted it with a life characterized by the Spirit's power. And that's where we find ourselves today.

## Lesson 19: Galatians 5:25-6:5

The first thing Paul does is connect back to 3:2-3. There he had written, "I only want to learn this from you all: Did you all receive the Spirit by works of Law or by faithful hearing? Thusly you all are mindless: After beginning by [the] Spirit, are you all now being completed by [the] flesh?" And here, in 5:25, Paul answers that question:

> If we live by [the] Spirit, we should also order [our lives] by [the] Spirit.

John MacArthur understands "live by [the] Spirit" to refer to the new life that believers have because of Christ, and "order [our lives] by [the] Spirit" to refer to their new way of life.[1] Thus, Paul makes it clear that a person who claims to be a Christian, but whose life remains unchanged, is deceived, and actually not alive at all. He is actually still under the curse of the Law. John Calvin says of this verse, "The apostle draws from the doctrine a practical exhortation. The death of the flesh is the life of the Spirit. If the Spirit of God lives in us, let him govern our actions."[2] And that's precisely what the next eleven verses (cf. 5:26-6:10) focus on.

Paul starts with the negative exhortation to conclude chapter 5:

> We must not become conceited, provoking one another, envying one another.

There are many things to say about this verse. MacArthur notes one aspect: "The pursuit of holiness can be perverted into self-righteous, proud piosity. No sin does greater damage to the church or is more offensive to God than self-righteousness."[3] However, it doesn't need only to refer to self-righteousness. According to one dictionary, the word translated "provoke," literally means, "to *call forth to oneself (challenge)*, i.e. (by implication to *irritate*)."[4] Paul wants believers in the Galatian church, and us in our churches today, to refuse to be irritants to other people.

Now don't hear what I'm not saying. I'm not saying that if someone in your church has an annoying habit or annoying hobby that Paul is saying they need to stop. That's not it at all. Paul is saying that if something is being

---

[1] John MacArthur, *Galatians*, 171.
[2] John Calvin, *Commentaries on the Epistles of Paul to the Galatians and Ephesians*.
[3] John MacArthur, *Galatians*, 175.
[4] James Strong, *Strong's Talking Greek & Hebrew Dictionary*. Emphasis in original.

done habitually that causes another brother or sister to stumble into sin, then the person with the habit needs to seriously consider rooting that habit out of their life (or at least refuse to partake around the person who is stumbling). However, at the same time, the one who is stumbling must grow angry at the person who is troubling her. She must actually raise the concern to the one troubling her so that something can be done to fix it and so that anger and bitterness are not allowed to fester. You can't get mad about something that you refuse to try to help fix.

Paul then writes 6:1-5, where he explains the positive practical application:

> Brothers, if indeed a person might be caught in any transgression, you all who are spiritual must yourselves restore such a one in a gentle spirit, watching yourselves lest you also might be tempted. You all must carry one another's burdens, and thusly you all will fulfill the Law of the Messiah. For if someone might consider [himself] to be something, being nothing, [then] he deceives himself. But let each man's work show for himself, and then for his [work] alone he will have reason for boasting, and not for another's [work], for each one will have to carry his own burden.

If we act like the Legos in the first picture above, then we will only practice this passage with the believers of whom we approve. However, true unity and fulfillment of the Spirit's fruits look like the second picture. John MacArthur writes, "Though a Christian's first concern must be for his own holiness and purity of life, God's Word makes clear that he also has a responsibility for the holiness and purity *of the rest of the church*."[5] Note that he does not say "part of the rest of the church," but rather "the rest of the church." This is huge! Paul's exhortation to real love can be broken into two subsections: Bearing with others and watching ourselves.

Verses 1-2 explain bearing with others:

> Brothers, if indeed a person might be caught in any transgression, you all who are spiritual must yourselves restore such a one in a gentle spirit, watching yourselves lest you also might be tempted. You all

---

[5] John MacArthur, *Galatians*, 175. Emphasis added.

## Lesson 19: Galatians 5:25-6:5

> must carry one another's burdens, and thusly you all will fulfill the Law of the Messiah.

Here's a mind-blowing thought: This should be what the church is known for. It should be happening day in and day out in the lives of church members. And what follows is a saddening truth: It doesn't happen like it should, even though many churches claim that they preach love. Too often, we're okay with our group of like-minded—like-dressed—Lego friends—be them hipsters or thugs, black or white, or old or young—and we force the ones who are different than us to take care of themselves. Paul's words in 1 Corinthians 1:10 should sting our ears into change, "Now I urge you, brothers, in the name of our Lord Jesus Christ, that all of you agree in what you say, *that there be no divisions among you, and that you be united with the same understanding and the same conviction.*"[6]

In churches these days, people think it's a good idea to have "foot-washing services" in order to demonstrate love for fellow believers, and it's because they'd rather do a ritual that is totally meaningless in our day than actually get their hands dirty "bearing with each other" (cf. Ephesians 4:2). When this passage says, "Thusly you all will fulfill the Law of the Messiah" (6:2), Paul is saying, "This is how you fulfill the Law—loving one another." And just to take it even one step farther, when Jesus says in Matthew 11:28-30, "Come to Me, all of you who are weary and burdened, and I will give you rest. All of you, take up My yoke and learn from Me, because I am gentle and humble in heart, and you will find rest for yourselves. For My yoke is easy and My burden is light," and when Paul says, "Carry one another's burdens," they are together saying that Jesus carries our burdens in life when other believers carry our burdens. If you don't get involved in the lives of other believers, and if you don't bear their burdens with them, then you are painting a blasphemous picture of what Jesus is like. We must all repent of our failures in this area!

Galatians 6:1 ends by saying, "watching yourselves lest you also might be tempted," and verses 3-5 explain what this looks like:

> For if someone might consider [himself] to be something, being nothing, [then] he deceives himself. But let each man's work show for himself, and then for his [work] alone he will have reason for boasting,

---

[6] Emphasis added.

<u>and not for another's [work], for each one will have to carry his own burden.</u>

I initially understood the charge in Galatians 6:1 to mean that, for instance, helping a struggling brother try to overcome a pornography addiction might open me up to that temptation, and while I don't doubt that reality, I think it works itself out differently. Paul is saying, "When you help someone else overcome a sin or temptation, you need to watch out for temptations toward pride because you don't struggle with that specific sin; if you allow pride to creep in, remember that <u>'pride comes before destruction'</u> (Proverbs 16:18)."

This is where verse 3 comes into effect. You deceive yourself if you think you're too good to be tempted to certain sins. Then verses 4-5 explain that the only person we're ultimately responsible for is ourselves. For this reason, we should desire others to help us bear our loads, and we should eagerly seek to help others carry theirs.

Before closing out this post, I want to demonstrate how every fruit of the Spirit is manifested through these six verses. Love is very clearly shown through the phrase, "<u>Thusly you all will fulfill the Law of the Messiah</u>" (6:2) By interacting with believers in this way, we can't help but show love. Martin Luther said, "The Law of Christ is the Law of love. Christ gave us no other law than this law of mutual love: 'A new commandment I give unto you, That ye love one another.' To love means to bear another's burdens."[7]

Joy is shown in the fact that 1) it should bring us joy to love others in this way, 2) we should be joyful in our practicing this task, and 3) doing this helps others to have joy.

Peace is shown because if we all bear with each other and carry each other's troubles, we won't consider ourselves to be what we are not (cf. 6:3).

Patience is shown by continually "bearing with each other" (cf. Ephesians 4:2) and "<u>carrying one another's burdens</u>" (6:2) even after months of already doing so.

Kindness was discussed last time as being from the same root as Christ, and as such, kindness is shown by being Christ to others by fulfilling His Law of love.

Goodness is shown because it is good to love others.

---

[7] Martin Luther, *A Commentary on St. Paul's Epistle to the Galatians*.

Lesson 19: Galatians 5:25-6:5

Faithfulness is shown as a pattern of life that seeks to be faithful to the Spirit (cf. 5:25), and that is done in no more explicit way than by habitually bearing with one another in love.

Gentleness is shown if we do this rightly; the same word as the manifestation of the Spirit (cf. 5:23) appears in 6:1 ("in a gentle spirit").

Self-control is shown because we are supposed to watch ourselves for pride in our hearts. Paul has now commanded believers to practice the fruit of the Spirit through the act of bearing with one another in love.

In conclusion, as believers in a local church, we must interact in each other's lives. There is no such thing as a church member who doesn't deserve your care and concern. Be the Legos in the second picture; don't let the first picture describe you!

## The One Who Bore Our Burdens

Now maybe you read this, and you think, "Yeah, wouldn't that be nice. I feel like I have literally no one to carry my burdens, and the people in the churches I've gone to are fake and judgy."

The church is full of broken people, imperfect people, people in need of grace—just like you.

This is why Jesus came to earth. He came to bear our burdens in His body on the cross. He died for the sins of whoever might believe in Him. He's there with you every step of the way—if you believe. Even when no one else wants to live out their Christian calling of bearing each other's burdens, He will live up to it. He loves you. Place your faith in Him today!

And if you are already a believer, but you have become convicted of your lack of love for others, know that Jesus paid for that sin too. Replace your faith in Him. He lived a perfect life in your place to pass in every way that you fail. Recommit to Him, believe the Gospel anew, and be freed to love like Christ!

## Reflection Questions

1. How does today's text show Paul's love for the church?
2. Can you point to anyone whose burdens you carry?
3. Can you point to anyone who is carrying your burdens?

4. How diverse is your church? Do you spend too much time in one group as opposed to another?
5. Have you placed your faith in Jesus yet?

# Praying the Text

*Jesus,*
*Thank You for being my example of burden-carrying. Please help me to follow in Your steps and carry someone else's burdens. I want to be a spiritual person. Help me, please! I love You.*

# Lesson 20

## Galatians 6:6-10

⁶The one who is being taught the word must fellowship in all good things with the one who is teaching. ⁷Do not be deceived; God is not [able to be] mocked. For whatever a person might sow, this also a person will reap: ⁸"The one who is sowing to the flesh will himself, from the flesh, reap corruption, but the one who is sowing to the Spirit will, from the Spirit, reap eternal life." ⁹And we should not become weary while doing good things, for in [the] right season we will reap, not fainting. ¹⁰Therefore, as we have season, we should work for the good of all people, but especially for the ones of the household of faith.

# Sowing and Reaping Reassessed

> I'm probably gonna catch some flak man
> But ima swallow this pill like pac-man
> Some of these folks won't tell the truth
> too busy tryina get them racks man
> Church tryina rob my paychecks
> Choir members probably having gay sex
> Pastor manipulating, hurting women
> I wonder what he's gonna say next
> Bookstore pimpin them hope books
> Like God don't know how broke looks
> And tellin me that I'm gonna reap a mil
> If I sow into these low crooks
> Plus I know ol' girl a freak, now how she sing the solo
> I walked into church with a snapback and they tellin' me that's a no-no
> That's backwards and I lack words for these actors called pastors
> All these folks is hypocrites and that's why I ain't at church.[1]

And if there's ever been a song written by a Christian artist that genuinely made me uncomfortable, it would be this one. Especially the line about pastors. The first time I heard it, I felt dirty for listening to it. The pastors who discipled me for the first three years of my Christian life were not at all actors. They were some of the most authentic men I've ever known. However, if I'm being candid, I've turned to these lyrics several times since 2014 (in times of anger and frustration) to say, "This is what is wrong with the American church." However, the last time I heard this song, the heavy emphasis on money and the specific words "reap" and "sow" got me thinking.

Additionally, a news article I found on Facebook this week[2] explained that one of the primary reasons why 59% of millennials have left the church is

---

[1] Lecrae, "Lecrae - Church Clothes (Music Video)," *YouTube* (May 10, 2012), https://www.youtube.com/watch?v=tlWvx0wdySk.

[2] This Lesson was originally published as a blogpost on March 11, 2017.

because of "distrust and misallocation of resources." The author explains, "Over and over we've been told to 'tithe' and give 10 percent of our incomes to the church, but where does that money actually go? Millennials, more than any other generation, don't trust institutions, for we have witnessed over and over how corrupt and self-serving they can be."[3] While I don't agree with the solutions proposed by the article, the point stands that the common "Give your money, and God will bless you" teaching has done much damage to the church's reputation. I say this upfront because today's passage has Paul talking about sowing and reaping. Let's look at the context.[4]

So we've finally come to the end of this super long section (cf. 5:13-6:10). Paul has proven that the Law is fulfilled through love for one another, but he has also explained that the flesh wars against the Spirit. He's described the results of following the flesh and the results of following the Spirit, and he's commanded that believers bear with one another in love, and it has been shown how bearing in love displays the Spirit's fruit and successfully wars against the flesh. Today, Paul wants to show us how we bear with those who teach us the Word, and in so doing, he shows us another way to resist the desires of the flesh and encourages pastors to remain faithful in their ministry at the same time.

Paul begins in verse 6 by saying:

<u>The one who is being taught the word must fellowship in all good things with the one who is teaching.</u>

John MacArthur writes, "The seemingly obvious interpretation, and the one that is most common, is that Paul is exhorting congregations to pay their pastors fairly. But although that principle is taught in the New Testament . . . it does not seem to be what Paul is teaching here."[5] However, I must lovingly

---

[3] Sam Eaton, "59 Percent of Millennials Raised in a Church Have Dropped Out—And They're Trying to Tell Us Why," *Faith It* (April 4, 2018), http://www.faithit.com/12-reasons-millennials-over-church-sam-eaton.

[4] And before tying it all together, let me just explain one thing I'm happy about from the past three years: Learning how to properly interpret Scripture. Three years ago, I would have said, "The beginning talks about bearing in love, and this talks about sowing and reaping; I'll tell what the text says without keeping them connected." However, that's faulty Bible study. Paul wrote this whole letter. From the first word to the last. It's one complete argument. We can't chop it and take what we want where we want and call it exegesis. We have to read all of it as a unit.

[5] John MacArthur, *Galatians*, 182.

## Lesson 20: Galatians 6:6-10

disagree. Especially when Calvin, Luther, and another modern commentator all see monetary giving being spoken of here. Cole states,

> It is, as often, difficult to decide whether this is the final verse of this section or the opening verse of the next. As usual, it will be best to take it as a "bridge verse," whichever group it is considered as falling under . . . When Paul says *koinōneito*, share, or "have fellowship," it is a Christian euphemism for "make a financial contribution."[6]

Now, lest I dismiss MacArthur too quickly, his explanation must be discussed, because it is helpful to understand the full meaning of our text today. MacArthur sees verse 6 as going with verses 1-5, and he wants to equate "the one who is teaching" of verse 6 with one of the ones "who are spiritual," in verse 1. He helpfully explains that the word translated "share"[7] in verse 6 is commonly translated "fellowship," and the word translated "good things" speaks primarily of things that have "spiritual or moral excellence," and thus, "The spiritual Christian who has picked up and held up his fallen brother also builds him up in the word, in whose good things they fellowship together."[8] Thus MacArthur sees the spiritual believer and the recovering believer as being able to share fellowship together in the good fruit that results from the recovering believer heeding the teaching of the spiritual believer.

I take the time to explain that because it helps add an extra layer to the following verses, even if we understand fellowship primarily as "monetary support." In verses 7-8, Paul explains the spiritual truth behind his command to share with the teacher:

> Do not be deceived; God is not [able to be] mocked. For whatever a person might sow, this also a person will reap: "The one who is sowing to the flesh will himself, from the flesh, reap corruption, but the one who is sowing to the Spirit will, from the Spirit, reap eternal life."

He starts by commanding them not to be deceived. Paul knows that the flesh wants to hold on to every dollar it is given. He also knows that the flesh wants to isolate itself and not fellowship with other believers. He says that you can't

---

[6] R. Alan Cole, *Galatians*, 228.
[7] Cf. *Holman Christian Standard Bible* on Galatians 6:6.
[8] John MacArthur, *Galatians*, 182.

trick God; the law of nature—reaping what you sow—can not be undermined. If a person refuses fellowship with other believers, then they will reap from the flesh; if a person hoards every dollar they are given, then they will reap from the flesh. God cannot be mocked. I want to give two examples of how this process works in the life of Christianity today: One in the context of the local church and one in the context of the wider Christian world.

First, in the local church, we are called to share with those who teach us the Word. We share with them by giving our money—tithe/10% is never called for in the New Testament. The model is actually to give until it hurts. Listen to this from Luke 21:1-4:

> He looked up and saw the rich dropping their offerings into the temple treasury. He also saw a poor widow dropping in two tiny coins. "I tell you the truth," He said. "This poor widow has put in more than all of them. For all these people have put in gifts out of their surplus, but she out of her poverty has put in all she had to live on."

She gave 100%.

Paul will connect this act of giving to the Spirit's manifestation of love in 2 Corinthians 8:8-9, "I am not saying this as a command. Rather, by means of the diligence of others, I am testing the genuineness of your love. For you know the grace of our Lord Jesus Christ: Though He was rich, for your sake He became poor, so that by His poverty you might become rich." This is what our giving to the ministry should look like. (And in Galatians 6:6 it *is* a command.) Because we reap what we sow, the teaching will reflect itself in our lives. If the teaching is all talk and no action, then the lives will be all talk and no action. If the teaching is judgmental and degrading, then the hearers will become judgmental Pharisees.

For this reason, the pastor should teach accurately, so people keep giving. He shouldn't have to preach one sermon a month on giving to keep people convicted about the need to give; they should do it willingly because he teaches accurately and models it in his own life. In the same way, if a ministry is fruitless, there is no need to sow monetary funds into it to keep it going, especially if it is doctrinally off or failing in the Christian living it produces.

In much the same way, as Christians, we read books written by other Christians. When we do this, we are sowing into their ministry, and thus fellowshipping with them. Since the teaching becomes the living, and since we reap what we sow, it follows that we should not spend time in worthless Christian media. If we do, it will come out in our life. If Christians only purchased biblically sound, Gospel-centered works, it would spur pastors worldwide to be accurate, biblical, and Christ-centered, and a revival of sorts would take place in the church, which could then lead to a revival in the world.

We must sow to the Spirit so that we can reap eternal life and avoid fulfilling the desires of the flesh. We must not sow to the flesh because if we do, then we will reap corruption. This is first shown in a lack of salvation assurance. People—like the majority of millennials today—who avoid church are sowing to the flesh and reaping corruption. I personally believe the biggest problem with millennials[9] is their pride: They can't take it if someone says they are wrong, and since the first premise of the Gospel is that everyone is wrong, no millennial—or really anyone else—wants to hear it. Thus, they avoid the church and put up smokescreens so they can continue to sow to their flesh.

In verses 9-10 we see an exhortation for believers to persevere in love—summing up the whole section:

> And we should not become weary while doing good things, for in [the] right season we will reap, not fainting. Therefore, as we have season, we should work for the good of all people, but especially for the ones of the household of faith.

It is hard work to bear with each other. It is hard to give our resources away sacrificially. It is often tough to resist the desires of the flesh. However, we must rest in the Spirit and let Him manifest Himself in our lives. The truth is there: We will reap if we don't give up sowing. This earthly life is the opportunity to sow. Sowing to the Spirit—the sowing we must not give up—is done through bearing with one another, fellowshipping with one another, not hoarding resources from one another, and by resisting the desires of the flesh. We also sow by doing the exact opposite, but that will result in corruption, and we must give that up immediately!

If your pastor is faithful to the Word and regularly points you toward Christ, give of your resources. Especially if he is a fulltime pastor who is employed by the church. He relies on you for support. If he is taking care of your spiritual needs, then you owe it to him to help support him. If you don't give of your resources, then you want to reap corruption from the flesh.

---

[9] In the realm of full disclosure, the fact that I was born in 1992 means that I am also, technically (unfortunately), a millennial.

However, if your pastor is not faithful to the Word, you are not sowing to the Spirit by giving to his ministry. Unfaithfulness to the Word—and neglect of the Gospel as presented in Galatians—leads to unhealthy situations like the one that Paul had to correct in this letter. The reason he's spent so much time on the difference between the flesh and the Spirit is that legalism and lawlessness both lead to fleshly corruption, and not to the Spirit's eternal life. If your pastor does not preach the Gospel, you will not reap eternal life by giving to him, but rather corruption from the flesh.

It is important to note what Paul says at the end of verse 10. We must work for the good of all, but especially for believers. When millennials are all about causes in the world, that's great, but when they neglect to come to church because they feel that the church isn't doing enough for those "out there," they are missing the point. We—as the church—owe love first and foremost to our own. Only after loving believers to the nth degree are we to show love to the world. And the primary way we'll show the world love is by telling them they're wrong and that only in Jesus can they be made right.

Why do you neglect to give to the church? Is it because you don't belong there because you have yet to be made a part of it by the blood of Jesus? I would plead with you to believe in Him today. Find a church that points you to Him and get involved. Love others well, which includes giving up your resources, and sow to the Spirit for eternal life.

In conclusion, the church has done a lot of damage in the name of "sowing and reaping." However, that is because they have separated the act of giving from the fruit of living. The teaching is promoted by the giving. The teaching shows its true colors through the living that follows. If you want to live a life of love to God and others, then give to teaching that accurately represents who God is. This will lead to eternal life, and it is another way in which we win the war against the flesh, walk by the Spirit in freedom, and prove that we are not under Law but rather fulfilling Christ's Law by bearing with one another in love.

# Another Type of Sowing

There is another type of sowing in Scripture as well, and I am still not referring to the joke of "Sow into my ministry, and you'll reap monetary/physical benefits." The type of sowing I am referring to is what all worthy pastors should be known for doing.

## Lesson 20: Galatians 6:6-10

It's based on Jesus' parable in Mark 4:3-8, 14-20. Jesus says:

> Listen! Consider the sower who went out to sow. As he sowed, this occurred: Some seed fell along the path, and the birds came and ate it up. Other seed fell on rocky ground where it didn't have much soil, and it sprang up right away, since it didn't have deep soil. When the sun came up, it was scorched, and since it didn't have a root, it withered. Other seed fell among thorns, and the thorns came up and choked it, and it didn't produce a crop. Still others fell on good ground and produced a crop that increased 30, 60, and 100 times [what was sown] . . . The sower sows the word. These are the ones along the path where the word is sown: when they hear, immediately Satan comes and takes away the word sown in them. And these are the ones sown on rocky ground: when they hear the word, immediately they receive it with joy. But they have no root in themselves; they are short-lived. When pressure or persecution comes because of the word, they immediately stumble. Others are sown among thorns; these are the ones who hear the word, but the worries of this age, the seduction of wealth, and the desires for other things enter in and choke the word, and it becomes unfruitful. But the ones sown on good ground are those who hear the word, welcome it, and produce a crop: 30, 60, and 100 times [what was sown]."

The sower scatters the seed of the Gospel, not caring where it lands. It isn't his job to say, "Oh, she certainly isn't worthy of hearing this message," or "he is too far gone to believe; I'll save this seed for someone else." No, he scatters it everywhere and leaves it to God's sovereign preparation of the soil.

This is why I end every Lesson[10] with a specific Gospel call. I want you to hear it. And I want you to hear it repeatedly if you've never believed.

Have you trusted Christ?

You see, there is yet another biblical form of sowing. Jesus came to earth, was crucified on the cross, and His dead body was planted (sown) in the grave. Three days later, God raised Him from the dead (reaped), and it was done to show that when we believe in Christ, we are spiritually buried for the spiritual reaping that will occur when Jesus returns. We won't stay dead. We will be raised to stand before Christ—believer and unbeliever.

---

[10] And every blogpost article and every novel I write...

The question is: When your spirit is reaped on that day, what will you receive? Blessing? Or cursing?

Those that don't believe in Christ are under a curse (Galatians 3:10). Those that do believe in Christ are blessed (Galatians 3:9).

Is your faith in yourself or in Jesus? I pray it's in Jesus. Give your life to Him today! He died to free you from the Law and sin. Place your faith in Him today, be sown in Him today, and reap spiritual blessing and life for eternity.

Trust Christ today!

# Reflection Questions

1. How does today's text show Paul's love for the church?
2. How generous are you with your money?
3. Based on this Lesson, do you sow more to the flesh or the Spirit?
4. Do you take advantage of your opportunities to do good to/for others? Or are you growing weary of doing good? Why?
5. Have you placed your faith in Jesus yet?

# Praying the Text

*Jesus,*

*I want to sow to the Spirit. Please help me to do it. I need to become more generous so that I am more willing to bear with others in love. I need to study the truth of the Gospel so that I am more confident of my standing in You. I need to resist the flesh so that the Spirit can grow stronger. I need You! Help me to love You more so that these actions become muscle memory for me.*

# Lesson 21

## Galatians 6:11-18

[11]Notice I wrote to you with large letters by my hand. [12]The ones who are wanting to make a good showing in [the] flesh are the ones compelling you all to be circumcised, only in order that they might not be persecuted for the cross of the Messiah. [13]For not even the ones being circumcised are keeping [the] Law themselves, but they are wanting you all to be circumcised in order that they might boast about [the] flesh of each of you. [14]But may it never be for me to boast unless about the cross of our Lord Jesus [the] Messiah, through which [the] world has been crucified to me, and I [have been crucified] to [the] world! [15]For neither circumcision nor uncircumcision is anything, instead a new creation. [16]And as many as will walk according to this standard: Peace [be] upon them and mercy also [be] upon the Israel of God.
    [17]For the remainder [of my life], let no one give me troubles, for I myself carry the marks of Jesus on my body.
    [18]The grace of our Lord Jesus [the] Messiah be with you all's Spirit, brothers. Amen.

# Milestones

There is one weekend of my life that I still clearly remember thirteen years after the fact. And while there's a lot of childhood birthday parties and sleepovers that could vie for the most memorable weekend of my life, the one I'm thinking of is neither a birthday nor a sleepover. But it did occur while I was in eighth grade, my childhood best friends were all there, and it was two nights long.

It was an event known as Milestones that was put on by the church in which I was raised. And out of all the events that were put on by that church throughout my childhood, if there is one that I'll carry into my future ministry, then it would be this one. The point of the event was to commission eighth-graders for high school. High school, for the child raised in the church, is a scary time. It is when a person starts becoming the person they will be for the rest of their life. For the child who is raised in the church, it will typically make or break their faith. That's what the event was for: Preparing eighth-grade boys to be strong men of God who stand firm despite what others say. It was centered around three virtues: Strength, courage, integrity. Everything that we did over the weekend fit into one of those three categories. Strength being initially seen in our 5 a.m. run the first morning there. Integrity being most memorable from our purity talk. Courage being very ingrained in our minds through several nighttime activities.

But, out of all of these virtues, I think the most important one is integrity. In my personal opinion, integrity gives you strength and helps you have courage. Lack of integrity leaves you weak and worried. And integrity isn't just about standing against sexual sin. Integrity also means that what you say is what you mean. And beyond that, it means that what you do is what is right to do, and you don't try to hide your mistakes.

So with that background, I'll share the specific story. On Saturday morning, we woke up before the sun and went for a run. Then we did push-ups. (I, being a skinny eighth-grader, had serious troubles here.) All we had for breakfast was a fruit-filled breakfast bar. Then we did more strenuous activity for the rest of the morning. When lunchtime finally rolled around, we were all hoping for something delicious, but we were sorely disappointed when we were served gruel. I don't remember what all it was made of, but I do remember it having oatmeal, beans, and little pieces of pickles in it. (I also remember it not being as bad as I initially expected.) However, one of the students disagreed with my assessment and decided to through the pickle pieces onto the ground. (If I remember correctly, some of us knew who had done it because he'd bragged about it.) When asked by the leadership, no one would come clean, so we all had to run. After like twenty minutes of extra running, he finally came clean. Integrity.

I share this because it was a quote from MacArthur that reminded me of that weekend. He says, in summary of the book of Galatians, that there are only

> Two forms of religion that man has ever known. There is grace/faith/Spirit religion, known as Christianity, and there is law/works/flesh religion, which identifies all the rest . . . It is as if, on the market shelf of world religions, there are hundreds of attractive packages, with a great range of shapes, sizes, labels, claims, and prices. But inside all of them is the same tasteless, nutritionless sawdust of works righteousness. Standing alone, unattractive and repulsive to the natural man, is the Gospel, which alone contains real food.[1]

It's the repulsive-looking gruel that actually provides nourishment. It's much better for you than processed pizza rolls or hot pockets.

Paul writes in Galatians 6:11-18,

> Notice I wrote to you with large letters by my hand. The ones who are wanting to make a good showing in [the] flesh are the ones compelling you all to be circumcised, only in order that they might not be persecuted for the cross of the Messiah. For not even the ones being circumcised are keeping [the] Law themselves, but they are wanting you all to be circumcised in order that they might boast about [the] flesh of each of you. But may it never be for me to boast unless about the cross of our Lord Jesus [the] Messiah, through which [the] world has been crucified to me, and I [have been crucified] to [the] world! For neither circumcision nor uncircumcision is anything, instead a

---

[1] John MacArthur, *Galatians*, 194.

## Lesson 21: Galatians 6:11-18

> new creation. And as many as will walk according to this standard: Peace [be] upon them and mercy also [be] upon the Israel of God. For the remainder [of my life], let no one give me troubles, for I myself carry the marks of Jesus on my body. The grace of our Lord Jesus [the] Messiah be with you all's Spirit, brothers. Amen.

Here we look at Paul's concluding sign-off from this letter. As such, Paul will review all of his key points before wishing his readers well. He starts in verse 11, by saying:

> Notice I wrote to you with large letters by my hand.

Cole explains,

> Paul takes the pen from his scribe (assuming that he has not written the whole letter himself) to write 'The Grace' in his own handwriting (cf. 2 Thess. 3:17), to assure them of the genuineness of the letter. But as he looks at the sprawling letters which he has written, he muses whimsically that they certainly make no fine outward show, and this becomes to him a parable of the whole of his life and ministry, and indeed of the Christian faith. As far as he is now concerned, there is nothing 'fine' in life but the cross of Christ; and he brushes the last vestiges of the Galatian quarrel from him in the knowledge of his own close relation to the crucified Messiah. On that note of peace the battle-scarred veteran ends the tortured letter.[2]

It is relatively well recognized that Paul employed a scribe to write his letters, and whether Paul told him the exact words to write or gave him the topics he wanted written allowing for a little freedom for the scribe, Paul remained ultimately responsible for the content of the letter, so we can say that it was written by Paul.[3]

---

[2] R. Alan Cole, *Galatians*, 233.

[3] Cf. David B. Capes, Rodney Reeves, and E. Randolph Richards, *Rediscovering Paul: An Introduction to His World, Letters and Theology* (Downers Grove, IL: IVP Academic, 2011); E Randolph Richards, *Paul and First-Century Letter Writing: Secretaries, Composition, and Collection* (Downers Grove, IL: IVP Academic, 2004).

Richards explains that the person behind the scribe could authenticate a letter in three ways (listed in descending order of value; ascending order of commonness): A seal pressed into clay, a summary of contents, a word of farewell in author's handwriting. "An author was held responsible for every word of the letter. The personal handwriting at the end of a letter indicated the author had seen the letter and consequently assumed responsibility for its contents."[4] However, Richards notes that "it is impossible to verify a postscript from Paul in his own handwriting," because we only have copies today. "Paul, however, on more than one occasion drew attention to his handwriting."[5] Richards also explains, "There is one clear example of a *summary* postscript among the letters of Paul (Philem 19-21)."[6] He then writes two pages later, "There are ample examples that Paul used a postscript as a 'signature' to his letters. Galatians 6:11-18 is the most commonly cited example."[7]

In this Lesson, I seek to show that Galatians 6:11-18 is, in fact, a summary postscript, summing up all the main points of the letter, even though Paul breaks from the standard norm of repeating "the material in the same order as the body of the letter."[8]

Paul summarizes 4:8-6:10 in verses 12-13:

> The ones who are wanting to make a good showing in [the] flesh are the ones compelling you all to be circumcised, only in order that they might not be persecuted for the cross of the Messiah. For not even the ones being circumcised are keeping [the] Law themselves, but they are wanting you all to be circumcised in order that they might boast about [the] flesh of each of you.

Paul was very clear in chapters 5-6 about not being under the Law anymore. He clearly showed the Galatians that the Judaizers were trying to put them back under a yoke of slavery. He explained that being under that yoke of slavery meant that Christ was pointless to them and that outside of Christ, they had no hope of keeping the Law. It is only in Christ—through love—that the Law is fulfilled (cf. 5:6, 5:13-6:10). The Judaizers' goals were explained clearly in 4:17: "They are zealous for you all, but not for good;

---

[4] E Randolph Richards, *Paul and First-Century Letter Writing*, 171.
[5] Ibid., 173.
[6] Ibid., 173. Emphasis in original.
[7] Ibid., 175.
[8] Ibid., 172.

## Lesson 21: Galatians 6:11-18

instead they want to shut you all out in order that you all might be zealous for them." They wanted to feed their egos because others had followed them, as Paul summarizes in 6:14. However, just like Paul said that the children of promise were persecuted by the child according to the flesh (cf. 4:29), he says the Judaizers preach circumcision to avoid persecution. Paul is saying, "Flee this false Gospel of Law-keeping and follow Jesus, who will truly enable you to keep the Law by the power of His Spirit."

Paul summarizes 2:11-4:7 in verses 14-15:

> But may it never be for me to boast unless about the cross of our Lord Jesus [the] Messiah, through which [the] world has been crucified to me, and I [have been crucified] to [the] world! For neither circumcision nor uncircumcision is anything, instead a new creation.

Paul took great pains in 2:11-4:7 to describe and prove theologically that we are not to follow the Law as believers. Paul is contrasting the Judaizer's hope to boast in the Galatians' flesh, by saying his sure boast is in the cross. Paul here strikes on the fact that the curse of the Law was defeated by Christ on the cross, and in Christ's victory—and His alone—Paul boasts. Christ's victory is the only thing that brings the freedom in Christ that Paul heralds in 5:1. Galatians 6:14 easily sums up Paul's theological claim in 3:10-14. It also brings added meaning to Paul's statement in 5:24. The victory is sure, even if not yet fully realized. We boast in Christ's sure work, not our own feeble attempts.

Because of this, and because it's a promise and not circumcision that makes a person right with God, neither circumcision nor uncircumcision matters. This is good news for women everywhere, and it is why Paul said what he did in Galatians 3:28, "There is not a Jew or a Greek, there is not a slave or a free [person], *there is not male and female*; for you all, yourselves, are one in [the] Messiah Jesus."[9] This new creation model is thoroughly explained by Paul in 5:13-6:10.

Paul hones in on and enhances 3:16 in verse 16:

> And as many as will walk according to this standard: Peace [be] upon them and mercy also [be] upon the Israel of God.

---

[9] Emphasis added.

The standard he is speaking of is the new creation standard laid out in 5:13-6:10. If a person is walking by this model, then Paul wishes peace upon him, whether or not he is circumcised. MacArthur explains, "To walk by this rule is to accept the Gospel of divine accomplishment through Christ's sacrifice on the cross and to walk by faith in the power of His Spirit, rather than by sight in the power of the flesh."[10]

The way the Greek sentence is structured, it makes the most sense to equate the ones who are wished peace with the ones who are wished mercy. In this case, those who are walking by this rule are the Israel of God. Paul had written in Galatians 3:16, "Now the promises were spoken to Abraham and to his seed. It does not say, 'And to seeds,' as [though] to many, but as to one, 'And to your seed,' which is [the] Messiah." Christ is the ultimate fulfillment of Israel, and those who are members of His body, by faith in His promise and no external religious symbol, are rightly called members of Israel, or the Israel of God. Cole explains clearly,

> While there is place for the believing Christian Jew in the kingdom of God, there is no place for the unbelieving, Jew or Gentile. Paul would go even further than that. He would say that the 'believing Jew' belongs to God's Israel, but that the Judaizer who does not *walk by this rule* does not belong. There cannot therefore be two groups within the church; there can only be one. That was why Paul was fighting at Antioch, for 'table fellowship' between Jewish and Gentile Christians.[11]

And thus, we also tie 2:11-21 into this concluding summary.

Paul summarizes 1:11-2:10 in verse 17:

For the remainder [of my life], let no one give me troubles, for I myself carry the marks of Jesus on my body.

And Paul is not talking about the marks of crucifixion that Jesus had on His body appearing on his own body. Mysticism, even Christian mysticism, is foolish. Saint Francis of Assisi was less than orthodox, as well as the whole

---

[10] John MacArthur, *Galatians*, 210.
[11] R. Alan Cole, *Galatians*, 237.

concept that has flown out of his lousy understanding of Galatians 6:17.[12] This is why devotional interpretations of Scripture fall short because it removes passages from their original context and is capable of making them say things they never intended to say.[13] It's no wonder the focus of this passage has been on what the scars are. I don't think that was Paul's point at all.

As a writer—and an ex-English major—verbs propel sentences. A better story is written with multiple verbs than with piles of adjectives. For this reason, I firmly believe that the emphasis in verse 17 is in the verb "carry," which happens to be the same word used in 5:10, 6:2, and 6:5—the only other three occurrences in the book. When Paul uses it in 5:10, he is talking about the false teachers being responsible for their teaching and bearing the judgment of God. In 6:5, he is talking about everyone on earth being held accountable for the fruit of their life. In 6:2, he commands us to bear one another's' burdens. In 2 Corinthians 11:28, amid a list of physical difficulties—visible proofs of which were probably present on his body—Paul says, "Not to mention other things, there is the daily pressure on me: my care for all the churches."

Jesus was marked for His church on the cross (Hebrews 12:2). The members of churches are His bride (Ephesians 5:22-32). Jesus identifies Himself with His bride (Acts 9:4-5). Therefore, the pains of the church are the pains of Jesus. If Paul bears the marks of Jesus in his body, then Paul is saying that he is bearing in love with the members of the church.

This can be further proven to be a likely interpretation. As a summary statement, Paul is not bringing anything new into his discussion at this point. The first phrase of the verse is especially telling: "Let no one give me troubles." We have long been away from any discussion about those who were causing Paul trouble. It was what he spent 1:11-2:10 discussing. He had to prove that he was qualified to preach Christ. Ultimately, what Paul is saying in verse 17 is that he is totally qualified to preach Christ because he practices what he preaches. By bearing with the saints in love, he is clearly walking by the Spirit and proving that his theology is real; he is a worthy apostle. One of the earliest Christian documents, known as the Didache, or "The Teaching of the Twelve"

---

[12] For more information on the topic, check out this page: https://en.wikipedia.org/wiki/Stigmata.

[13] And yes, you are right. This is a devotional commentary. But the interpretations presented within are contextually careful. When I called this *A devotional commentary on Galatians*, I wanted to emphasize that this book seeks to further spiritual life, rather than getting bogged down in technicalities. I pray that I achieved this goal.

clarifies about discerning who is a true or false teacher: "And every prophet who teaches the truth, if he does not do what he teaches is a false prophet" (11:10).[14] Paul practiced what he preached; he could be trusted; no one needed to trouble him about that fact anymore.

Paul concludes with only slight derivations from his typical sign-off in verse 18:

> The grace of our Lord Jesus [the] Messiah be with you all's Spirit, brothers. Amen.

The conclusions of all of Paul's epistles are very similar. And here, there are three parts to notice that make it slightly unique.

First, he calls them brothers. This is likely to comfort them, lest they have been scared about the state of their position in Christ by the content of the letter.

Second, he asks that the grace of Christ be with their Spirit.[15] This is a wish that those who genuinely are believers would be comforted by Christ's grace.

And third, he concludes by saying, "Amen." Cole explains,

> Paul, with full meaning, sets his *Amen*, common at the end of Hebrew blessings and prayers, from which it has passed into Christian usage (1 Cor. 14:16). But it is really an *Amen* to the uniqueness of Christ and the sufficiency of his cross for salvation, so that it is also an *Amen* to the whole letter, and indeed to Paul's whole theological position, since God himself has already set his *Amen* to Christ (2 Cor. 1:20).[16]

---

[14] Charles, Hoole, trans, *The Didache: The Teaching of the Lord to the Gentiles through the Twelve Apostles* (London: David Nutt, 1894), WORDsearch. I slightly modified the grammar and wording for modern readers.

[15] I could write an entirely separate chapter parsing out the fact that Paul is talking to a whole group of people, but he says that they all (together) only have one Spirit. This is why Christian unity is actually possible, and why it is such a problem if you are refusing to be unified in submission with fellow believers under the Gospel/Law/Cross of the Messiah (cf. Galatians 1:7, 6:2, 12 — the only three occurrences in Galatians where Χριστος has the definite article). Attempting to be unified under anything besides these three themes (better: this one theme) is also problematic.

[16] R. Alan Cole, *Galatians*, 241.

# Lesson 21: Galatians 6:11-18

And with that, we've come to the end of Galatians. I think that my following lyrical summary of the book would pretty well state the main points of the letter:

> *And if we take a close look at Galatians we'll see*
> *That Paul wants us to be clear—not in any way deceived*
> *If we follow law we've fallen from grace*
> *And it's up to us to hold our place*
> *Cuz Jesus became a curse for us*
> *And His life is what makes us righteous*
> *For that reason stand firm—resist the yoke*
> *Of slavery that will just leave you choked*
> *Instead walk in love and truly fulfill the Law*
> *Christ did first and His Spirit enables us all.*[17]

But, if I just end it there, then I've not done my job.[18]

# The Gospel According to Paul

This whole book points to the Gospel. John MacArthur explains, "The book of Galatians has been called 'The Crucifixion Epistle,' not only because it directly mentions the cross or crucifixion some seven times . . . but because God's redemptive grace, the theme of the epistle, became efficient for men only through the cross of Christ."[19] And thus, since the song is titled, "Christ Crucified," I'll let Shai Linne call you to faith in Christ.

> *When I say "Trust in Jesus", cats look at me like I'm crazy, yet*
> *This song is your "wake-up show" like Sway and Tech*
> *'Cause sin's problem is much greater than human hurts*
> *You owe a debt to the Creator of the universe*
> *And trust me son, He'll do much more than dial your number*
> *The Lord is gonna track you down like a bounty hunter*

---

[17] liL fytr, "Ammunition," *Welcome to da Faith* (Victorville, CA: FYTR records, 2017), Spotify.

[18] The following heading was originally part of the same section, but as this is the final section of the book, I wanted to conclude with a "whole book" Gospel presentation, so I separated it with the heading.

[19] John MacArthur, *Galatians*, 198.

*Live Free or Die Lawfully*

> *On judgment day, coppin' pleas ain't gonna work*
> *'Cause God is like a shower drain, He sees all your dirt*
> *The evil you do with your devious crew*
> *You're rotten to the core, He's knocking at your door*
> *Your weed and your brew, the freaks that you screw*
> *You're shopping at the store; you should be dropping to the floor*
> *If you make it your business to pray for forgiveness*
> *The Savior of misfits will take you from His hit list*
> *But say you dismiss this- it shows you're misled*
> *'Cause like "The 6th Sense" you don't even know that you're dead.*[20]

I pray that you wouldn't wait one more day to trust Christ with your life and that you would refuse to trust yourself any longer.

The book of Galatians was one that played a crucial role in helping to lead to the milestone in Christian history known as the Reformation. As such, I'll let Martin Luther close us out with the closing words of his commentary because I second them:

> The Lord Jesus Christ, our Savior, who gave me the strength and the grace to explain this Epistle and granted you the grace to hear it, preserve and strengthen us in faith unto the day of our redemption. To Him, the Father and the Son and the Holy Spirit, be glory, world without end. Amen.[21]

# Reflection Questions

1. How does today's text show Paul's love for the church?
2. How would you summarize the book of Galatians?
3. What part of today's passage do you most need to remember as you go about your life from this point forward?
4. What new things have you learned throughout this study?
5. Have you placed your faith in Jesus yet?

---

[20] Shai Linne, "Christ Crucified," *The Solus Christus Project* (Philadelphia: Lampmode Recordings, 2005), Spotify.

[21] Martin Luther, *A Commentary on St. Paul's Epistle to the Galatians*.

Lesson 21: Galatians 6:11-18

# Praying the Text

*Jesus,*

*Thank You for giving Paul the words for this book. Please help me to put it into practice each and every day. I need to walk by the Spirit. I need to trust in Your name. I need to walk in love. I need to walk by faith. I need to avoid yokes of both sin and Law. Please help me walk more closely with You every single day. I can't do this alone.*

# EXCURSUS: Tough Love – liL fytr[1] in Galatians

Having a day off work is super helpful, especially when your cat has a vet appointment early in the morning the same day because it forces you to get up early and be productive. As such, I decided to return to Galatians, and look specifically at the following question: "Is Paul really living in love when he talks harshly against the people who are leading the Galatians astray?"

Statements that could be taken harshly occur as early as 1:8. "<u>But even if we or an angel from heaven might evangelize to you all different from what we evangelized to you all, *let [such a one] be cursed.*</u>"[2] Then in 4:30, Paul says, "<u>Throw out the servant-girl and her son; for the son of the servant-girl will not inherit with the son of the free-woman.</u>" [3] And then Paul goes off (for lack of a better phrase) in 5:2-12:

> <u>Behold, I, myself—Paul—say to you all that if you might get circumcised then [the] Messiah is of no benefit for you all. Now I testify again that every man who is getting circumcised is obligated to keep the whole Law. *You all were cut off from [the] Messiah, the ones of you all who are trying to be made righteous by Law; you all fell away from grace.* For we ourselves are eagerly awaiting faith, hope, and righteousness by [the] Spirit. For in [the] Messiah Jesus neither circumcision nor uncircumcision is any influencer, instead faith working itself out through love. You all were running well, [so] *who cut in on you all to persuade you all to disobey the truth?* The persuasion [is] not from the One who called you all. "A little yeast spreads throughout the whole lump [of dough]." I myself have confidence in

---

[1] liL fytr stands for "live in Love; find your true reward." For more information check out https://www.lilfytr.com.

[2] Emphasis added.

[3] If your reading this book in order, then you will remember that this analogy refers directly to Paul's antagonists.

[the] Lord that you all will think nothing different, but *the one who is troubling you all will bear the judgment,* whoever he might be. But if I myself, brothers, still preach circumcision, then why am I still being persecuted? Then the scandal of the cross has been abolished. *I wish that the ones who are troubling you all might also emasculate themselves.*[4]

I hold to this statement: "The whole point of the Bible is love. Each of the 66 books in our canon emphasizes a different aspect, but they all describe and promote love."[5] As such, I hold that the Gospel of God's love for sinful man can be expressed clearly from each passage (rightly exegeted and exposited), and I hold that the personal application of every passage should have something to do with love (either for God or man) as well. So the question for today is: "How do we apply love from the above passages that show Paul blasting dudes?"

The first thing to say is that love is not defined as telling people that they're great no matter what they do or say. Proverbs 22:6 says, "Teach a youth about the way he should go; even when he is old he will not depart from it," and it is better translated/interpreted, "The way you train a child is the way he will turn out." The point being: "Love your child enough to discipline them." While discipline may seem harsh to some, it teaches valuable lessons that will prove invaluable later in life. Proverbs pulls no punches when it says, "The one who will not use the rod hates his son, but the one who loves him disciplines him diligently" (13:24). Love is therefore defined as thinking of others ahead of yourself. It would be much easier to let someone go on in their destructive behavior, especially when society says, "Physical discipline isn't good for a child's self-esteem."[6]

---

[4] Emphases added.

[5] Joshua Wingerd, "Living to Love (3 of 3)," *live in Love; find your true reward* (May 20, 2016), http://www.lilfytr.blogspot.com/2016/05/living-to-love-lil-fytr-explanation-3.html.

[6] Staff Writer, "Spanked Children more likely to have low self-esteem," *Guelph Mercury Tribune* (January 7, 2011), http://www.guelphmercury.com/living-story/2685238-spanked-children-more-likely-to-have-low-self-esteem. Excerpt from article:

> "Spanking a child is not a quick fix for bad behaviour. Spanking teaches children not to trust their parents. It hurts the parent-child relationship as fear, anger and resentment builds up. Fear of being spanked along with a weak parental bond can damage a child's self-esteem. Children who are spanked are more likely to have screaming tantrums, get into fights, hurt animals and refuse to share. Using spanking to correct behaviour distracts the child from learning to resolve conflict effectively. What he or she is learning is that when adults get mad, they use hitting as a way to express anger and solve problems."

## EXCURSUS: Tough Love

If you genuinely love your children, then you will teach them that bad decisions cause pain (and a spanking is a lot less pain then a gunshot wound to the head because a lack of physical discipline allowed your child to join a gang [cf. Proverbs 1:8-18]).

By way of comparison, Paul loved the Galatians enough to rebuke them and say, "You're wrong if you listen to these other people." And, as Paul made clear throughout his letter, theology matters because wrong thinking leads to wrong living. Paul wanted the Galatians to prove that their salvation was real, but they couldn't do this if they reverted back to the Law. Paul said, "You all were cut off from [the] Messiah, the ones of you all who are trying to be made righteous by Law; you all fell away from grace." (5:4). MacArthur explains, "To attempt to be justified by law is to reject the way of grace ... Law and grace cannot be mixed. As a means to salvation they are totally incompatible and mutually exclusive. To mix law with grace is to obliterate grace . . . Legalism does not please God but offends Him."[7] Earlier, he explained, "Whether before or after conversion, trust in human works of any kind is a barrier between a person and Christ and results in unacceptable legalism."[8]

Paul didn't want anyone to be separated from Christ. He made this truth abundantly clear in Romans 9:1-3, "I speak the truth in Christ—I am not lying; my conscience is testifying to me with the Holy Spirit— that I have intense sorrow and continual anguish in my heart. For I could almost wish to be cursed and cut off from the Messiah for the benefit of my brothers, my own flesh and blood." As such, he boldly rebuked people who were apostatizing from the faith (cf. Galatians 1:6) and pleaded with them to return to the truth (cf. 5:1). It takes real love to actually be willing to tell someone that they are wrong—to risk alienating yourself from them. False love—which is not love at all—tells people precisely what they want to hear.

"But what about the people that Paul said should be cursed (cf. 1:8) or thrown out (cf. 4:30) or castrated (cf. 5:12)?" you object. "How is that loving?"

And I will admit that you bring up a good point. But the first thing to note is that the recipients of this letter were not those people. Those statements were written to the deceived, not the deceivers, to show the deceived the gross error of their heeding the teaching of the deceivers. Paul's love is primarily reaching out to the deceived to set them back on the right path so that they can end up at the right destination.

---

[7] John MacArthur, *Galatians*, 135.
[8] Ibid., 134.

However, I firmly believe that Paul expected the Judaizers (deceivers) to hear/see the content of the letter. And I also firmly believe that while they probably were greatly offended at what Paul wrote, he was no doubt hoping for conversion from them. I back up this thought by quoting Titus 1:13, where Paul says rebuke is to make someone more sound in faith: "Rebuke them sharply, *that they may be sound in the faith*."[9]

The most literal translation of Galatians 5:10 says, "The one who is troubling you all *will bear the judgment*, whoever he might be."[10] Paul is warning the false teacher(s) of the fact that judgment awaits them. This judgment was described in 1:8 when Paul said that the one who teaches a different Gospel is to be cursed. One scholar explains that the word translated "judgment" "means the 'decision' of the judge . . . as the result of the action, the sentence . . . Usually the decision is unfavorable, and it thus bears the sense of condemnation."[11] As such, Paul wants the Judaizers to know that they are standing over the pit of hell, and unless they turn from their ways, they will be damned eternally.

A problem with many who call themselves Christians today is that they are too comfortable with the fact that millions of people who don't know Jesus are headed to hell. Jesus taught, "Love your enemies and pray for those who persecute you" (Matthew 5:44), and there's nothing more loving than telling someone that they are in danger of hell. Even secular society would agree with me; check out the following quote from atheist Penn Jillette, of the famous magician duo, Penn & Teller:

> I've always said that I don't respect people who don't proselytize. I don't respect that at all. If you believe that there's a heaven and a hell, and people could be going to hell or not getting eternal life, and you think that it's not really worth telling them this because it would make it socially awkward—and atheists who think people shouldn't proselytize and who say just leave me alone and keep your religion to yourself—how much do you have to hate somebody to *not* proselytize? How much do you have to hate somebody to believe everlasting life is possible and not tell them that?

---

[9] Emphasis added. Our hope and prayer should always be that false teachers would repent and return to the straight and narrow path of the Gospel. This was Paul's hope and prayer.
[10] Emphasis added.
[11] Kittel, *TDNT*, III:942.

## EXCURSUS: Tough Love

> I mean, if I believed, beyond the shadow of a doubt, that a truck was coming at you, and you didn't believe that truck was bearing down on you, there is a certain point where I tackle you. And this is *more* important than that.[12]

Paul does not hate the false teachers. He hates the spiritual terrorism they are inflicting on the converts whom he loves deeply. He hates the fact that they are undermining the work of his Lord and Savior, Jesus Christ. He hates the fact that they are blind to their error. And he loves them enough to try to help them see their need for repentance. He points out the coming judgment as the curse of God, and he trusts God to awaken those whom He will. Paul's whole letter is a call to wake up, regardless of who the reader might be.

He told the Galatians to throw the deceivers out (cf. 4:30) because he wants his readers to separate from false brothers. If the Judaizers were allowed to stay, then they would think that there was no need for them to change, and they would continue to influence the Galatians harmfully. By telling the Galatians to throw them out, it forced everyone involved to ask themselves, "Do I trust Christ or my works?" Isolation gives people time to think, and Paul wanted everyone in Galatia to think about the foundation of their faith. He risked sounding hateful because he loved them enough to counsel them for the best.

And then, we come to Galatians 5:12, which I did not do enough justice to in my original post on 5:2-12. Here Paul says, "I wish that the ones who are troubling you all might also emasculate themselves." I do not believe that Paul was so angry that he was telling them that he hoped they would accidentally neuter themselves. Instead, I think he was challenging their assumed spirituality based on works. Cole explains,

> If they are so enthusiastic about circumcision, one 'mutilation' of the flesh, why not go the whole way and castrate themselves, as did the indigenous eunuch priests of Asia Minor in honour of their strange, barbarous gods? That is the only possible meaning of *apokopsontai*, *mutilate themselves*. The language is bitter, but it is not merely a 'coarse jest', as is sometimes said. It is designed to set circumcision in its true

---

[12] Penn Jillette, quoted in Justin Taylor, "How Much Do You Have to Hate Somebody to Not Proselytize?" *The Gospel Coalition* (November 18, 2009), https://www.thegospelcoalition.org/blogs/justin-taylor/how-much-do-you-have-to-hate-somebody-to-not-proselytize. Emphasis in original.

light as but one of the many ritual cuttings and markings practised in the ancient world. True, God had once used circumcision as the 'sign of the covenant' in Israel; but, since he was not now using it in the Christian church, it had no more relevance to the Gentile Christians than any other of these strange customs. Indeed, the eunuch priests of paganism undoubtedly thought that they were acquiring great 'merit' by their action. In this sense at least, therefore, there is a real comparison.[13]

If they were to heed this advice by Paul, which no one in their right mind would, it would still accomplish nothing for them. This is yet a final attempt by Paul to say, "To add *any* human effort or act to God's gracious provision through the death of His Son is to exchange the saving Gospel of Jesus Christ for the damning falsehood of paganism."[14] Trust Christ! Don't trust works.

So, with that, I argue that Paul's whole underlying motivation throughout the letter of Galatians is love. He wants people to be reconciled to God in the only way possible: The blood of Christ!

Now when I go to pick up my cat from the vet, I'll ask him if the Judaizers really should get themselves castrated because he'll know firsthand what it's like. I guarantee that he'll say, "Meow," which I'll translate as "No!" And I think that Paul would say the same because his point was only to show the Judaizers the foolishness of trusting the work of circumcision when other pagans were "much more devoted."

---

[13] R. Alan Cole, *Galatians*, 203.
[14] John MacArthur, *Galatians*, 142.

# EXCURSUS: Seeking the Seed – a treatise on Galatians 3:16

*Galatians 3:16b (NASB)*
*He does not say, "And to seeds," as referring to many, but rather to one, "And to your seed," that is, Christ.*

Jesus.[1] The main topic of the Christian's holy Scriptures—all twenty-seven books.

Right?

Wrong.

Jesus is the topic of all *sixty-six* books of the Christian's holy Scriptures. He said so Himself in Luke 24:44, "These are My words which I spoke to you while I was still with you, that all things which are written about Me in the Law of Moses and the Prophets and the Psalms must be fulfilled." Even before this point, Luke explains, "Beginning with Moses and with all the prophets, He explained to them the things concerning Himself in all the Scriptures" (Luke 24:27). The point is that Christ is both present in the Old Testament, and He is, Himself, the theme of the Old Testament. John records Jesus telling the Pharisees, "You search the Scriptures because you think that in them you have eternal life; it is these that testify about Me" (John 5:39).

---

[1] This treatise is formatted differently from the rest of this book, except that Scripture quotations are still underlined. You will notice that there are no citations from other authors to help prove my claims within this treatise. The point of this treatise is to allow the Scripture to speak for itself, to take everything in its plainest sense, and to allow the Scripture to interpret the Scripture.

I have utilized *New American Standard Bible* throughout due to its commitment to literalness. When *NASB* adds a word not present in the original language, they *italicize* it so that it is clear to us. When a Scripture in the New Testament is quoting from the Old Testament, they render the quotation in ALL CAPS so that it is clear to us. If I have tried to clarify something, like changing a pronoun to its antecedent or making the text even more literal, then I have used [brackets], but I am still primarily following *NASB*. I have also altered the capitalization at the beginning of lines in poetic sections and aligned them in the center to show poetic style.

I hope you are led to a deeper love and appreciation for both the Gospel and Jesus Christ Himself as a result of this lengthy treatise.

*Live Free or Die Lawfully*

If this is the case—and coming straight out of our Lord's mouth, we can know that it *is* the case—then why do so many preachers seem to forget that the first three-quarters of their Bible is there?

Paul wrote, "All Scripture is [breathed out] by God and profitable for teaching, for reproof, for correction, for training in righteousness; so that the man of God may be adequate, equipped for every good work" (2 Timothy 3:16-17). The Scripture Paul here refers to *is* the Old Testament, and while the New Testament is certainly also included in Paul's statement, the Old Testament is what he had in mind when he wrote it. There is a ton of benefit to be gleaned from hearing sermons preached from Old Testament texts; when we don't preach/listen to sermons on these texts, we give/receive no more than a quarter of the truths contained in the Christian's holy Scriptures.

But how should we properly go about understanding, knowing, and loving Christ even from Old Testament passages? And what about the obvious fact that the Old Testament seems to be primarily about Israel? How do we relate to Israel as the church? Paul gives us the answer to these questions in Galatians 3:16 when he says—under the inspiration of the Holy Spirit:

> Now the promises were spoken to Abraham and to his seed. He does not say, "And to seeds," as *referring* to many, but *rather* to one, "And to your seed," that is, Christ.

## I. Paul's understanding in Galatians 3:16

This passage forces us to ask several questions before continuing:

1) What are the promises?
2) Who is Abraham?
3) Who is "He"?
4) Where'd these seeds come from?
5) Is Christ really the one who was promised to Abraham?

**1.** The promises are messages of certainty that God spoke to Abraham, which can be found in Genesis 12:7, 13:15, 17:8, 24:7, but are most fully found in 12:1-3 (which will be exposited more fully throughout this treatise). Genesis 12:7 says, "The LORD appeared to Abram and said, 'To your

## EXCURSUS: Seeking the Seed

[seed] I will give this land.'" Genesis 13:15, 17:8, and 24:7 all repeat this same promise. Genesis 12:1-3 explains:

> The LORD said to Abram, "Go forth from your country, And from your relatives And from your father's house, To the land which I will show you; And I will make you a great nation, And I will bless you, And make your name great; And so you shall be a blessing; And I will bless those who bless you, And the one who curses you I will curse. And in you all the families of the earth will be blessed."

In this lengthy statement, Abram (God will change his name to Abraham in Genesis 17) is only told to do one thing. But God makes seven promises to him. Additionally, there's nothing in the text to lead one to believe that if Abram disobeys God's singular command, then the promises will fail to be realized. God simply makes seven unconditional statements about Abram's future. These are the promises of which Paul speaks in Galatians 3:16. Paul says the promises were spoken to Abraham and to his seed, and he says the seed is Christ. This means, if true, that all Old Testament promises find their fulfillment in Jesus Christ (cf. 2 Corinthians 1:20).

**2.** Abraham is the father of three world religions. Judaism, Islam, and Christianity all find their roots in Abraham (though it is important to note that only Christianity claims a spiritual, God-wrought connection to Abraham; cf. Galatians 3:6-7, 29). He was the father of Isaac, who was the father of Israel, who was the father of Judah (cf. Matthew 1:2). He was also the father of Ishmael (cf. Genesis 16:15) through whom the Arabic peoples who invented Islam came. And, being the great-grandfather of Judah, Abraham was the distant ancestor of Jesus Christ, in whom all Christians are spiritually.

Before all that, though, Abraham was a pagan. His life was changed—as was world history—when God called him to leave his country and follow Him (cf. Genesis 12:1). Abraham is also the father of faith, as Genesis 15:6 shows: [Abram] believed in the LORD; and He reckoned it to him as righteousness. It is important to know what he believed, though. Genesis 15:4-5 explains:

> "[Eliezer, your servant] will not be your heir; but one who will come forth from your own body, he shall be your heir." And He took him outside and said, "Now look toward the heavens, and count the stars,

*if you are able to count them." And He said to him, "So shall your descendants be."*

The simple fact that Abram was reckoned righteous when he believed God's promise to him about one son from [his] own body proves that Abram was placing his faith in the promise of Christ because faith in any other name will not lead to righteousness.

**3.** The "He" referred to in Galatians 3:16—as already assumed in the discussion of **1** and **2**—is God. God is the one who made the promises to Abraham and his seed. God, the One who cannot lie (cf. Numbers 23:19; Titus 1:2; Hebrews 6:18), made promises to Abraham, and He would live up to His word and so prove Himself trustworthy.

**4.** Seed comes from the Hebrew word *zera'*. In the Septuagint (LXX, the Greek translation of the Hebrew Scriptures), the word is translated with the Greek word *sperma*. In Genesis 12:7, the LXX uses *spermati* (dative singular). In Paul's argument in Galatians 3:16, he emphasizes that it does not say *spermasin* (dative plural).

His point is made crystal clear in Galatians 3:28-29. *There is neither Jew nor Greek, there is neither slave nor free man, there is neither male nor female; for you are all one in Christ Jesus. And if you belong to Christ, then you are Abraham's [seed], heirs according to promise.* Because Christ is the promised seed, all who are in Christ are also Abraham's seed. In a way, this is saying not that the church has replaced Israel, but that the church is viewed by God as equal to Christ. He sees Christ when He sees the church. Physical Israel never had that status, and it never will either. A Jew may become a Christian and may become part of Abraham's seed, but the nation of Israel will never be wholly saved. It is not a matter of God not being able to save them, but instead that it was never a part of His plan.

Note: Just because both Christ and the church are referred to as Abraham's seed (Galatians 3:16, 29), and just because that insinuates that God sees them as equal, it does not follow that we should look at the church and say, "Oh look, it's Jesus." That would be gross idolatry and blasphemy. Jesus is holy; on earth, before Christ returns, the church is anything but holy in practice. In God's eyes, it is, but we must never be guilty of bringing our gloriously holy Savior down by calling the church Jesus. The two will become one (cf. Genesis 2:24; Revelation 19:7-8), but until that day, Christ should always be elevated much more highly than His bride.

# EXCURSUS: Seeking the Seed

**5.** Christ really is the one promised to Abraham, though certainly Abraham's mind was put at ease when Isaac was born (cf. III.A.1). God's promise was fulfilled to Abraham in Isaac, but it had a greater fulfillment to come, found in Christ. This is common in biblical prophecy. It is similar to looking at a mountain range from a specific angle: You think you are only looking at one peak, but when you get there, you realize that behind one small ridge is actually a wide valley followed by a towering mountain. Isaac was the small peak; Jesus is the towering mountain.

Genesis is actually pretty clear about the Isaac/Jesus dichotomy. God promised Abraham the following in Genesis 21:12, "Through Isaac your [seed] shall be named." If Isaac was the seed, then why would Abraham's seed still need to come through Isaac? In fact, there are plenty of places throughout the New Testament that would lend credence to the fact that Christ is the seed promised to Abraham: John 15:1 and the Gospel of Matthew are primary examples.

## A. "The true vine" (John 15)

We read the following words from Jesus in John 15:1-8.

> I am the true vine, and My Father is the vinedresser. Every branch in Me that does not bear fruit, He takes away; and every *branch* that bears fruit, He prunes it so that it may bear more fruit. You are already clean because of the word which I have spoken to you. Abide in Me, and I in you. As the branch cannot bear fruit of itself unless it abides in the vine, so neither *can* you unless you abide in Me. I am the vine, you are the branches; he who abides in Me and I in him, he bears much fruit, for apart from Me you can do nothing. If anyone does not abide in Me, he is thrown away as a branch and dries up; and they gather them, and cast them into the fire and they are burned. If you abide in Me, and My words abide in you, ask whatever you wish, and it will be done for you. My Father is glorified by this, that you bear much fruit, and *so* prove to be My disciples.

What Jesus is saying here is so much more than that He is the source of the fruitful Christian life (though He is certainly saying that as well). The primary point for the purpose of this discussion is the very first statement: "I am the true vine, and My Father is the vinedresser."

Jesus is building on imagery from Isaiah 5, where God, through Isaiah, likens Israel to a vine that He planted and for which He cares. (Jesus uses this imagery in Matthew 21, and Paul picks it up in Romans 11; we will discuss both before the end of this treatise.) Isaiah writes,

> Let me sing now for my well-beloved
> A song of my beloved concerning His vineyard.
> My well-beloved had a vineyard on a fertile hill.
> He dug it all around, removed its stones,
> And planted it with the choicest vine.
> And He built a tower in the middle of it
> And also hewed out a wine vat in it;
> Then He expected *it* to produce *good* grapes,
> But it produced *only* worthless ones.
> (Isaiah 5:1-2)

Isaiah then goes on in verses 3-6 to interrogate Jerusalem about whether or not the vineyard keeper could have taken better care of his vineyard; Isaiah concludes that he could not have. And then Isaiah begins 5:7 by clearing up all confusion: For the vineyard of the LORD of hosts is the house of Israel and the men of Judah His delightful plant.

So when Jesus says in John 15:1, "My Father is the vinedresser," He is making an explicit reference to Isaiah 5, and when He says, "I am the true vine," He is calling Himself the real vine—He is the ultimate meaning of the vine discussed in Isaiah 5. And since the vine clearly represents Israel, Jesus is claiming to be the true Israel, the real Israel, the ultimate meaning of what Israel was supposed to be.

Jesus goes on to talk about fruit production in John 15:2-8 because, as the real vine, He produces fruit. He explains in verse 5, "Apart from Me you can do nothing," because, ultimately, we are not the ones bearing fruit; He bears fruit through us. (This also proves that Jesus is the true vine and the church is not. Jesus does not say, "Apart from the church you can do nothing" because the church is not on the same level as Christ. Let's fight against idolatry!) As such, the church is to find its identity in Christ, saying, "Jesus is the fulfillment of Israel," and not see Jesus as removed from us, asking, "Does the church replace Israel?"

EXCURSUS: Seeking the Seed

Jesus said, "I am the true vine, and My Father is the vinedresser," and that should settle the discussion. Jesus is the fulfillment of Israel; the church is simply a consequence of Jesus being the fulfillment of Israel. (Remember that both Jesus and the church are the seed of Abraham according to Galatians 3:16, 29. But only Jesus is the seed to whom the promises were spoken.)

## B. Matthew's argument in his Gospel (Matthew 1:1)

One of the main thrusts of Matthew's Gospel is proving that Jesus is the fulfillment of God's promises to Abraham that Paul refers to in Galatians 3:16. This is proven explicitly in Matthew 1:1 when he writes, "The record of the genealogy of Jesus the Messiah, the son of David, the son of Abraham." While the word son is literally different than the word seed (*huios* versus *sperma*, respectively, in Greek), the point is still synonymous. Son refers to a descendant just as much as seed refers to a descendant.

And as we move forward from that first verse, we see multiple references to Jesus being the fulfillment of Israel (better: Son of Abraham). When Mary and Joseph flee to Egypt with the infant Jesus, Matthew comments on their return with a verse from Hosea originally referring to the nation of Israel: OUT OF EGYPT I CALLED MY SON (Matthew 2:15, cf. Hosea 11:1). John the Baptist's words in 3:9 are also telling, "Do not suppose that you can say to yourselves, 'We have Abraham for our father'; for I say to you that from these stones God is able to raise up children to Abraham." Considering that this is what the Jewish nation presumes, one wonders if maybe this statement was more prophetic than it appears on the surface.

Jesus then gets baptized (think Israel crossing the Red Sea; cf. 1 Corinthians 10:1-2) and enters the wilderness for forty days to be tempted, much like Israel was tested for forty years in the wilderness (cf. Numbers 14-26). Jesus is greater because He never succumbed to temptation (cf. Matthew 3:13-4:11).

Fast-forward to chapter 5, where Jesus climbs a mountain and preaches a sermon that gets at the heart of the Law Moses delivered from Mount Sinai (cf. Exodus 19:18-20:21). Even more interesting is how Jesus' sermon highlights the points of the Law expounded in Matthew 22:37-39,

> YOU SHALL LOVE THE LORD YOUR GOD WITH ALL YOUR HEART, AND WITH ALL YOUR SOUL, AND WITH ALL YOUR

MIND. This is the great and foremost commandment. The second is like it, YOU SHALL LOVE YOUR NEIGHBOR AS YOURSELF.

After His sermon, a crowd that desires healing meets Jesus. One of the most notable individuals healed is a Roman centurion's servant who was sick at home. The centurion tells Jesus, "Lord, I am not worthy for You to come under my roof, but just say the word, and my servant will be healed." At this statement, Jesus turns to the crowd and probably shocks them when He says, "Truly I say to you, I have not found such great faith with anyone in Israel. I say to you that many will come from east and west, and recline *at the table* with Abraham, Isaac and Jacob in the kingdom of heaven; but the sons of the kingdom will be cast out into the outer darkness; in that place there will be weeping and gnashing of teeth." Jesus then goes on to heal the centurion's servant from a distance (cf. 8:5-13). Matthew's point including this story in his narrative is that Jesus again points away from the nation of Israel as the source of heaven's occupants. He says He has not found faith like that in Israel, and then He says the nation of Israel (sons of the kingdom) will end up outside. It is faith, not forefathers, that gets a person into God's kingdom.

After more stories of healing and teaching in chapter 9, we are presented with a list of names in chapter 10. The list contains twelve names. Where else is a list of twelve names? The twelve tribes of Israel. But in Matthew 10 we have the twelve disciples of Jesus (cf. 10:2-4). The twelve were, in a matter of speaking (minus Iscariot; plus Mattathias and Paul), the first believers and fathers of the Christian faith. In fact, it is notable that immediately following this naming, Jesus sends them out to preach about the coming Kingdom of Heaven (cf. 10:7). Jesus goes on to say, "But beware of men, for they will hand you over to *the* [Sanhedrin] and scourge you in their synagogues; and you will even be brought before governors and kings for My sake, as a testimony to them and to the Gentiles" (10:17-18). The initial perpetrators of betrayal named here are the Jews, the them that the disciples will testify to along with the Gentiles.

Even here we start to see a shift in the focus. Jesus paints the nation of Israel as mostly hostile to His mission. The fruit of the twelve Apostles' preaching was new birth and spiritual fatherhood (cf. 1 Timothy 1:2) that would eventually grow to the point where it could be said that there are twelve tribes of believers all descending spiritually from one of the twelve Apostles (cf. III.B).

## EXCURSUS: Seeking the Seed

Fast forward to Matthew 13. Jesus gives several parables about the kingdom. What do we see in verses 14-15?

He quotes Isaiah and says,

> YOU WILL KEEP ON HEARING, BUT WILL NOT UNDERSTAND;
> YOU WILL KEEP ON SEEING, BUT WILL NOT PERCEIVE;
> FOR THE HEART OF THIS PEOPLE HAS BECOME DULL,
> WITH THEIR EARS THEY SCARCELY HEAR,
> AND THEY HAVE CLOSED THEIR EYES,
> OTHERWISE THEY WOULD SEE WITH THEIR EYES,
> HEAR WITH THEIR EARS,
> AND UNDERSTAND WITH THEIR HEART AND RETURN,
> AND I WOULD HEAL THEM.

It's plain from a surface reading that Jesus is saying two things here. First, by quoting Isaiah—a prophet to Israel—He is making a statement about Israel and their lack of faith. Second, He says that if they return, He will heal them. The Greek sentence structure states the healing as a future certainty *if* the people return (which is not expressed as a command or a certainty, but as a subjunctive, "might return").

In chapter 14, Jesus feeds the five thousand, which is a fulfillment of what Israel experienced in the wilderness for forty years under Moses (cf. 14:13-21). John's Gospel helps fill this in and make it clear, also pointing out just how much greater Jesus is than Moses (cf. John 6:1-13, 22-58).

In chapter 15, Jesus goes into Canaanite territory. While there, a Canaanite woman approaches Him. Much like Rahab in Joshua 2 (also a Canaanite, cf. Matthew 1:5), she exhibits saving faith and is even complimented by Jesus with the words, "Your faith is great" (15:28). It is reminiscent of the compliment Jesus paid the centurion in Matthew 8.

In chapter 16, we start to see a dichotomy drawn between God's people and the people of Israel when it comes to the leaders of these two people groups. First, in verses 1-12, the Pharisees and Sadducees test Jesus, and Jesus responds; and second, in verses 13-20, the disciples display wisdom by recognizing who Jesus truly is (something Israel's religious leaders were blind to). Peter announces, "You are the Christ, the Son of the living God" (16:16). In recognizing this dichotomy, it is essential to point out that Jesus responds to Peter in verse 17, "Blessed are you, Simon Barjona, because flesh and blood did not reveal *this* to you, but My Father who is in heaven." God reveals His Son to whom He will, and not all who are descended from Israel are Israel (cf. Romans 9:6; more on this under II.B).

When we move into chapter 17, we quickly realize that Jesus isn't just claiming that He is the Son of God to the disciples in chapter 16; He proves it to them in 17:1-13. This is where we read of the Transfiguration, where Jesus, while on earth, is given for a brief moment the glory He will have for eternity in heaven. A voice from heaven confirms Peter's words from a chapter earlier: "This is My beloved Son, with whom I am well-pleased; listen to Him!" (17:5). What was hidden from the teachers of Israel was revealed to the disciples of Jesus.

Fast forward to chapter 21, skipping three chapters of Jesus proving by teaching (primarily) and actions that His Kingdom is upside down from the kingdom s of the world—even Israel. (Only one comment needs to be made before moving to chapter 21. The rich, young ruler is turned away, and the disciples wonder who can be saved if a rich person [blessed by God according to the Law] is almost impossible to save. Jesus says, "With people this is impossible, but with God all things are possible" [19:26]. Salvation belongs to God. If He wants to save national Israel, He can; if He doesn't want to, He need not. [We will come back to this later.] The point remains that Jesus is the perfect fulfillment of Israel as He says in John 15:1.)

At the opening of Matthew 21, Jesus comes into Jerusalem on a donkey, and Matthew explains that it fulfills biblical prophecy: "SAY TO THE DAUGHTER OF ZION, 'BEHOLD YOUR KING IS COMING TO YOU, GENTLE, AND MOUNTED ON A DONKEY, EVEN ON A COLT, THE FOAL OF A BEAST OF BURDEN.'" (21:5, cf. Zechariah 9:9). Matthew's point is to show explicitly that Jesus is the King who Israel was waiting for, which draws a sharp contrast with Israel's actions a few chapters later.

Jesus then comes into the temple and proves that it had been defiled by people trying to make a profit off of the sacrificial system. "It is written, 'MY HOUSE SHALL BE CALLED A HOUSE OF PRAYER'; but you are making it a ROBBERS' DEN." (21:13). Even the Jewish religious/sacrificial system had been polluted.

In 21:33-45, Jesus tells a scathing parable that also connects explicitly to John 15:1 because Jesus is the true Israel, the true vine. In verses 37-39, Jesus says that the vineyard owner sends his son to check out the production of the vineyard, but the tenants kill him. In verse 43, Jesus states it plainly, "Therefore I say to you, the kingdom of God will be taken away from you and given to a people, producing the fruit of it." It is of note that Jesus here speaks

## EXCURSUS: Seeking the Seed

of the kingdom of God. Matthew is the only Gospel writer who uses the phrase Kingdom of heaven, which occurs thirty-one times in his Gospel, whereas the phrase, kingdom of God, only occurs four times (five if you are utilizing the Textus Receptus [KJV]). Whenever Matthew uses kingdom of God, he is using it to shame the nation of Israel, or its leaders, for their lack of belief:

- **Matthew 12:28**
  "But if I cast out demons by the Spirit of God, then the kingdom of God has come upon you."
- **Matthew 19:24**
  "Again I say to you, it is easier for a camel to go through the eye of a needle, than for a rich man to enter the kingdom of God."
- **Matthew 21:31**
  "Truly I say to you that the tax collectors and prostitutes will get into the kingdom of God before you."
- **Matthew 21:43**
  "Therefore I say to you, the kingdom of God will be taken away from you and given to a people, producing the fruit of it."

When Jesus wants to emphasize what the nation of Israel has missed, He uses kingdom of God, which is a much more explicit statement than kingdom of heaven.

Matthew records Jesus saying that the kingdom would be taken away from the Jewish nation. Instead it will be given to those described in Matthew 5:3-12, and if we remember that Jesus described the Jewish nation as persecutors in 10:17, then it follows that the nation of Israel is not the inheritor of the kingdom, as Jesus explicitly stated in 21:43.

In chapter 22, the Jewish leaders are playing off 21:45-46 and are now trying to find an excuse to get rid of Jesus. In so doing, Jesus has an irrefutable answer for everything.

In chapter 23, Jesus gives a scathing review of Jewish religion, repeating seven times (excluding verse 14 and "blind guides" in verse 16), "But woe to you, scribes and Pharisees, hypocrites." In so doing, Jesus is warning the Jewish people to escape their false, damning influence. Jesus says, in verses 2-4,

> The scribes and the Pharisees have seated themselves in the chair of Moses; therefore all that they tell you, do and observe, but do not do

according to their deeds; for they say *things* and do not do *them*. They tie up heavy burdens and lay them on men's shoulders, but they themselves are unwilling to move them with so *much as* a finger.

Jesus proves Himself to be a greater teacher in 11:28-30, when He says,

> Come to Me, all who are weary and heavy-laden, and I will give you rest. Take My yoke upon you and learn from Me, for I am gentle and humble in heart, and YOU WILL FIND REST FOR YOUR SOULS. For My yoke is easy and My burden is light.

In chapter 24, Jesus continues to plead with the Jews to see Him as He truly is before it is too late. In 24:2, He prophesies the destruction of the temple that came about in AD 70 when Titus besieged Jerusalem: "Truly I say to you, not one stone here will be left upon another, which will not be torn down." From there, Jesus embarks on His eschatology discussion, warning Israel of the end. Just because God is done with Israel as a nation (cf. 21:43) does not mean that He does not want the Jewish people to come to Christ.

In chapter 25, Jesus gives two parables about the second coming (kingdom of heaven will be comparable to, 25:1; it is just like, 25:14). In 25:31-46, He stops giving parables and instead gives a prophecy; the only parable-like feature in this text is that He uses a simile in verse 32 to describe the way believers and unbelievers will be separated (as the shepherd separates the sheep from the goats).

I said before that one of Matthew's main thrusts in writing his Gospel is to prove that Jesus is the fulfillment of the Abrahamic promise. In Genesis 12:3, God says, "I will bless those who bless you, and the one who curses you I will curse." In Matthew 25:31-46, we see this become a reality. In verses 34-36, we read the following words from Jesus:

> Come, you who are blessed of My Father, inherit the kingdom prepared for you from the foundation of the world. For I was hungry, and you gave Me *something* to eat; I was thirsty, and you gave Me *something* to drink; I was a stranger, and you invited Me in; naked, and you clothed Me; I was sick, and you visited Me; I was in prison, and you came to Me.

## EXCURSUS: Seeking the Seed

Notice the fifth word in the passage. Blessed. Now look at Jesus' words in verses 41-43:

> Depart from Me, accursed ones, into the eternal fire which has been prepared for the devil and his angels; for I was hungry, and you gave Me *nothing* to eat; I was thirsty, and you gave Me nothing to drink; I was a stranger, and you did not invite Me in; naked, and you did not clothe Me; sick, and in prison, and you did not visit Me.

Notice the fourth word in the passage. Accursed. Verses 42-43 read exactly the opposite of verses 35-36, just like the second part of Genesis 12:3 is exactly the opposite of the first.

From this, it becomes clear that Jesus was the one God was speaking the promise to in Genesis 12, as Paul explained in Galatians 3:16. It does not ultimately matter what one's relationship is with Israel; the question is: What is your relationship to Jesus Christ?

And Israel as a collective whole gives their answer to this question in Matthew 27:25, "His blood shall be on us and on our children!" Jesus had prophesied this decision clearly in Matthew 21:33-44, specifically verse 38, and He had told the result in 21:43, "The kingdom of God will be taken away from you and given to a people, producing the fruit of it." It is especially interesting that Matthew's Gospel is the only one where the Jewish nation is recorded as saying that they are responsible for Christ's blood. Matthew wants to show that as a nation they are no longer unique; if anything, he wants to portray them as worse off, since they had the prophecies and everything, but they still killed Jesus.

The good news is that Jesus did not stay in the grave! Matthew 26-27 describes His death, but Matthew 28 describes His resurrection. In the last two verses of the book, Jesus sends His followers on a mission. This mission is laid out as follows in verse 19: Make disciples of all the nations. That word all is important. Israel is a nation. As a nation, they should be evangelized too. The point of this treatise is not to say that Israel is damned, but rather that their rights and privileges as a nation were fulfilled in Christ, and now they need Him and His grace the same as a nation in Africa, Asia, Europe or America. Second Corinthians 1:20 says, For as many as are the promises of God, in [Jesus] they are yes.

To wrap up this section, Jesus fulfills God's promises to Abraham and Israel, and as such, it was never specifically about Israel. This leads us to the next section: Paul's understanding of the issue in Romans 9-11.

## II. Paul's understanding in Romans 9-11

Funnily enough, when I was working on my undergrad, I took a class with a highly Arminian professor that included a discussion of the book of Romans. This professor summed up his discussion of Romans 9-11 by quoting a commentary that said something along the lines of, "Paul's argument becomes incoherent, inconsistent, and contradictory in these chapters." In an effort to hunt down the source of the quote, I discovered that it was actually misquoted by my professor. In reality, the author was not making that judgment against Paul, but describing a consensus among many scholars.

> The opinion of many interpreters, who think that Paul is inconsistent, incoherent, or even contradictory in these chapters . . . Attempts have been made to solve this alleged contradiction by stressing that Paul, in beginning his discussion at 9:1, did not yet realize the solution to which he was to come in 11:25–32.[2]

When it comes to modern attempts to claim that Israel as a nation is still under the blessing of God—though that blessing is currently postponed—I must agree that these three chapters are incoherent and that Paul doesn't know his argument at the outset.

However, if we let Scripture speak for itself, and if we keep in mind the discussion above—beginning with Galatians 3:16 and extending through Matthew's Gospel—Paul's argumentation will prove to be both clear and convincing.

### A. The problem (9:1-5)

In Romans 9:1-5, Paul describes the problem that is confronting him. In verses 1-2, he emphasizes the seriousness of the problem:

---

[2] Joseph. A. Fitzmyer, *Romans*, Anchor Yale Bible (London: Yale University Press, 2008), Logos, 609.

## EXCURSUS: Seeking the Seed

> I am telling the truth in Christ, I am not lying, my conscience testifies with me in the Holy Spirit, that I have great sorrow and unceasing grief in my heart.

He states in three different ways that what follows is the truth, and then in verse 2, he explains that it brings him grief. These two verses control the remainder of these three chapters. If his grief is removed, it is merely because of joy and meditation on a much more significant fact!

In verses 3-5, he describes what it is that brings him grief:

> For I could wish that I myself were accursed, *separated* from Christ for the sake of my brethren, my kinsmen according to the flesh, who are Israelites, to whom belongs the adoption as sons, and the glory and the covenants and the giving of the Law and the *temple* service and the promises, whose are the fathers, and from whom is the Christ according to the flesh, who is over all, God blessed forever. Amen.

There are several things to point out in these verses.

First, we see the phrase kinsmen according to the flesh in verse 3, and then verses 4-5 contain a list of things that are also true according to the flesh. Israel's sonship, glory, covenants, Law, temple service, promises, and fathers only are such because the people of Israel are physically descended from Abraham. He will expand upon this fact in verses 6-8.

Second, though closely connected with the first, Christ came from Israel in a fleshly way. This is the only claim that the nation of Israel—Jews of today—has on Christ. (Paul is clear to whom belongs the list in verse 4 and the first item in verse 5, but he explicitly states that Christ does not belong to them; He came from them.) Paul is clear, though, to explain that while Israel can only claim Christ as one of their physical relatives, in truth, He is over all humanity—Israel included—and more than just being a human Jew, Jesus Christ is God! Interestingly, it was this claim that ultimately led the Jews to order His crucifixion. If we turn back to Matthew 26:63-66, we read:

> The high priest said to Him, "I adjure You by the living God, that You tell us whether You are the Christ, the Son of God."
> Jesus *said to him, "You have said it *yourself*; nevertheless I tell you, hereafter you will see THE SON OF MAN SITTING AT THE

RIGHT HAND OF POWER, and COMING ON THE CLOUDS OF HEAVEN."
Then the high priest tore his robes and said, "He has blasphemed! What further need do we have of witnesses? Behold, you have now heard the blasphemy; what do you think?"
They answered, "He deserves death!"

Third, before we move to verses 6-8, a word must be said about Paul's mindset in verse 3. Despite the clear fact that all the promises of God are fulfilled in Christ (cf. 2 Corinthians 1:20) and nothing remains to be fulfilled for national Israel, Paul's heart is for his nation. This comes out clearly in at least three other places in Romans:

- **Romans 1:16**
  For I am not ashamed of the Gospel, for it is the power of God for salvation to everyone who believes, to the Jew first and also to the Greek.
- **Romans 10:1**
  Brethren, my heart's desire and my prayer to God for them is for *their* salvation.
- **Romans 11:13-14**
  But I am speaking to you who are Gentiles. Inasmuch then as I am an apostle of Gentiles, I magnify my ministry, if somehow I might move to jealousy my fellow countrymen and save some of them.

Also, all throughout Acts, whenever Paul entered a new town, he taught in the synagogue first: "They came to Thessalonica, where there was a synagogue of the Jews. And according to Paul's custom, he went to them" (Acts 17:1-2).

It must be asked: Does your heart break for your relatives who do not know Christ? Would you rather go to hell so your family could be saved, or would you rather be in heaven with your family cursed to hell?

Paul would rather be cut off from Christ so his relatives could be saved. And he lived this mindset out. We know he was telling the truth (cf. 9:1). Would your life evidence the same, or would your life call you a liar? This is a primary point to be proven throughout this treatise: If we want all Israel to be saved (which we should, whatever that phrase might mean), then we must evangelize! And this is true whether you agree 100% with my conclusions or disagree 95% with my conclusions. (If you disagree 100%, you would also say that evangelism is not necessary for Israel to be saved, but since that is anti-Scripture, I pray that you do not hold that view.)

## B. The solution = election (9:6-26)

In this section, Paul lays out the solution and works through it very systematically. The logic he sets down in this section, especially verses 6-8, is indispensable for understanding the remainder of Romans 9-11.

### 1. Paul's thesis (9:6-8)

Paul lays out his thesis for all three chapters in verses 6-8. In verse 6a, he removes a huge burden from our thinking:

> But *it is* not as though the word of God has failed.

In that short sentence, Paul tells us that any perceived problem with what follows is not the Scripture's fault but man's interpretation. In other words, for the Jewish people to think they are in because they are descended from Abraham, and because God made a promise to Abraham, does not mean that God owes the Jewish people anything, but rather that they eisegeted the text and made it about them when it was really about Christ (cf. Galatians 3:16).

Paul goes on in verses 6b-8:

> For they are not all Israel who are *descended* from Israel; nor are they all children because they are Abraham's descendants, but: "THROUGH ISAAC YOUR DESCENDANTS WILL BE NAMED." That is, it is not the children of the flesh who are children of God, but the children of the promise are regarded as descendants.

In the immediate, original context, this is describing the difference between Ishmael, born from Abraham's lack of faith (cf. Genesis 16), and Isaac, born according to God's promise (cf. Genesis 18, 21). Two things must be said regarding verses 6-8.

First, someone could try to say that Paul contradicts himself between 6b and 7. In 6b he says, "They are not all Israel who are *descended* from Israel."

In 7 he continues, "Nor are they all children because they are Abraham's descendants." Israel was Abraham's grandson. Someone could say that just because all of Abraham's descendants are not part of the promise (due to Ishmael), all those descended from Isaac (cf. 7b) are part of the promise, and as such, all of Israel's children would be part of the promise too. Paul will elaborate even on the Isaac point in the verses to come (cf. 9-13). Regardless, in verse 6, Paul is laying out an absolute truth about the many physical descendants of Israel, and then going back two generations to prove the point with specific examples.

Second, we come to the fact that in verse 8, Paul literally says, "the children of the promise are regarded as [a seed]." It is singular, and in this instance, it works out to smooth it out to "descendants" because children is plural (but cf. Galatians 3:29). However, in verse 7b, when Paul quotes from Genesis 21:12, it is inaccurate to smooth it out. Paul writes literally as God spoke to Abraham, "THROUGH ISAAC A SEED WILL BE NAMED TO YOU." This harks back to the promise Paul wrote about in Galatians 3:16. "The promises were spoken to Abraham and to his seed. He does not say, 'And to seeds,' as *referring* to many, but *rather* to one, 'And to your seed,' that is, Christ." Paul's theology of the Old Testament and Israel has not changed between writing Galatians and Romans; his point is the same, though further expounded in Romans. To carry the quote of Genesis 21:12 in Romans 9:7 as Paul wrote in Galatians 3:16, we could rewrite it thus: "THROUGH ISAAC A SEED WILL BE NAMED TO YOU, that is, Christ." And what do seeds do? They get buried, and they grow, producing fruit. And thus, Paul concludes 9:8 by writing, "the children of the promise are regarded as descendants." As Paul wrote of the Gospel in Romans 1:16, "it is the power of God for salvation to everyone who believes." A person must believe the promises of God as fulfilled in Christ to be counted as a descendant of Abraham (thus, to be in Christ—the fulfillment and reality of Israel—and ultimately, to be a child of God).

## 2. Jacob, not Esau (9:9-13)

As mentioned previously, Paul elaborates on the fact that just because someone is descended from Abraham's son Isaac does not necessitate that he be part of Israel. This discussion occurs in 9:9-13.

## EXCURSUS: Seeking the Seed

> For this is the word of promise: "AT THIS TIME I WILL COME, AND SARAH SHALL HAVE A SON." And not only this, but there was Rebekah also, when she had conceived *twins* by one man, our father Isaac; for though *the twins* were not yet born and had not done anything good or bad, so that God's purpose according to *His* choice would stand, not because of works but because of Him who calls, it was said to her, "THE OLDER WILL SERVE THE YOUNGER." Just as it is written, "JACOB I LOVED, BUT ESAU I HATED."

In this section, Paul compares and contrasts two promises of God found in Genesis, ultimately proving without a doubt that what happens is God's purpose according to His choice.

In verse 9, Paul concludes his discussion of Abraham, Sarah, and Isaac by quoting God's promise to Sarah as regards Isaac's certain birth (cf. Genesis 18:14).

In verse 12, we read the promise that God spoke to Isaac's wife, Rebekah: "THE OLDER WILL SERVE THE YOUNGER." As such, we see that God chose Jacob and left Esau to his devices. Paul then throws in Malachi 1:2-3 to clear up any confusion, where we read, "JACOB I LOVED, BUT ESAU I HATED."

In verses 10-11, between the records of these promises, we see a contrast between the situations described. Rebekah also, when she had conceived *twins* by one man, highlights that Jacob and Esau were born at the same time, sharing the same parents. It contrasts with Isaac and Ishmael, who were born to two different mothers, a decade apart.

Verse 11 highlights the importance of this fact. God's choice of Jacob over Esau had nothing to do with anything either had done. When God promised Rebekah that THE OLDER WILL SERVE THE YOUNGER, they were both still in her womb. Essentially, Paul says, "God chooses whom He will, and it has nothing to do with their choices; it's all His good pleasure!"

Even within the same family, God can choose one person for Himself and pass over another. For Paul's purposes, this ultimately refers to the family (read: nation) of Israel. Just because Jacob was chosen by God does not necessitate that all of his descendants be chosen by God, just like the fact that Isaac being chosen by God did not necessitate that both Jacob and Esau be chosen.

This leads me to a question: Just like Paul pleads for his nation (read: family) to be saved, even though he knows they were not all chosen by God, how much do you plead with God to save the unsaved people in your immediate family? I posit that we don't plead enough. We are not enough described by Paul's words in 9:1-3.

## 3. Nations included (9:14-18)

When Paul quotes Malachi in 9:13, it leads us to another question and another layer of this discussion. Paul states this question in 9:14.

> What shall we say then? There is no injustice with God, is there? May it never be!

This is a very logical question. Why would God love one person and hate another? Doesn't that make God less than just? Paul uses the strongest words possible when he says, "May it never be!"

Now, Paul is smart. He knows he can't just say, "No!" and leave it at that. So instead, he quotes Scripture to prove his point, essentially saying, "If you don't like it, you don't have a problem with me; you have a problem with God" (cf. 9:20 for close to this exact statement). He quotes Exodus 33:19 in 9:15, "I WILL HAVE MERCY ON WHOM I HAVE MERCY, AND I WILL HAVE COMPASSION ON WHOM I HAVE COMPASSION." Paul's point is that it matters little what we think God should do as regards peoples' salvation; God is in control. And when it comes to Jacob and Esau, God was never indebted to show mercy and love to Esau or Jacob. He graciously chose to show it to Jacob, and that is how God works.

In 9:16 Paul writes, "So then it *does* not *depend* on the man who wills or the man who runs, but on God who has mercy." Paul is saying that no one can add anything to or subtract anything from the equation. Everything is ultimately in God's hands.

Paul then expands the focus in verse 17. We must keep in mind that this whole section is seeking to prove the statement of 9:6 (But *it is* not as though the word of God has failed. For they are not all Israel who are *descended from* Israel). When Paul puts pen to the page for verse 17, he is still ultimately seeking to prove that statement true, while at the same time defending against the charge of God being unjust (cf. 9:14). The focus widens from Israel to Egypt, from Israel to other nations, from Israel to the Gentiles. This is where the focus remains, essentially, through the end of chapter 11 (but most assuredly through 11:6).

EXCURSUS: Seeking the Seed

In 9:17 Paul writes, "For the Scripture says to Pharaoh, 'FOR THIS VERY PURPOSE I RAISED YOU UP, TO DEMONSTRATE MY POWER IN YOU, AND THAT MY NAME MIGHT BE PROCLAIMED THROUGHOUT THE WHOLE EARTH.'" This is a quotation from Exodus 9:16. This statement comes from God, through Moses' lips, to Pharaoh after six plagues have brutalized Egypt.

We must not miss the fact that God put Pharaoh in his position of power so that he would not let Israel go; so that God could send plagues, ultimately ruining Egypt; so that Rahab and other peoples of the world might say, "For we have heard how the LORD dried up the water of the Red Sea before you when you came out of Egypt." (Joshua 2:10).

The first half of the answer to the question, "What is the chief end of man?" according to the Westminster Shorter Catechism is, "Man's chief end is to glorify God" (WCF 1.1). And the fact of the matter is that even if a person decides not to glorify God, God will get glory from that person somehow or another. This is the story of Pharaoh in a nutshell. It's also where I must ask, "Are you going to glorify Him on your own, by believing in Jesus, or will you wait until He breaks your legs on Judgment Day? I pray it's the former!

Paul's conclusion in verse 18 means that if you do decide to glorify God on your own, it is due solely to His mercy, and if you don't, then you can't pat yourself on the back for being too "wise" to believe in God. Paul says, "So then He has mercy on whom He desires, and He hardens whom He desires." Before moving on, I must point out that this verse clarifies that there are two types of people. For this reason, when he writes in 11:32, "For God has shut up all in disobedience so that He may show mercy to all," regardless of what else it means, we must know that the all to whom God shows mercy cannot include those—like Pharaoh—whom He has hardened eternally. But we'll get there soon enough.

## 4. The Gentiles are Israel (9:19-26)

Paul anticipates another question/objection from his words so far, and he jots it down. In verse 19, Paul writes,

You will say to me then, "Why does He still find fault? For who resists His will?"

And it is a good question. Simply put, this objection acknowledges God as sovereignly controlling all. Unfortunately, most objectors in our day are not this theologically astute. However, Paul's response in verses 20-21 silences any and all objections like this:

> On the contrary, who are you, O man, who answers back to God? The thing molded will not say to the molder, "Why did you make me like this," will it? Or does not the potter have a right over the clay, to make from the same lump one vessel for honorable use and another for common use?

Paul is clear. Taking issue with God's sovereign plan (for salvation no less) is like a lump of clay arguing with the potter. It's ridiculous even to imagine. God is God; we are not. God is in heaven; we are not. God is holy and good; we are not. We must submit in faith; we must not argue and rage (cf. Psalm 2).

As we move into verses 22-26, we must keep in mind that this whole discussion is not primarily about personal salvation, but rather about God's plan for Israel as a nation. This topic will come full and center by the end of verse 24, and then verses 25-26 will prove it beyond a doubt.

But first, Paul gives a metaphor to help us understand something of God's sovereign plan. In verses 22-24, we read:

> What if God, although willing to demonstrate His wrath and to make His power known, endured with much patience vessels of wrath prepared for destruction? And *He did so* to make known the riches of His glory upon vessels of mercy, which He prepared beforehand for glory, *even us*, whom He also called, not from among Jews only, but also from among Gentiles.

Three things are worth noting in these verses.

First, Paul starts by saying, "What if?" This demonstrates that this might not be exactly how God did it, but it does give us something substantial to fit our minds around. And if we think about it, the whole Old Testament is a demonstration of God's patience. He is patient for 800+ years before the exile to Babylon finally happens.

Second, notice the difference in verbal tenses in verses 22 and 23. In 22, God endured with much patience those who were prepared for destruction. God doesn't take credit for their preparation. By contrast, in verse

EXCURSUS: Seeking the Seed

23, when it comes to vessels of mercy, we read that He prepared them Himself for glory. It is not God's fault that people die in their sin, but it is 100% because of God that anyone is saved. If you object to this, I kindly point you back to verse 20.

Third, verse 24 makes it clear that vessels of mercy are not just Jews. Praise God! The nations (Gentiles) are included too!

And then we move to verses 25-26, where Paul quotes Scripture to prove that Gentile inclusion is part of God's plan.

> As He says also in Hosea, "I WILL CALL THOSE WHO WERE NOT MY PEOPLE, 'MY PEOPLE,' AND HER WHO WAS NOT BELOVED, 'BELOVED.'" "AND IT SHALL BE THAT IN THE PLACE WHERE IT WAS SAID TO THEM, 'YOU ARE NOT MY PEOPLE,' THERE THEY SHALL BE CALLED SONS OF THE LIVING GOD."

The Gentiles were not God's people; now they are. The Gentiles were not beloved; now they are. The Gentiles were refused access to God; now God sees them as His children. This is the Gospel! This is God's plan! This is the story of the Bible. And it is only possible through Jesus (cf. Ephesians 2:11-22).

## C. A remnant? (9:27-29)

Now that Paul has proven that the Gentiles belong, he reverts back to his question in 9:1-5. What happened to national Israel? Are they to be forever prepared for destruction? The transition here is abrupt. Verse 26 talked about Gentiles being called SONS OF THE LIVING GOD, and verses 27-29 read thus:

> Isaiah cries out concerning Israel, "THOUGH THE NUMBER OF THE SONS OF ISRAEL BE LIKE THE SAND OF THE SEA, IT IS THE REMNANT THAT WILL BE SAVED; FOR THE LORD WILL EXECUTE HIS WORD ON THE EARTH, THOROUGHLY AND QUICKLY." And just as Isaiah foretold, "UNLESS THE LORD OF SABAOTH HAD LEFT TO US A POSTERITY, WE WOULD HAVE BECOME LIKE SODOM, AND WOULD HAVE RESEMBLED GOMORRAH."

One moment, Paul is proving that the Gentiles belong, and before even totally coming to terms with that fact, he introduces the idea of a remnant. These three verses are made up of two quotes from the prophet Isaiah.

In the first, Isaiah essentially says, "It doesn't matter if Israel grows to number one trillion people—only some of them will be saved." Isaiah then reminds us that God's word never returns to Him void (Romans 9:28; cf. Isaiah 55:11). We can trust God when He speaks in His Word.

A reflection thought: It matters little how many (or how few) people we have in our churches; there is no guarantee that all (or even most) of them are genuinely saved. The remnant simply means "less than all." The point is that we must always preach the Gospel because we don't know who is in and who is out. Paul will hit on this more in 10:14-15.

In the second Old Testament quotation, Paul quotes Isaiah as essentially saying, "If it weren't for the remnant of Israel, God would have destroyed them like He had destroyed Sodom and Gomorrah, only saving Lot." That's quite a statement about Israel's wickedness! Paul will spend the entire next chapter discussing modern Israel's failure to understand God rightly. But in verse 29 specifically, Paul is highlighting God's grace. Paul understands Isaiah's words here as basically saying that if it were not for this remnant, then God's plan would have already crashed and burned. Therefore, the remnant is part of God's sovereign plan. (More on the specifics of that later, as Paul will greatly elaborate on it in 11:7-26.)

But before moving on, this demands one more thought. When Martin Luther—mostly alone—stood up to call the church out of its superstitious slumber, God was in control even before Luther believed the Gospel. When Jesus was crucified—true Israel, as I've already discussed in this treatise—God was in control. When Judah—virtually the only remaining Israelite tribe—went into exile to Babylon, God's sovereign control over and care for a remnant was shown in minor by verses like 2 Kings 25:27-30 (cf. 24:6-16). When the church—even today—seems like it is dying, whether due to prosperity liars or the many cults that have arisen or even the fact that many who claim Christ want to live as they did in Judges (lone-ranger like), God is still in control and protecting His remnant. If He were not, Judgment Day—much like Genesis 19—would have already occurred.

## D. Israel prefers the Law to faith (9:30-10:21)

# EXCURSUS: Seeking the Seed

In 9:30-10:21, Paul spends a whole chapter discussing why Israel has only been left with a remnant. They refuse to obey the call of the Gospel of Jesus Christ.

## 1. A question concerning Israel's failure (9:30-33)

Paul continues his thought by asking a hypothetical question:

<u>What shall we say then?</u>

In essence, this question ties everything together from 9:19-26 (about Gentiles being children of God) to 9:27-29 (about how national Israel only has a remnant left). Paul is pretending to be someone reading this and wondering about it.

He answers the question in 9:30b-31.

<u>That Gentiles, who did not pursue righteousness, attained righteousness, even the righteousness which is by faith; but Israel, pursuing a law of righteousness, did not arrive at *that* law.</u>

Paul will elaborate on this fact in chapter 10, and even in the last two verses of chapter 9, but for now we must keep in mind what Paul has said prior in this chapter:

- <u>But *it is* not as though the word of God has failed</u> (9:6).
- <u>God's purpose according to *His* choice would stand</u> (9:11).
- <u>So then He has mercy on whom He desires, and He hardens whom He desires</u> (9:18).

God is in control, and nothing happens apart from His plan. If Gentiles are called His children, it is because He chose them; if national Israel has fallen away, it's because God allowed it.

But then Paul asks another question:

<u>Why?</u> (9:32a).

I pointed out that the ultimate answer is, "God willed it," which we will see more clearly in chapter 11, but for now, Paul wants to give the practical, human-observation-level answer.

In verses 32-33, he answers his question.

> Because *they did* not *pursue it* by faith, but as though *it were* by works. They stumbled over the stumbling stone, just as it is written, "BEHOLD, I LAY IN ZION A STONE OF STUMBLING AND A ROCK OF OFFENSE, AND HE WHO BELIEVES IN HIM WILL NOT BE DISAPPOINTED."

These verses are amazing! I say that because they tie back to Jesus. Jesus is the reason both why Israel has disappeared (read: fallen away) and why the Gentiles have appeared (read: believed). If we think back to Matthew 21:42, Jesus quoted this very verse about Himself. The parable that He had told before getting to verse 42 is proof that He was a stumbling stone for Israel. In verse 43, He had said that He would give the vineyard to those who will produce its fruit: Gentiles.

The fruit of Christianity, the fruit Jesus wants to see, can only come by faith. Paul spent the end of Romans 3 and all of Romans 4 discussing how faith—not works—makes you a child of God. Earlier in his life, he had written Galatians—a whole book about how the Law cannot save you, only faith.

Paul wrote and preached so that people would come to faith in Jesus and stop stumbling over Him. This should be the heart of every Christian—especially pastors. The Gospel should never be far from our lips: "Believe in Him, and you will never be disappointed!"

## 2. Paul's desire for their salvation (10:1-4)

As Paul opens chapter 10, so also he opens his heart, much like in the first verses of chapter 9, and he further expounds on why Israel is out and the Gentiles are in. Paul writes,

> Brethren, my heart's desire and my prayer to God for them is for *their* salvation. For I testify about them that they have a zeal for God, but not in accordance with knowledge. For not knowing about God's righteousness and seeking to establish their own, they did not subject

## EXCURSUS: Seeking the Seed

themselves to the righteousness of God. For Christ is the end of the law for righteousness to everyone who believes (10:1-4).

There are two main thoughts in these four verses: One on verses 1-2, and one on verses 3-4.

First, Paul is clear that he wants his countrymen to be saved. He desires it in his heart, and he prays for it to be a reality. Simply put, despite what looks clear to us—our loved one might never believe—we must plead with God to change them, trust Him that He knows what He is doing, and live our lives like Paul: Eager to speak the message of salvation.

Paul says in verse 2 that they are very close to getting it, but just far enough that, apart from divine intervention, they will never find Him. It's like an angle. You can take the smallest angle possible, but as the lines extend away from the origin point, the slightest of angles will always end up with the individual lines farther and farther apart from each other. Paul says that their zeal is actually ignorance. God must bless Israelites with real knowledge, or they will not be saved.

Second, Paul explains the knowledge they need, and he explains that ultimately, the knowledge they need is the knowledge that leads to Christ. Any other knowledge is a waste of time. A right study of God's Law and God's righteousness will lead to Christ every time.

Romans 1:16-17 explains that in the Gospel of Jesus, "the righteousness of God is revealed." With this in mind, Romans 10:3 explains that the Jewish people did not subject themselves to the [Gospel]. If we study the entirety of Romans, we will discover that Paul makes the case that God's righteousness is given to people by faith in Christ = imputation (cf. Romans 3:21-30, 4:1-8). For the Jewish people to work for righteousness—as Paul clearly states here—they are missing Christ, missing the Gospel, and completely falling short of God's righteousness.

## 3. The only hope for their salvation (10:5-17)

In Romans 10:5-17, Paul lays out the only hope for Israel's salvation. Now, regardless of what Paul might say in this section, we must keep in mind that the Scripture does not contradict itself. So, whatever we come to learn in these verses will not be overturned by something we read farther on in Romans (e.g., chapter 11). Paul begins this section by drawing a distinction between faith and works of Law in verses 5-13. Then he explains how to be made righteous by faith in verses 14-15. And then he tells us that Israel ignored these plain facts, but even so, it doesn't change the facts, in verses 16-17.

## a. The difference between faith and works (10:5-13)

Let's begin by looking at the distinction between legal (Law) righteousness and imputed (faith) righteousness. Paul writes in 10:5-8,

> For Moses writes that the man who practices the righteousness which is based on law shall live by that righteousness. But the righteousness based on faith speaks as follows: "DO NOT SAY IN YOUR HEART, 'WHO WILL ASCEND INTO HEAVEN?' (that is, to bring Christ down), or 'WHO WILL DESCEND INTO THE ABYSS?' (that is, to bring Christ up from the dead)." But what does it say? "THE WORD IS NEAR YOU, IN YOUR MOUTH AND IN YOUR HEART"—that is, the word of faith which we are preaching.

The Law of Moses was never the answer. Paul says as much in Galatians 3:10, 24. If you want to be saved by the Law, you have to practice it perfectly, or you will die. Paul turns in verses 6-8 and says, "Faith is better." He does this in two primary ways. First, he tells us what faith is not in verses 6-7. Second, he tells us what faith is in verse 8.

Faith is not doing anything to add to or increase our standing with God or the merit of Christ. There is nothing we can do to build on what Christ has done for us.

Faith believes in the message about Christ. Paul elaborates on this theme in verses 9-13. He writes:

> If you confess with your mouth Jesus *as* Lord, and believe in your heart that God raised Him from the dead, you will be saved; for with the heart a person believes, resulting in righteousness, and with the mouth he confesses, resulting in salvation. For the Scripture says, "WHOEVER BELIEVES IN HIM WILL NOT BE DISAPPOINTED." For there is no distinction between Jew and Greek; for the same *Lord* is Lord of all, abounding in riches for all who call on Him; for

EXCURSUS: Seeking the Seed

"WHOEVER WILL CALL ON THE NAME OF THE LORD WILL BE SAVED."

There are three observations to make on this text in this context. This is probably the pinnacle of Romans 9-11.

First, Paul's whole discussion is centered around confession and belief. In verses 9-10, he explains that confession flows from a person's mouth, and belief flows from a person's heart. Then in verse 11, he quotes from Isaiah 28:16, where Isaiah says that no one who believes (heart) will ever be lost. And in verse 13, he quotes from Joel 2:32, where Joel says that everyone who confesses (calls on vocally) will be saved.

Second, in verse 12, Paul defines what the Scripture passages he quotes mean by whoever. Both Jew and Gentile are held to this standard. (Here it is clear that Jew is referring to national Israel.) God doesn't change His criteria because someone is of Jewish descent. All must confess and believe. And of all who believe and confess, they are counted in the whoevers of verses 11 and 13, and they will be saved. The all in verse 12 must be interpreted in context!

Third, what is curiously absent here is any mention of repentance. As preachers—as will be apparent throughout the next few paragraphs—our job is to call people to believe the Gospel. Belief is what saves. Repentance does not save a person. Repentance is the first sign of genuine faith because to believe in Jesus is to repent of unbelief. But repenting of specific, petty sins is not the task of the unbeliever.

## b. How to be made righteous by faith (10:14-15)

In verses 14-15a, Paul poses several questions that this line of thinking raises.

> How then will they call on Him in whom they have not believed? How will they believe in Him whom they have not heard? And how will they hear without a preacher? How will they preach unless they are sent?

Verse 13 ended by promising that WHOEVER WILL CALL ON THE NAME OF THE LORD WILL BE SAVED. As such, verses 14-17 serve as Paul's necessary transition between how people are saved and why Israel is not. But we must unpack verses 14-15, and their rhetorical questions, first.

Paul is a genius here. He first states WHOEVER WILL CALL ON THE NAME OF THE LORD WILL BE SAVED. He then asks how a person can call on God if he doesn't believe in God. Rhetorically, the answer is, "He can't." (Calling on God is the first fruit of true heart belief; Jesus said, "But the things that proceed out of the mouth come from the heart" in Matthew 15:18.) Paul then draws the application of salvation back a step and asks how they can believe if they can't hear. Rhetorically, again, "They can't." (This is why if a sermon is to be a Christian sermon, Christ must be proclaimed *and* hearers must be urged to believe.) Paul then goes back, yet another step, and asks how people can hear without someone preaching. Rhetorically, "They can't." (This is why even everyday Christians must thoroughly know the Gospel, because it isn't preaching if you aren't using words,[3] and Paul here says that people can't hear to believe if people aren't preaching with their mouths.) But then Paul takes it back a final step. He asks how preachers will go if they aren't sent. Rhetorically, surprise, the answer is: "Jesus sent every Christian on this mission when He gave the Great Commission in Matthew 28:19-20)."

And then at the end of verse 15, Paul quotes from Isaiah as a way of encouraging obedient Christians:

Just as it is written, "HOW BEAUTIFUL ARE THE FEET OF THOSE WHO BRING GOOD NEWS OF GOOD THINGS!"

This is how we prove our repentance from our murderous, hateful hearts (cf. Matthew 5:21-26). Paul said in Romans 3:15, "THEIR FEET ARE SWIFT TO SHED BLOOD," and what we have in 10:15 is transformed feet. Instead of spreading death, we spread life. This should be an encouragement for every Christian, but alas, most of us would rather that our Israelology be right so our eschatology can be right, than study the glorious truths of the Gospel so that we can be complimented by God. (Remember that all this talk of Gospel, belief, and salvation is in a portion of Scripture that is discussing both Israelology and eschatology; we can't be right on other ologies if our gospelology is wrong.)

---

[3] Sorry, not sorry, Saint Francis.

EXCURSUS: Seeking the Seed

### c. Israel does not have faith (10:16-17)

In verse 16, Paul shares the bad news:

> However, they did not all heed the good news; for Isaiah says, "LORD, WHO HAS BELIEVED OUR REPORT?"

If there was any question about the identity of all in verse 12, then verse 16 explains that it does not include those who fail to believe. Paul also proves, by this verse, that not everyone who hears, believes. He concludes by summing up the section in verse 17:

> So faith comes from hearing, and hearing by the word of Christ.

These statements set the groundwork for the rest of the chapter, in which Paul will prove that Israel has no excuse for its lack of belief.

## 4. An excuse for Israel? (10:18-21)

At this point, it seems as though Paul is saying that the only way to be saved is by believing in Christ, and that the only way to believe is by hearing the Gospel, and that national Israel has rejected God's provision in Christ. It seems that way because it is that way. And in verses 18-21, Paul will try to let Israel off the hook for their lack of belief, but in the end, he can't.

His first rhetorical question comes in verse 18a.

> But I say, surely they have never heard, have they?

Paul figures that someone might reason thus, or maybe he himself tried to reason thus until God spoke to him otherwise (through Scripture—as proved in the paragraph to follow).

Quickly put, the answer is negative. Israel did hear. Paul proves it through Scripture, and with this Scripture, I think it is safe to infer that no person on earth can claim, "But I didn't hear, though" (cf. Romans 1:18-20, which concludes by saying they are without excuse). The passage Paul quotes to answer his question says,

> Indeed they have: "THEIR VOICE HAS GONE OUT INTO ALL THE EARTH, AND THEIR WORDS TO THE ENDS OF THE WORLD" (10:18b).

The fact that the text says <u>earth</u> and <u>world</u> proves that beyond just claiming Israel is without excuse, Paul is saying that even Gentiles who refuse to believe are without excuse.

And in verse 19a, Paul asks a follow-up question:

> But I say, surely Israel did not know, did they?

In essence, he is asking, "Is ignorance an excuse?" Some people do hear the Gospel and do not know that they are hearing it. Paul proves, from verse 19b-21, that at least in Israel's case, this excuse will not work. He quotes three passages:

> First Moses says, "I WILL MAKE YOU JEALOUS BY THAT WHICH IS NOT A NATION, BY A NATION WITHOUT UNDERSTANDING WILL I ANGER YOU." And Isaiah is very bold and says, "I WAS FOUND BY THOSE WHO DID NOT SEEK ME. I BECAME MANIFEST TO THOSE WHO DID NOT ASK FOR ME." But as for Israel He says, "ALL THE DAY LONG I HAVE STRETCHED OUT MY HANDS TO A DISOBEDIENT AND OBSTINATE PEOPLE."

There are several things to note.

First, the talk of <u>jealousy</u> and <u>nations</u> will recur in Romans 11:7ff. We will get there in due time.

Second, Paul asks if Israel's not-knowing is an excuse. In verse 19, he quotes Moses as saying, <u>A NATION WITHOUT UNDERSTANDING</u>. As will be clear in 11:7ff., this ignorant nation is the Gentiles. Plain fact: God gives saving knowledge to those He will save. Lack of knowledge is no excuse.

Third, in verse 21, Paul tells us that ignorance isn't even Israel's problem. Their problem is disobedience. The last words of Romans 10 describe Israel as <u>A DISOBEDIENT AND OBSTINATE PEOPLE</u>.

# E. The remnant again? (11:1-6)

## EXCURSUS: Seeking the Seed

But, lest you fear, Paul has one more whole chapter answering the question he first posed in 9:6 and again raised in 10:1. A similar statement will be made in 11:1a,

> I say then, God has not rejected His people, has He?

And Paul immediately answers his question in strong language:

> May it never be!

And whether we look at it as the physical people of God (Israel) or spiritual Israel (cf. 9:6), the statement is true. But let me qualify that.

Obviously, God could never reject the spiritual people He redeemed by the blood of His Son (cf. 8:38-39). But the text (cf. 10:21) is clear that God has not rejected national Israel: I HAVE STRETCHED OUT MY HANDS; instead, national Israel has rejected Him: A DISOBEDIENT AND OBSTINATE PEOPLE. Remember the dichotomy in 9:22-23? God endured with much patience vessels of wrath, but He prepared beforehand for glory those He would save. And 9:24 makes an interesting point directly related to 11:1ff. Those He prepared beforehand were the ones He called not from among Jews only, but also from among Gentiles. This text is clear that physical Jews are part of the Kingdom of God. Paul uses himself as an example in 11:1b of this very fact:

> For I too am an Israelite, a descendant of Abraham, of the tribe of Benjamin.

There are physical Israelites who make up spiritual Israel—God's people.
There is a double meaning in 11:2a.

> God has not rejected His people whom He foreknew.

First, God will never reject His spiritual people. Second, God need not reject physical Israel for them to reject Him and His provision in Christ. As Paul will show in verses 2b-5, historically, the majority of national Israel has regularly rejected God, but there is still hope. Paul writes:

> Or do you not know what the Scripture says in *the passage about* Elijah, how he pleads with God against Israel? "Lord, THEY HAVE KILLED YOUR PROPHETS, THEY HAVE TORN DOWN YOUR ALTARS, AND I ALONE AM LEFT, AND THEY ARE SEEKING MY LIFE." But what is the divine response to him? "I HAVE KEPT for Myself SEVEN THOUSAND MEN WHO HAVE NOT BOWED THE KNEE TO BAAL." In the same way then, there has also come to be at the present time a remnant according to *God's* gracious choice.

There are at least four observations to make on this text.

First, Paul says that Elijah was pleading against Israel. Against. This is not a quotation from the Old Testament. This is Paul's interpretation of the Old Testament context from which the quote of verse 3 flows. Paul sets Israel up as Elijah's enemies. National Israel was Elijah's antagonist.

Second, Elijah thought he was the only faithful one left, but God is clear that He actually has SEVEN THOUSAND faithful men. Simply put, we will be surprised by the number of faithful—nationally Jewish—people who are redeemed by Christ's blood in the end, whether or not there actually is a Jewish revival before Christ's return. (We will return to that question before the end of this treatise.)

Third, Paul explains that there is a remnant at the present time. If the Scripture is true (hint: It is!), then we don't need to look for a day in the future when the Jewish remnant suddenly appears. It is here at the present time. (The question of revival and remnant of national Israel is still to be discussed in this treatise.)

Fourth, Paul says that this remnant is according to *God's* gracious choice. This is a beautiful word. Anyone who believes ultimately believes because of God's gracious choice. Paul had written in 9:11, *God's purpose according to His choice would stand*. If a physically Jewish person comes to Christ and is turned into a spiritual Jew, it is because of God's gracious choice, not because he is a Jew physically. The Jews cannot say, "Because we are God's people, God owes us salvation." Paul agrees in 11:6,

> But if it is by grace, it is no longer on the basis of works, otherwise grace is no longer grace.

(It must be said before moving on: Christianity is grace from beginning to end. If Ephesians 2:8 says, *For by grace you have been saved,* then we should never think that we are now being perfected by the flesh [Galatians 3:3]. Paul said, I do not nullify the grace of God, for if righteousness comes through the Law, then Christ died needlessly [Galatians 2:21]. If salvation has anything to do with works, then grace is no longer grace and Christ died needlessly. I'll echo Paul. May it never be! If Christ died needlessly, then we should just call ourselves Ians, because there would be no need for Christ. Christian, please see grace as grace—not as an excuse for sin but as the motivation and power to overcome sin.)

## F. Separating Israel from the elect (11:7-10)

In verses 7-10, Paul pokes a massive hole in the prevailing, modern theory that Israel as a nation will be restored (come to Christ). In verse 7, he states the fact, and in verses 8-10, he proves it through Scripture.

## 1. The fact (11:7)

Verse 7 begins with Paul asking a rhetorical question on the heels of verse 6. Verse 6 says, "But if it is by grace, it is no longer on the basis of works, otherwise grace is no longer grace." This harks back to 9:31-32. Israel, pursuing a law of righteousness, did not arrive at *that* law. Why? Because *they did* not *pursue it* by faith, but as though *it were* by works. In essence, before we get to 11:7, Paul is saying that God's choice is not by works, Israel is trying to work, and as such, they are disobeying God. Paul says as much in verse 7:

> What then? What Israel is seeking, it has not obtained, but those who were chosen obtained it, and the rest were hardened.

Israel, as a collective nation, is seeking/pursuing righteousness/reconciliation with God by works. They will never get it if they keep employing the strategy of works. Paul then makes a colossal contrast: But. He says that the individuals from both Israel and the nations who were chosen by grace did obtain righteousness/reconciliation with God. And the verse concludes with a damning phrase: The rest were hardened. This phrase brings back to mind 9:18. He has mercy on whom He desires, and He hardens whom He desires. God takes the credit for hardening national Israel.

## 2. The Scriptures (11:8-10)

Paul proves through two Old Testament quotations 1) that God takes the credit for hardening Israel, and 2) precisely what this hardening looks like. He writes in verses 8-10:

> Just as it is written, "GOD GAVE THEM A SPIRIT OF STUPOR, EYES TO SEE NOT AND EARS TO HEAR NOT, DOWN TO THIS VERY DAY." And David says, "LET THEIR TABLE BECOME A SNARE AND A TRAP, AND A STUMBLING BLOCK AND A RETRIBUTION TO THEM. LET THEIR EYES BE DARKENED TO SEE NOT, AND BEND THEIR BACKS FOREVER."

God hardened Israel, and the text says that even DOWN TO THIS VERY DAY the hardening is in effect. We can know that this is a certainty by just looking at the nation of Israel. Even today, national Israel is more concerned about their land in the Middle East than they are about believing in Jesus as the Messiah.

Interestingly, 11:9 is attributed to David. David writes that THEIR TABLE will BECOME A SNARE... A TRAP... A STUMBLING BLOCK AND A RETRIBUTION. This originally comes from Psalm 69:22-23, but it is quite interesting that David also brings up the TABLE in Psalm 23:5, You prepare a table before me in the presence of my enemies. This table is Christ. Christ is sustenance for the weary soul, even in the midst of the worst situations. So, when Paul says that THEIR TABLE has BECOME A SNARE AND A TRAP, AND A STUMBLING BLOCK AND A RETRIBUTION TO THEM, he's merely reiterating what he said in 9:32-33. They stumbled over the stumbling stone, just as it is written, "BEHOLD, I LAY IN ZION A STONE OF STUMBLING AND A ROCK OF OFFENSE, AND HE WHO BELIEVES IN HIM WILL NOT BE DISAPPOINTED."

If you're reading this, and you've never believed, what are you waiting for? I don't care if you're Jewish or Muslim, atheist, or "carnal Christian," you need to believe. If you believe, then you will not be disappointed. If you fail to believe, Paul's words in 11:10 will come true: [Your] EYES will BE DARKENED TO SEE NOT, AND [your] BACKS will be bent FOREVER. Please heed the call of the Gospel! Christ was crucified. I know it sounds crazy, but this is why He is a STONE OF STUMBLING. Don't stumble over Him any longer!

EXCURSUS: Seeking the Seed

That last word of 11:10 seals the deal. The hardening is FOREVER. This is hardening on a national level. Individuals can be saved by Christ—like Paul was—but Israel as a nation is forever hardened. And it's not just Israel: In reality, any nation that thinks God owes them salvation has been hardened. I'll go farther: Every nation of this world is already hardened. The Apostle John would agree. Spiritual Israel is not made up of any whole nation. Instead, John writes in Revelation 5:9,

> Worthy are You to take the book and to break its seals; for You were slain, and purchased for God with Your blood *men* from every tribe and tongue and people and nation.

No nation stands out above any other in spiritual Israel. God doesn't redeem nations; He hardens nations, and He chooses individuals from the nations to soften and save by His sovereign grace. (I anticipate rebuttals as regards Revelation, so know that I will get there as soon as we finish working our way through Romans 9-11.)

## G. Watch out for pride (11:11-24)

There is something that needs to be pointed out before plunging forward in chapter 11. Romans 11:7 says, What Israel is seeking, it has not obtained, but those who were chosen obtained it, and the rest were hardened. The rest of the chapter focuses on those who were chosen, and the word Israel does not recur until verses 25-26 where it refers not to national Israel, but to spiritual Israel—because the rest were hardened. Verse 10 concluded by saying that national Israel would be hardened forever.

This leads Paul to a rhetorical question in 11:11a,

> I say then, they did not stumble so as to fall, did they?

Israel, as a nation, is—grammatically—a singular noun; they is plural. Paul is not asking about national Israel here. He is talking about individuals from national Israel—likely a remnant according to God's gracious choice (11:5). This is why he can answer his question as he does:

> May it never be!

The remnant from Israel, elected by God's grace, will never permanently fall. It harks back to the thought that initiated this whole discussion in Romans 9-11; Romans 8:37-39 is as true for physically Jewish believers as it is for Gentile believers:

> But in all these things we overwhelmingly conquer through Him who loved us. For I am convinced that neither death, nor life, nor angels, nor principalities, nor things present, nor things to come, nor powers, nor height, nor depth, nor any other created thing, will be able to separate us from the love of God, which is in Christ Jesus our Lord.

Paul then breaks out in a discussion of the sovereign plan of God in Romans 9-11 (though at this point we are two-thirds of the way through it). In 11:11-24, Paul's overarching point is that his readers watch out for pride. In verses 11-16, he explains his role in God's sovereign plan, and in 17-24, he warns his converts about being conceited because of their being chosen by God.

## 1. Paul's role (11:11b-16)

Paul says in 11:5 that there is a remnant *at the present time*. However, he also says in 11:7, What Israel is seeking, it has not obtained, but those who were chosen obtained it. This harks back to 8:30, "These whom He predestined, He also called; and these whom He called, He also justified; and these whom He justified, He also glorified." No one has been glorified yet. But because of God's gracious choice in predestination, glorification is an inevitable reality. Meaning, in 11:7 (those who were chosen obtained it) not that they already did, but rather that it is a certainty. Paul's ministry proves this fact.

Paul says in 11:11b-12,

> But by their transgression salvation *has come* to the Gentiles, to make them jealous. Now if their transgression is riches for the world and their failure is riches for the Gentiles, how much more will their fulfillment be!

The they/their/them in these verses is speaking of elect Jewish individuals who have yet to believe in Christ. Their transgression is their stubborn unbelief. In

## EXCURSUS: Seeking the Seed

Paul's ministry, this is clearly shown in Acts 13:46, Paul and Barnabas spoke out boldly and said, "It was necessary that the word of God be spoken to you first; since you repudiate it and judge yourselves unworthy of eternal life, behold, we are turning to the Gentiles."

Because of the Jews' response (or lack thereof) to Paul's preaching, Paul turned to the Gentiles, and they found salvation. Salvation from God is better than all the riches in the world! Paul looks forward to a day when all the elect Israelites are as spiritually wealthy as he and the Gentile believers are.

Paul continues to clarify the goal of his ministry in verses 13-14.

> But I am speaking to you who are Gentiles. Inasmuch then as I am an apostle of Gentiles, I magnify my ministry, if somehow I might move to jealousy my fellow countrymen and save some of them.

Paul brags on his ministry to the Gentiles in the hopes that it will spur his countrymen to believe. Note that he doesn't say Israel, and also note that he doesn't attempt to save all of them. He is trying to save some of them. The some is the same as the they/their/them from 11:11-12. Namely, elect Jews who currently do not believe.

Paul continues in verse 15, concluding his explanation of his ministry by looking forward to the hopeful result:

> For if their rejection is the reconciliation of the world, what will *their* acceptance be but life from the dead?

Simply put, elect national Israelites are still rejecting Christ, even today. When the last elect Israelite is saved, Christ will return and bring the dead to life. Verse 16 proves this:

> If the first piece *of dough* is holy, the lump is also; and if the root is holy, the branches are too.

These illustrations are parallel, both describing the same concept. The first harks back to Numbers 15:17-21 and the law of first fruits. Interestingly enough, Paul calls Christ the firstfruits in 1 Corinthians 15:22-23. For as in Adam all die, so also in Christ all will be made alive. But each in his own order: Christ the first fruits, after that those who are Christ's at His coming. So, in

Romans 11:16, Christ is the *first piece of dough*, and His followers are the lump; Christ is the root, and His followers are the branches.

Paul will expand on the branch metaphor in verses 17-24, but suffice it to say that Christ's people are secure only by the merits of Christ. The reason Paul gives for the lump and branches being holy is that Christ—the first piece and the root—is holy. There is no other reason. And thus, Paul is ready to ask the Gentile believers some pointed questions.

## 2. The convert's position (11:17-24)

This next section lends further support to the fact that national Israel is out. I'll elaborate and explain after I quote verses 17-18a.

> But if some of the branches were broken off, and you, being a wild olive, were grafted in among them and became partaker with them of the rich root of the olive tree, do not be arrogant toward the branches.

If Israel were to be restored, then there would be no reason for arrogance. In essence, Paul is here saying, "Check your response to this teaching." He continues in verse 18b:

> If you are arrogant, *remember that* it is not you who supports the root, but the root *supports you*.

Remember that the root is Christ.

It is imperative to note that, in verse 17, Gentile believers are grafted in among branches that are broken off. Not only that, but Paul says the Gentile believers became partaker with them. How can someone become a partaker of the rich root of the olive tree with branches that were broken off?

In verse 16, Paul wrote, if the root is holy, the branches are too. Gentile believers become partakers with the broken off branches because all the branches are holy, *not* because every Jewish person is a branch.

The metaphor here is not exactly the same as the one in John 15. There, the chopped off branches are burned; here, the chopped off branches will be regrafted in when they believe in Christ (cf. 11:23). Paul will further explain how all of this works in verse 25.

Paul anticipates an objection to his warning against arrogance. In verses 19-21, he writes:

## EXCURSUS: Seeking the Seed

> You will say then, "Branches were broken off so that I might be grafted in." Quite right, they were broken off for their unbelief, but you stand by your faith. Do not be conceited, but fear; for if God did not spare the natural branches, He will not spare you, either.

Paul makes it clear that Gentile salvation is not due to anything in the Gentiles. At the same time, he attributes the Jews' apparent loss of salvation not to God's power, but to the Jews' failure to believe the Gospel. God graciously allowed the Gentiles to believe the Gospel (cf. 11:5-7). And just like the Jews were cut off for disobeying the Gospel, Paul warns Gentiles that sin can also disqualify them.

**OBJECTION:** Isn't salvation permanent, like Romans 8:38-39 says?

**ANSWER:** Yes. Most assuredly, yes! But this section of Scripture is still seeking to answer the question posed because of Romans 8:38-39. It appears on the surface that something can prevent salvation, and the Jews are exhibit-A. As will be made clear from 11:24 though, all the dismembered branches will be regrafted into Christ so no elect Jew will lose his/her salvation eternally. And when it comes to Gentiles, the same is true. But as Paul said in Romans 6:1-2, What shall we say then? Are we to continue in sin so that grace may increase? May it never be! How shall we who died to sin still live in it? Sin is not fitting for a believer, and when tied back to Romans 11:20, this includes arrogance and conceit.

So, if you call yourself a Christian, and if you love sin of any type, please check yourself. You may be an elect branch, but love of sin is not compatible with Christianity. Check yourself! You don't want to find out too late that you don't belong to Christ. Believe in Him today!

Paul offers a complex picture of God and salvation in verse 22. In fact, Paul commands us to pay attention by using the word behold.

> Behold then the kindness and severity of God; to those who fell, severity, but to you, God's kindness, if you continue in His kindness; otherwise you also will be cut off.

There are four things to note in this text.

First, Paul wants us to understand that God is kind. The Bible is replete with this theme, and it is not just a New Testament theme. As early as Adam and Eve in Genesis 3, we see that The LORD God made garments of skin for Adam and his wife, and clothed them (3:21). He would have been just to strike them down, but instead, He covered their sinfulness by providing—Himself—the first animal sacrifice. This occurred after they believed His preaching of the first Gospel of Jesus Christ (cf. Genesis 3:15; note: Their belief is not explicitly stated, but it is easy to infer from the text).

Second, Paul wants us to understand that God is severe. To put it simply, God is severe toward those who take His kindness for granted. For instance, the physically Jewish people thought God owed them salvation, so He became severe toward them, and now only a remnant will be saved, and some are still not yet believing, so God is still severe toward them.

Third, salvation is not merely a past event. Paul says that believers must continue in His kindness, or else they will also be cut off. God doesn't care if you prayed a prayer when you were six. He wants to know if you believe NOW in Jesus. John 3:16 says literally, For God so loved the world, that He gave His only begotten Son, that whoever [is believing] in Him shall not perish, but have eternal life. Do you believe currently? If not, you are in danger of being cut off.

Fourth, as I discussed above, this cutting off could be permanent—as John 15 describes—or it could be temporary—as our text describes. The answer to which kind of cutting off it is depends on your response—or a Jewish person's response—to the questions: Do you believe in Jesus? Do you have a new relationship with sin?

Paul says as much in 11:23,

> And they also, if they do not continue in their unbelief, will be grafted in, for God is able to graft them in again.

If a nationally Jewish person believes, it proves that she is part of spiritual Israel. Not all Jews will believe, but those who do are part of spiritual Israel. And Paul further proves his point in verse 24:

> For if you were cut off from what is by nature a wild olive tree, and were grafted contrary to nature into a cultivated olive tree, how much more will these who are the natural *branches* be grafted into their own olive tree?

It is more than just that God can bring national Jews—the elect ones—to Christ, but instead that it is right for Him to do so. If He can turn wild Gentile

EXCURSUS: Seeking the Seed

branches into a fruitful, cared-for vine, then it is only right for Him to bring wild, rebellious Jews back. Paul calls it their own olive tree, because of 9:5, whose are the fathers, and from whom is the Christ according to the flesh. Christ is Jewish. Thus, the vine is "Jewish." Therefore, the vine must contain Jewish people, if even only a handful—an elect remnant.

## H. "All Israel will be saved" (11:25-32)

Paul sums up the whole discussion in 11:25-32. Paul explains once and for all that national Israel will not be spiritually restored as a whole.

## 1. Important Definitions (11:25-27)

In verses 25-27, Paul defines all Israel as he did both in 9:6 and earlier in 2:28-29. Paul writes in verse 25-27:

> For I do not want you, brethren, to be uninformed of this mystery—so that you will not be wise in your own estimation—that a partial hardening has happened to Israel until the fullness of the Gentiles has come in; and so all Israel will be saved; just as it is written, "THE DELIVERER WILL COME FROM ZION, HE WILL REMOVE UNGODLINESS FROM JACOB." "THIS IS MY COVENANT WITH THEM, WHEN I TAKE AWAY THEIR SINS."

There are three extensive comments to be made on this text, but first, it is necessary to point out that the two occurrences of Israel in this text are 1) the first since 11:7, and 2) the last in the whole epistle. (In fact, the word Israel only occurs from 9:6-11:26 in Romans; it is confined to this discussion.)

First, Paul starts out verse 25 by saying that he wants his readers to understand a mystery. Mystery doesn't mean in the Bible what it means to us today. We read mystery novels where we are trying to solve something. Mystery in the Bible is something that though formerly secret, has now been revealed. So, in essence, Paul is saying that the future of national Israel was a secret, but now that Jesus has come, the secret has been revealed, because typically, all biblical mysteries were revealed in Jesus. Paul doesn't want his readers to be ignorant of this mystery. So, after a parenthesis (that we will look at in the next paragraph), Paul states the explanation of the mystery: A partial hardening has happened to Israel until the fullness of the Gentiles has come in. We will dive into this in a moment.

Second, the parenthesis Paul gives is huge. So that you will not be wise in your own estimation. The word you is plural in Greek. This means that Paul is not talking about one individual's interpretation of his words; instead, it is a command to the church that ties back to 11:18. Do not be arrogant. The church should not think it is better than Israel—or wiser than Israel—just because the nation of Israel is cursed forever (cf. 11:10).

Third, the mystery is immense! A partial hardening has happened to Israel until the fullness of the Gentiles has come in; and so all Israel will be saved. A partial hardening can be more literally translated: A hardening away from a part. Again, Israel was said in 11:7 to have not obtained what it was seeking, but those who were chosen obtained it, and from there until this verse, we had not seen the word Israel. The part that is away from hardening is the elect Israelites. The rest of the nation is hardened eternally, but the separate part—the remnant according to God's gracious choice at the present time (11:5)—will be saved before the last Gentile is saved.

Look at what Paul writes: The fullness of the Gentiles has come in; and so all Israel will be saved. The timeline doesn't allow for a period between the last Gentile being saved and all Israel being saved. You have to eisegete a seven-year tribulation into the text at this point. No translations[4] take the word so in verse 26 as a chronological marker, then, even though the HCSB has a footnote that reads, "Or and then all."[5] Many translations actually read, "in this way," meaning that it is due to all the Gentiles coming in that all Israel will be saved. This is because Paul's final definition of Israel in Romans is a spiritual definition that includes both Jews and Gentiles.

Romans 2:28-29 says, For he is not a Jew who is one outwardly, nor is circumcision that which is outward in the flesh. But he is a Jew who is one inwardly; and circumcision is that which is of the heart, by the Spirit, not by the letter; and his praise is not from men, but from God. This is no different than one of Paul's final statements in Galatians. He writes, "Peace and mercy be upon them, and upon the Israel of God" (6:16). It would make no sense for Paul to wish peace upon national Israel at the end of a letter attacking the legalism of national Judaism. Paul's view of Israel is that it is the faithful people of God, the ones found in Christ—the true Israel (cf. John 15:1), the true seed of Abraham (cf. Galatians 3:16).

---

[4] I checked NIV, HCSB, NASB, KJV, NKJV, CSB, NRSV, ESV.
[5] Cf. *Holman Christian Standard Bible* on Romans 11:26.

EXCURSUS: Seeking the Seed

The two Old Testament Scriptures Paul pulls from in 11:26-27 seek to prove that all Israel will be saved when the fullness of the Gentiles has come in. Paul quotes:

"THE DELIVERER WILL COME FROM ZION, HE WILL REMOVE UNGODLINESS FROM JACOB." "THIS IS MY COVENANT WITH THEM, WHEN I TAKE AWAY THEIR SINS."

You might object: "Look! Paul quotes God saying He will remove ungodliness from Jacob. That means all Israelites must be restored in the end."

Nope. Not true. Consistency is key. In John 1:29, the Baptizer says, "Behold, the Lamb of God who takes away the sin of the world!" No interpreter worth his salt would take this to mean that Jesus took away the sin of every individual in the world. In the same way, there is no reason to understand Romans 11:26-27 as God taking away sin from every physical descendant of Jacob. What it does mean, though, is that God removes sin from every spiritual descendant of Jacob/Israel, and it will be experientially true the day Christ returns.

## 2. The position of elect non-believing Jews (11:28-29)

In verse 28, Paul returns to the present time. No more is he looking to the promise of Christ's certain return after all Israel (spiritual) is saved. Instead, he turns back to the topic of 11:11-16—that is they/their/them, the elect remnant according to God's gracious choice that has yet to believe. Paul writes in verses 28-29,

From the standpoint of the Gospel they are enemies for your sake, but from the standpoint of God's choice they are beloved for the sake of the fathers; for the gifts and the calling of God are irrevocable.

Simply put, all those chosen will eventually be irresistibly called and saved, even though present circumstances look like that is impossible. No matter how vocally resistant a Jewish person might be, if she was chosen, God will convert her before the end (of time or of her life).

Paul says the elect national Israelites are enemies from the standpoint of the Gospel because all Jews who fail to believe in Christ think that Christians worship a false god and are thus idolatrous blasphemers. He says the elect national Israelites are beloved for the sake of the fathers because of how he began this conversation in 9:3, 5-8.

> For I could wish that I myself were accursed, *separated* from Christ for the sake of my brethren, my kinsmen according to the flesh . . . whose are the fathers, and from whom is the Christ according to the flesh, who is over all, God blessed forever. Amen. But *it is* not as though the word of God has failed. For they are not all Israel who are *descended* from Israel; nor are they all children because they are Abraham's descendants, but: "THROUGH ISAAC YOUR DESCENDANTS WILL BE NAMED." That is, it is not the children of the flesh who are children of God, but the children of the promise are regarded as descendants.

When Paul says in 11:29 that the gifts of God are irrevocable, he is explaining the reason for why he brings up the sake of the fathers in verse 28. Gifts can be better translated as graces. God promised Abraham that his descendants would be more numerous than the sand on the seashore (Abraham is the father), and while many of his innumerable descendants are Gentiles (cf. 11:25-26), God must save all of His elect to keep His promise to Abraham. God will never say, "Oh, that person was elect, but they sinned and rebelled their election away." Remember that 11:17-24 proves that despite backsliding and falling away, all of the elect will be finally grafted into Christ.

## 3. Jew and Gentile are on a level playing field (11:30-32)

Paul turns to the Gentiles in verses 30-32 to tell them, "Don't think it's crazy that elect Jews who currently hate you can still be saved; you were also in a seemingly unsavable state." He writes,

## EXCURSUS: Seeking the Seed

> <u>For just as you once were disobedient to God, but now have been shown mercy because of their disobedience, so these also now have been disobedient, that because of the mercy shown to you they also may now be shown mercy. For God has shut up all in disobedience so that He may show mercy to all.</u>

Verses 30-31 are essential to understanding the <u>all</u> in verse 32, but verses 30-31 are also a recapitulation of 11:11-16 about God's sovereign plan and the mentality behind Paul's ministry to the Gentiles. Therefore, when verse 32 says <u>all</u>, the point is all the elect—whether nationally Jewish or Gentile. And again, verses 30-31 are not talking about every national Israelite; Paul says <u>their/these/they</u> referring to the <u>chosen</u> ones of 11:7.

God will get the glory in salvation. He saves the "unsavable" and passes over the "worthy" ones. This is why the <u>all</u> <u>that He may show mercy to</u> are the same as the <u>all</u> that He <u>has shut up in disobedience</u>. It blows our minds and leaves us confused and reeling, but it is part of God's perfect plan. We would do things differently if it were up to us, but this is part of why Paul closes the chapter as he does in verses 33-36 (cf. next heading).

The primary lesson to learn here is that the way things seem does not mean that that is how it is. Yes, national Israel is hardened, and even now, elect Israelites are still hardened, but so are many elect Gentiles. We can't say, "Oh, that person is too far gone for God's grace to change." Every individual could be elect; we don't know. God doesn't give us elect-dar to guide us to only preach the Gospel to those who are elect. We are to preach the Gospel to everyone, and we are to trust God to apply salvation to those who are His. In the end, He will fulfill His promises and get all that belongs to Him.

## I. God's ways are high (11:33-36)

Paul concludes the chapter (and his discussion) by praising God for His greatness and wisdom. In our "wisdom," we would do things differently, and we might be tempted to argue with God and accuse Him of unfairness or foolishness for His decisions, so Paul writes, likely drawing inspiration from Isaiah 55:8-9. There God declared, "<u>For My thoughts are not your thoughts, nor are your ways My ways," declares the LORD. "For as the heavens are higher than the earth, so are My ways higher than your ways and My thoughts than your thoughts.</u>"

*Live Free or Die Lawfully*

Paul writes, in Romans 11:33-36,

> Oh, the depth of the riches both of the wisdom and knowledge of God! How unsearchable are His judgments and unfathomable His ways! For WHO HAS KNOWN THE MIND OF THE LORD, OR WHO BECAME HIS COUNSELOR? Or WHO HAS FIRST GIVEN TO HIM THAT IT MIGHT BE PAID BACK TO HIM AGAIN? For from Him and through Him and to Him are all things. To Him be the glory forever. Amen.

There are several things to note in this text.

First, in the first Scripture that Paul quotes here (cf. 11:34, and Isaiah 40:13), Paul makes it clear that we can't change God's mind about His plan. It was set in stone before the foundation of the world (Ephesians 1:4), and as a result, Gentiles who were at that time separate from Christ, excluded from the commonwealth of Israel, and strangers to the covenants of promise, having no hope and without God in the world . . . have been brought near by the blood of Christ (Ephesians 2:12-13). When Paul speaks of the commonwealth of Israel and the covenants of promise, he is speaking of spiritual Israel—elect Jews and Gentiles. God's plan will not change, and there's nothing we can say, do, or claim to change it.

Second, Paul goes farther in the second Scripture he quotes (cf. 11:35, and Job 41:11). Simply put, God owes humanity nothing. Actually, that's not even totally true. He owes us all hell. But thanks be to God that He sent Christ to die for us. God doesn't have to save a single Gentile, and—for consistency sake—He doesn't have to save a single Jew either. He could leave every single human being in his/her sin—whether Jew or Gentile—and be perfectly just. The fact that He saves any of us is grace, and since no worthy interpreter will claim that every person in the world must be saved for God to be said to love the world, so also, God does not need to save every living Jewish person at a particular time in history in order for all Israel to be saved. Christ is true Israel, and all those elected in Christ will be saved by the last day, and so all Israel will be saved.

Third, all of this might boggle our minds, but the truth is: God will get the glory. God is the source and end of everything. Like the author of a book can do what he wants with the characters he creates, so also God—the Creator of the ends of the earth (Isaiah 40:28)—can do what He wants with His creation. And believers can trust that God causes all things to work together

EXCURSUS: Seeking the Seed

for good to those who love God, to those who are called according to His purpose (Romans 8:28). God will get the glory.

Paul ends the chapter (and his discussion) by saying, To Him be the glory forever. Amen.

## III. Anticipated objection: Revelation prophesies the national restoration of the Jews

But with what has been stated so far, I can anticipate a particular objection. "Okay, but Revelation is describing the future, and it describes Israel being restored. Your interpretation is wrong."

## A. Understanding Revelation

This is an important objection, and to answer it accurately, several discussions must occur before diving into Revelation 7. 1) How does biblical prophecy work? 2) What exactly is Revelation about? 3) Is Revelation truly prophecy? Once these three questions are discussed, we can dive into Revelation 7.

## 1. How does prophecy work? (Isaiah 7-8)

In Revelation 1:1, we read that God gave this vision to John to show to His bond-servants the things which must soon take place. If Revelation is truly prophecy (which we will discuss under III.A.3), then we need to make sure we understand the whole book in light of 1:1. We will look at the opening phrase under III.A.2, but first, we must understand what it means when John says things which must soon take place. Jesus gave the vision to John so that Jesus' bond-servants will know what must soon take place.

The book of Revelation was not a 2019 *New York Times* bestseller. It wasn't even a 1999 *New York Times* bestseller. Most scholars would agree that Revelation was written before AD 100. John wrote it to show his readers then—primarily—and us today—as a result—what must soon take place. So, it only makes sense that if Revelation is prophetic (again, we will answer this under III.A.3), then it has to offer something to the original audience. To prove this concept, let's look at Isaiah 7-8.

In Isaiah 7:10-16, we read the following:

> Then the LORD spoke again to Ahaz, saying, "Ask a sign for yourself from the LORD your God; make it deep as Sheol or high as heaven."
> But Ahaz said, "I will not ask, nor will I test the LORD!"
> Then he said, "Listen now, O house of David! Is it too slight a thing for you to try the patience of men, that you will try the patience of my God as well? Therefore the Lord Himself will give you a sign: Behold, a virgin will be with child and bear a son, and she will call His name Immanuel. He will eat curds and honey at the time He knows enough to refuse evil and choose good. For before the boy will know enough to refuse evil and choose good, the land whose two kings you dread will be forsaken."

Ahaz feared that they would try again and succeed, so God sent Isaiah to Ahaz to comfort him and reassure him of God's presence with him.

Now I know what you're thinking: "Isaiah 7:14 is the Christmas verse; it's about Jesus."

And you're right. But Isaiah was written about seven hundred years before Jesus was born. So how could this sign prove anything to Ahaz if Ahaz would be dead long before Jesus shows up on the scene?

So, God sends Isaiah to Ahaz and essentially says, "Since I want to encourage you in light of My presence with you, ask anything you can think of that I can do to prove My continued presence with you." Ahaz stubbornly refuses to ask anything, probably due to a lack of belief (cf. 7:9). God decides to give a sign, anyways. A virgin will be with child and bear a son, and she will call His name Immanuel. The prophecy continues in verse 16, which cannot be neglected in the original context: For before the boy will know enough to refuse evil and choose good, the land whose two kings you dread will be forsaken.

And then if we read Isaiah 8:1-8, we see the fulfillment of this prophecy in the original context:

> Then the LORD said to me, "Take for yourself a large tablet and write on it in ordinary letters: Swift is the booty, speedy is the prey. And I

## EXCURSUS: Seeking the Seed

will take to Myself faithful witnesses for testimony, Uriah the priest and Zechariah the son of Jeberechiah."

So I approached the prophetess, and she conceived and gave birth to a son.

Then the LORD said to me, "Name him Maher-shalal-hash-baz; for before the boy knows how to cry out 'My father' or 'My mother,' the wealth of Damascus and the spoil of Samaria will be carried away before the king of Assyria."

Again the LORD spoke to me further, saying, "Inasmuch as these people have rejected the gently flowing waters of Shiloah and rejoice in Rezin and the son of Remaliah; now therefore, behold, the Lord is about to bring on them the strong and abundant waters of the Euphrates, *even* the king of Assyria and all his glory; and it will rise up over all its channels and go over all its banks. Then it will sweep on into Judah, it will overflow and pass through, it will reach even to the neck; and the spread of its wings will fill the breadth of your land, O Immanuel."

The first thing to note in this text is that the words Swift is the booty, speedy is the prey that Isaiah writes on the scroll in 8:1 is an English translation of the Hebrew phrase Maher-shalal-hash-baz that Isaiah is told to name his son in 8:3. Also, God promises in 8:4 that this child will still be an infant when Damascus and Samaria are defeated by Assyria. This connects Isaiah's child (second child, cf. 7:3) Maher-shalal-hash-baz to the child prophesied in 7:14. Also, the concluding word of 8:8 makes the connection crystal clear—Immanuel. It wasn't that Immanuel would be the child's literal name, but rather that the child would be proof of God's presence with the people of the land despite the enemy.

"But," you insist, "Isaiah 7:14 has to be talking about Jesus because no other virgin ever had a baby."

You're right—in a sense. First of all, every woman who ever had a baby was a virgin at one point. And second, the Hebrew word (*almah*) need not always refer to a literal virgin.

- **Exodus 2:8**
Pharaoh's daughter said to her, "Go *ahead*." So the girl (*almah*) went and called the child's mother.

Context proves this as Miriam, Moses' older sister, so it is likely (though not necessary) that she was still a virgin at this point.
- **Proverbs 30:18-19**
There are three things which are too wonderful for me, Four which I do not understand: The way of an eagle in the sky, The way of a serpent on a rock, The way of a ship in the middle of the sea, And the way of a man with a maid (*almah*).
In the context, there is no reason to think this is talking about a literal virgin.

We know from the immediate context of Isaiah 7-8 that the prophetess was likely not a literal virgin. Isaiah 7:3 says, Go out now to meet Ahaz, you and your son Shear-jashub. So, Isaiah had a son before Maher-shalal-hash-baz. This would lend credence to the theory that (*almah*) doesn't necessitate a literal virgin.

I will admit that the overwhelming proof is that the word usually refers to a literal virgin. This is why Matthew ends up saying Isaiah 7:14 was fulfilled in Jesus in Matthew 1:21-23,

> "She will bear a Son; and you shall call His name Jesus, for He will save His people from their sins."
> Now all this took place to fulfill what was spoken by the Lord through the prophet: "BEHOLD, THE VIRGIN SHALL BE WITH CHILD AND SHALL BEAR A SON, AND THEY SHALL CALL HIS NAME IMMANUEL," which translated means, "GOD WITH US."

Notice that Jesus has two names, just like Maher-shalal-hash-baz. Again, IMMANUEL is used as a comfort; in Jesus, GOD [is] WITH US physically.

Now I am a huge proponent of seeking connections to Christ in the Old Testament, but something must be said at this point: Isaiah's prophecy in 7:14 had a dual fulfillment; Maher-shalal-hash-baz and Jesus, because the original audience needed comfort. This does not mean that Revelation 7 has a dual fulfillment. Matthew can do this because he was an inspired Scripture writer, and the Scriptures—such as the virgin birth reference in Genesis 3:15—were influencing him too. We can't twist Revelation 7 to mean that national Israel is restored because 1) we are not inspired, and 2) the Scriptures clearly teach the opposite—e.g., Romans 9-11.

EXCURSUS: Seeking the Seed

So, in the end, our interpretation of a passage of Scripture must be consistent with how the original audience would have understood it.

## 2. What is Revelation about? ("Jesus Christ" – Revelation 1:1a)

This leads us to our second question. What exactly is Revelation about? John tells us the simple answer to this question in the first words of the book: The revelation of Jesus Christ. John does not say, "The revelation of the end of the world." He does not say, "The revelation of the antichrist." He doesn't even say, "The revelation of the final week mentioned in Daniel 9:27." John says, The revelation of Jesus Christ. Revelation is our English translation of the Greek apocalypse, which literally means, unveiling. So, a better translation of Revelation 1:1 is The unveiling of Jesus Christ. It follows, then, that Revelation is ultimately about Jesus Christ, but specifically about the mystery which has been kept secret for long ages past (Romans 16:25). Paul's full statement fleshes out the truth of this statement: Now to Him who is able to establish you according to my Gospel and the preaching of Jesus Christ, according to the revelation of the mystery which has been kept secret for long ages past.

In short, the mystery has been unveiled in Christ, and this is the message John is delivering in Revelation. Also, to properly understand John's intention and use of frequently fantastic imagery, we must know the genre of this book. It is not seeking to describe literal dragons or beasts or pearly gates. Instead, it fully utilizes symbolism because it is an apocalypse.

Apocalyptic literature was popular in the ancient world, and—besides Revelation—Daniel, Ezekiel, and Zechariah in our Bibles contain apocalyptic portions. In Daniel, he makes it clear that the ram and the goat are kings (Daniel 8), and so also in Revelation, John explains the images that we would not know from other parts of Scripture (cf. 1:16, 20). In Revelation, to properly understand it, we must be well-versed in our Old Testament; the vast majority—if not all—of the allusions, symbols, and references in Revelation flow straight out of the Old Testament. The vision of Revelation 7 is no different. And again, because it is the unveiling of Jesus Christ, all of the symbols ultimately serve to acquaint us even better with the Gospel of Jesus Christ. This is how the original readers (hearers, cf. 1:3) would have understood it, and so must we.

## 3. Is Revelation truly prophecy? (Revelation 1)

This leads to the third and final question before diving into Revelation 7. Is Revelation truly prophecy? My answer is, "sort of."

The primary genre of Revelation is apocalyptic. As described above, it means that the book is full of fantastic symbolism and imagery, and it seeks to unveil a mystery. In ancient times, the primary use of apocalyptic literature was to portray the battle between good and evil on a cosmic scale. John tells us in 1:1, <u>The unveiling of Jesus Christ</u>, because, for the Christian, Jesus is the only hope in this cosmic struggle. Through an apocalyptic medium, John hopes to convince his readers (<u>hearers</u>) of this truth.

However, when we get to 1:4, we see another medium: <u>John to the seven churches that are in Asia: Grace to you and peace</u>. This reads like the start of any epistle we find in the New Testament. As such, epistle would be a secondary genre for this book. John is writing a personal letter—inspired by God (<u>which God gave Him . . . and communicated *it* by His angel to His bond-servant John</u>)—to the universal church (<u>seven</u> is the number of perfection) in order to encourage us to persevere in the faith/struggle between good and evil (cf. 2:7, 11, 17, 26; 3:5, 12, 21).

And in 1:19 we find the outline of the book. <u>Therefore write the things which you have seen, and the things which are, and the things which will take place after these things</u>. In other words, the outline boils down to 1) past, 2) present, and 3) future. However, this does not mean that Revelation is prophecy, but only that it contains prophecy. No one would say Matthew is prophecy because chapters 24-25 are prophetic; no one would say 1 Corinthians is prophecy because a good majority of chapter 15 is prophetic; we need not call Revelation prophecy just because most of chapters 17-22 are prophetic.

The outline boils down to 1) past [1:1-20], 2) present [2:1-16:11],[6] and 3) future [16:12-22:9]. Revelation 22:10-21 is the epilogue. And the present (2:1-16:11) can be broken into seven visions, beginning with the church as it has always stood throughout history (cf. Revelation 2-3). The majority of

---

[6] An argument could be put forward that 2:1-3:22 belong in the past, because they are addressed to actual, historical churches. I have placed them in the present because I want emphasize the fact that these churches represent all local churches at different periods in their life of ministry.

EXCURSUS: Seeking the Seed

Revelation is looking at the church and its struggle through the ages from different angles and via different symbols. The prophecy starts with the sure promise of Christ returning and dealing a death blow to evil (cf. 16:12ff.).

## B. Revelation 7:4-8 is a picture of spiritual Israel (the church)

Therefore, when we come to Revelation 7, it is an apocalyptic vision (better: auditory journey [cf. III.B.1.c]) of the present that must be interpreted in light of other Scripture.

## 1. Exposition of Revelation 7:4-8

John writes as follows in Revelation 7:4-8,

> And I heard the number of those who were sealed, one hundred and forty-four thousand sealed from every tribe of the sons of Israel:
> from the tribe of Judah, twelve thousand *were* sealed, from the tribe of Reuben twelve thousand, from the tribe of Gad twelve thousand,
> from the tribe of Asher twelve thousand, from the tribe of Naphtali twelve thousand, from the tribe of Manasseh twelve thousand,
> from the tribe of Simeon twelve thousand, from the tribe of Levi twelve thousand, from the tribe of Issachar twelve thousand,
> from the tribe of Zebulun twelve thousand, from the tribe of Joseph twelve thousand, from the tribe of Benjamin, twelve thousand *were* sealed.

In short, the tribes mentioned in these verses are as follows: Judah, Reuben, Gad, Asher, Naphtali, Manasseh, Simeon, Levi, Issachar, Zebulun, Joseph, Benjamin. This is important because the first thing that stands out in this list is how different it is from the Old Testament lists.

## a. Differences between Revelation 7:4-8 and other tribal references in Scripture

The first thing to notice is that Judah is Israel's fourth-born son (cf. Genesis 29:31-35).[7] Reuben is Israel's firstborn son (cf. Genesis 29:32), and in every list but three, Reuben is mentioned first. But in Revelation 7:4-8, Reuben is second, after Judah. Why? The three occurrences in which Judah comes first are Numbers 2 (arrangement of camp), Numbers 7 (dedication offerings), and 1 Chronicles 2-8 (genealogy of Israel). The Numbers 7 order is directly based on Numbers 2, and 1 Chronicles 2-8 goes from the kingly genealogy into Judah—the kingly tribe—before turning to Simeon. In none of the three examples of Judah coming before Reuben does Reuben come second. (We will return to the topic of Judah heading this list under the next heading.)

Reuben and Gad are the second and third tribes mentioned. These two tribes are often mentioned together, but usually, Manasseh is mentioned with them (half-tribe of Manasseh that is) as the tribes who settled east of the Jordan River (cf. Joshua 1:12-15). And Gad never occurs third in the lists, except in the censuses of Numbers 1 and 26.

However, Gad and Asher occurring together makes sense, because these two were brothers of the same mother—Zilpah, Leah's maid (Genesis 35:26). However, these two were the seventh and eighth sons of Israel and, as such, are never mentioned together in the top half of a list except in Revelation 7:4-8.

Naphtali is the fifth in John's list. Naphtali was Israel's sixth son, but the pattern of the Old Testament is to put him in the back of the list, not the top half. Another interesting feature of this list is seen when we compare Genesis 35:25, The sons of Bilhah, Rachel's maid: Dan and Naphtali. In Revelation 7:4-8, Dan is absent. He is also missing from the genealogy (his descendants, that is) in 1 Chronicles 2-8. (If John were trying to say all of national Israel will be restored, Dan would certainly appear on this list.)

Manasseh is sixth on the list. The peculiarity of this name will be clearly seen when we get to the eleventh name on the list, but again, it is important to note who is missing. Ephraim is absent. Ephraim is Manasseh's younger brother. However, this becomes very interesting when we read Genesis 48:13-14, 17-19:

---

[7] For easier reference, on page 323, I have compiled tables showing the tribal lists I reference in this section.

## EXCURSUS: Seeking the Seed

> Joseph took them both, Ephraim with his right hand toward Israel's left, and Manasseh with his left hand toward Israel's right, and brought them close to him. But Israel stretched out his right hand and laid it on the head of Ephraim, who was the younger, and his left hand on Manasseh's head, crossing his hands, although Manasseh was the firstborn.
>
> ...
>
> When Joseph saw that his father laid his right hand on Ephraim's head, it displeased him; and he grasped his father's hand to remove it from Ephraim's head to Manasseh's head. Joseph said to his father, "Not so, my father, for this one is the firstborn. Place your right hand on his head."
>
> But his father refused and said, "I know, my son, I know; he also will become a people and he also will be great. However, his younger brother shall be greater than he, and his descendants shall become a multitude of nations."

By John removing Ephraim from the list, it shows (at least in a way) that in God's economy being great doesn't matter. (Also, just like with Dan and Naphtali, the absence of Ephraim shows that John is not trying to say that all of national Israel will be restored.)

Simeon comes seventh. This is strange. In all but three Old Testament examples, Simeon is second. (Numbers 2 and 7 are counted as one occurrence because the order in 7 is due to the arrangement of the tribes in 2.) Simeon is fifth or seventh (Canaan-dwellers alone or including eastern settlements) in Joshua 13-19. The strangest occurrence (lack of occurrence) is in Deuteronomy 33 when Moses skips Simeon while blessing the tribes. Simeon's absence could be because the historian writes, *The second lot fell to Simeon . . . and their inheritance was in the midst of the inheritance of the sons of Judah* (Joshua 19:1). When the kingdom split in Rehoboam's day (cf. 1 Kings 12:16-17), Simeon was absorbed into the kingdom of Judah. For this reason, Simeon ceased being an independent tribe. By John including Simeon, he is at the very least showing us that God knows His people by name as He calls them from the surrounding peoples (cf. Revelation 2:17, 3:12, 18:4; 2 Corinthians 6:17).

Levi comes eighth. The inclusion of this name should raise eyebrows for anyone who thinks national Israel will be restored. Levi is always mentioned when the context is speaking of Israel's sons, and in these cases, he is always listed third, except in the genealogy of 1 Chronicles 2-8, where Judah, Reuben, and Levi are all swapped. (There, Judah is placed first instead of fourth, Reuben is placed third instead of first, and Levi is placed fourth [leaving out eastern tribes] instead of third. ["Instead of" refers to birth order.]) When it comes to "the tribes of Israel" proper, Levi is never included. There is no tribal leader for Levi in Numbers 1:5-15; Levi is not included in either census in Numbers 1 or 26 (though to be fair they do get their own census in Numbers 3 and 26:57-62); Levi does not bring gifts to the sanctuary in Numbers 7; Levi does not receive land in Canaan in Joshua 13-19. And the text itself is clear on this too:

- **Numbers 1:47**
  The Levites, however, were not numbered among them by their fathers' tribe.
- **Numbers 26:62**
  They were not numbered among the sons of Israel since no inheritance was given to them among the sons of Israel.
- **Deuteronomy 10:9**
  Therefore, Levi does not have a portion or inheritance with his brothers; the LORD is his inheritance, just as the LORD your God spoke to him.)
- **Deuteronomy 18:1**
  "The Levitical priests, the whole tribe of Levi, shall have no portion or inheritance with Israel; they shall eat the LORD'S offerings by fire and His portion."
- **Joshua 18:7**
  "For the Levites have no portion among you, because the priesthood of the LORD is their inheritance."

If Levi has no portion among Israel, then why does John include this tribe in his list in Revelation 7? Perhaps because—like the other eleven mentioned—it is not to be taken literally.

The last four tribes mentioned are the four youngest sons of Israel—in birth order: Issachar, Zebulun, Joseph, Benjamin. The only occurrences of these names in this order are in birth lists, though Issachar does receive the fourth from last lot for land in Joshua 13-19. Otherwise, apart from birth order, these four names never occur in this order.

EXCURSUS: Seeking the Seed

An important note to make on Zebulun goes along with that made on Naphtali. Zebulun was absent in 1 Chronicles 2-8, but in Revelation 7, he is back. Why? It's not to say national Israel will be restored, or else Dan would also be in Revelation 7, but at the very least it could show 1) they are not all Israel who are descended from Israel (Romans 9:6), and 2) those who were chosen obtained [God's grace] (Romans 11:5, 7). Again, if all of national Israel is going to be restored, shouldn't Dan be in Revelation 7? All of those whom God has elected will be saved.

Joseph is a son of Israel, but nowhere is he considered a tribe. Joseph's two sons, Manasseh and Ephraim, fill in spots eleven and twelve for Joseph and Levi. (This is explained in Genesis 48:21-22.) Occasionally, Joseph will stand in for his sons (cf. Deuteronomy 33:1-29), but if Joseph is mentioned, then Ephraim and Manasseh are not. Revelation 7 is an anomaly because both Joseph and Manasseh are mentioned in the same list.

## b. Reason for the tribes selected (and order thereof)

In essence, what John is doing in Revelation 7:4-8 is illustrating Paul's statement from Romans 11:26—all Israel will be saved—by describing, in essence, a census of Israel's tribes. Now, at this point, I've only really explained how the Revelation list differs from the Old Testament lists. Let's now look more closely at what might be going on with the names that were picked. I'll give you a hint. It has to do with names. Reasoning: Why else would Moses have been inspired to record the meanings of all of Jacob's sons' names? (cf. Genesis 29:32-30:24; 35:18; 41:51-52).

Again, Judah is the first tribe John mentions, so we must ask, "Why?" Part of the reason could be that Judah is the head of the army (based on camp order) in Numbers 2, and it shows up even more clearly in Judges 1:1-2.

> The sons of Israel inquired of the LORD, saying, "Who shall go up first for us against the Canaanites, to fight against them?"
> The LORD said, "Judah shall go up; behold, I have given the land into his hand."

Jesus Christ is the Messiah, or as John describes Him in Revelation 5:5, the Lion that is from the tribe of Judah. As the Messiah—"the anointed one"—He is King. In 1 Samuel 8:20, the people of Israel demand a king partly so that we also may be like all the nations, that our king may judge us and go out before us and fight our battles. And King David's great sin is set up in the following way: It happened in the spring, at the time when kings go out *to battle*, that David sent Joab and his servants with him and all Israel, and they destroyed the sons of Ammon and besieged Rabbah. But David stayed at Jerusalem (2 Samuel 11:1). All that to say that kings are expected to lead armies. Judah, as the royal tribe, is listed first because Christ leads His army.

Not only that, but the name Judah sounds very similar to the Hebrew word meaning, "Praise." When born, Judah's mother exclaimed, "This time I will praise the LORD" (cf. Genesis 29:35). Who else deserves praise, but Christ? No one!

But, at the same time, Paul had explained in Romans 9:3-5, My kinsmen according to the flesh, who are Israelites . . . whose are the fathers, and from whom is the Christ according to the flesh. As mentioned above, Jesus is descended from the tribe of Judah according to the flesh (cf. Matthew 1:1-17; Luke 3:23-34[38]). Paul also wrote, there has also come to be at the present time a remnant according to *God's* gracious choice [from national Israel] (Romans 11:5). For this reason, when it comes to national Israel, they are primarily included in the statement, from the tribe of Judah, twelve thousand were sealed (Revelation 7:5). (This does not mean that Old Testament saints failed to come from other tribes; a study of the names mentioned in Hebrews 11 would prove this beyond a doubt.) The reason we refer to Israelites as Jews is because the northern ten tribes split from Judah, and Simeon was absorbed by Judah. "Jew" comes from Judah. So another possibility for Judah being named first relates to Paul's words (and ministry example) in Romans 1:16,

> For I am not ashamed of the Gospel, for it is the power of God for salvation to everyone who believes, to the Jew first and also to the Greek.

Reuben is named second. His name means, "Behold, a son," but the statement his mother uses to explain his name is, "Because the LORD has seen my affliction; surely now my husband will love me" (cf. Genesis 29:32). If we look at the Hebrew original, Reuben sounds very similar to has seen my affliction. It is wordplay.

But why would this name show up in the census of Revelation 7?

## EXCURSUS: Seeking the Seed

John explains part of his reasoning for writing the book of Revelation in 1:9 when he writes, I, John, your brother and fellow partaker in the tribulation and kingdom and perseverance *which are* in Jesus. John, in the first-century, was already in the tribulation. For this reason, it is right to say that the whole history of the church can be summed up with the word tribulation. For this reason, Reuben's inclusion in the list of all Israel is meant to encourage God's people to persevere, because God has seen [our] affliction. God cares for His people, and Reuben's inclusion proves this.

Gad is mentioned third. Leah, his "adoptive" mother, said, "How fortunate!" at his birth (cf. Genesis 30:11). The word means fortunate. Who is more fortunate than God's people? No one! It is a reminder of our blessed station as God's people.

Asher is mentioned fourth. Leah, again his "adoptive" mother, said, "Happy am I! For women will call me happy," at his birth (cf. Genesis 30:13). The word means happy, and it is no wonder that this would describe God's people. Those most fortunate (Genesis 30:11) have the most reason to be happy. It is a reminder of the joyful attitude of God's people, even amid affliction and persecution.

Naphtali is mentioned fifth. Rachel, his "adoptive" mother, said, "With mighty wrestlings I have wrestled with my sister, and I have indeed prevailed," at his birth (cf. Genesis 30:8). The word means, "My wrestling." Interestingly, Jacob wrestles with God in Genesis 32:24-31, and due to this, we sometimes refer to serious praying as wrestling. Paul writes in Romans 15:30, Strive together with me in your prayers to God. John writes as follows in Revelation 5:8,

> When He had taken the book, the four living creatures and the twenty-four elders fell down before the Lamb, each one holding a harp and golden bowls full of incense, which are the prayers of the saints.

The inclusion of Naphtali is a reminder that God hears our prayers, values them like incense, and as His people, we must pray fervently—especially in line with the Bible's closing verse: Amen. Come, Lord Jesus (Revelation 22:20).

Manasseh is mentioned sixth. Joseph named his son thus, because he said, "God has made me forget all my trouble and all my father's household" (cf. Genesis 41:51). The word means, "To cause to forget." As God's people, despite persistent persecution and tribulation, the fact of being one of God's people should cause us to forget our past lives of sin. As Peter writes in 1 Peter

4:3, For the time already past is sufficient *for you* to have carried out the desire of the Gentiles. As God's people, we should forget our past and only think of it to thank God for His grace.

Simeon is mentioned seventh. His mother named him, saying, "Because the LORD has heard that I am unloved, He has therefore given me this *son* also" (cf. Genesis 29:33). Simeon sounds like the Hebrew word has heard. God hears His people's prayer. When we wrestle with God in prayer, He hears us, and as a result, we will forget our troubles—if not now, then in eternity. If he promises to hear, we must pray!

Levi is mentioned eighth. (It goes without saying that Levi was the priestly tribe, and Jesus has become a high priest forever [Hebrews 6:20]. The author of Hebrews goes on, It is evident that our Lord was descended from Judah, a tribe with reference to which Moses spoke nothing concerning priests [7:14]. But Jesus is a high priest forever according to the order of Melchizedek, and another priest arises according to the likeness of Melchizedek [6:20, 7:15].)

In addition to Jesus being our high priest, Peter explains that all of God's people are A CHOSEN RACE, A royal PRIESTHOOD, A HOLY NATION, A PEOPLE FOR *God's* OWN POSSESSION (1 Peter 2:9).

When Levi was born, his mother said, "Now this time my husband will become attached to me, because I have borne him three sons" (Genesis 29:34). Levi sounds like the Hebrew for "attached to." Here's a beautiful promise for all of God's people: Because Christ is our high priest, and because we form a PRIESTHOOD, the blood of Christ attaches us to God in a way unknown in the time of the Levitical priesthood (cf. Hebrews 10:1-10).

Issachar comes ninth. His mother named him, saying, "God has given me my wages because I gave my maid to my husband" (cf. Genesis 30:18). Issachar sounds like the Hebrew for "reward." A grand reward is promised to God's people. Paul described it in 2 Timothy 4:8,

> There is laid up for me the crown of righteousness, which the Lord, the righteous Judge, will award to me on that day; and not only to me, but also to all who have loved His appearing.

Further, John describes this reward in seven different ways—to churches—in Revelation 2:7, 10-11, 17, 26-28; 3:5, 12, 21. There is a reward awaiting God's people who persevere in the faith, those sealed.

Zebulun comes tenth. His mother named him, saying, "God has endowed me with a good gift; now my husband will dwell with me, because

# EXCURSUS: Seeking the Seed

I have borne him six sons" (cf. Genesis 30:20). Zebulun sounds like the Hebrew for "honored." If we look ahead to Revelation 21:9-11, we read the following:

> Then one of the seven angels . . . came and spoke with me, saying, "Come here, I will show you the bride, the wife of the Lamb." And he carried me away in the Spirit to a great and high mountain, and showed me the holy city, Jerusalem, coming down out of heaven from God, having the glory of God.

For proof that the bride is the church, let's hear Paul in Ephesians 5:31-32,

> FOR THIS REASON A MAN SHALL LEAVE HIS FATHER AND MOTHER AND SHALL BE JOINED TO HIS WIFE, AND THE TWO SHALL BECOME ONE FLESH. This mystery is great; but I am speaking with reference to Christ and the church.

(We will look at the connection between the bride and Jerusalem under heading III.B.2.b.) The Scripture is clear that God's people will be honored by God. This is a promise and an encouragement for believers tired of striving in this walk.

    Joseph comes eleventh. His mother named him, saying, "May the LORD give me another son" (cf. Genesis 30:24). Joseph means, "He adds." If you are a believer in Jesus, then you are a proof of this promise. God adds to His people. The Kingdom is growing. (We will understand the truth of this statement as soon as we look at Benjamin.)

    Benjamin is the last tribe mentioned. (All twelve of these tribes are sealed. This sealing is proof of the security of a believer's salvation, another glorious promise.) Benjamin's mother named him Ben-oni ["son of my sorrow"]; but his father called him Benjamin ["son of the right hand"] (cf. Genesis 35:18). Two notes must be made on the meaning of Benjamin's name.

    First, it is a pointer to Christ. The author of Hebrews explains that Jesus, having offered one sacrifice for sins for all time, SAT DOWN AT THE RIGHT HAND OF GOD (Hebrews 10:12). And, since Mark is clear that Jesus Christ [is] the Son of God (1:1), it follows that Jesus is the Son of the right hand of God. (Thus, we see a pointer to Christ both at the front [Judah] and back [Benjamin] of the list in Revelation 7.)

    Second, Jesus is clear in Matthew 25 that His people—"you who are blessed of My Father"—are on His right (25:34). Just as Jesus is the Son of the right hand of God, so also God's people—those in Christ (cf. Colossians 1:1, amongst many others)—are sons (and daughters) of the right hand of God. Paul is clear in Romans 8:14-16,

> For all who are being led by the Spirit of God, these are sons of God. For you have not received a spirit of slavery leading to fear again, but you have received a spirit of adoption as sons by which we cry out, "Abba! Father!" The Spirit Himself testifies with our spirit that we are children of God.

### c. John sees in Revelation 7:9-17 what he heard in 7:4-8

However, if we restrict Revelation 7 to verses 4-8, then we aren't being thorough enough. John continues in verses 9-10, 13-14; for context, I will quote beginning with 7:4 and then jump forward to verse 9 and following:

> And I heard the number of those who were sealed, one hundred and forty-four thousand sealed from every tribe of the sons of Israel:
>
> ...
>
> After these things I looked, and behold, a great multitude which no one could count, from every nation and *all* tribes and peoples and tongues, standing before the throne and before the Lamb, clothed in white robes, and palm branches *were* in their hands; and they cry out with a loud voice, saying, "Salvation to our God who sits on the throne, and to the Lamb."
>
> ...
>
> Then one of the elders answered, saying to me, "These who are clothed in the white robes, who are they, and where have they come from?"
>
> I said to him, "My lord, you know."
>
> And he said to me, "These are the ones who come out of the great tribulation, and they have washed their robes and made them white in the blood of the Lamb."
>
> (Revelation 7:4, 9-10, 13-14)

# EXCURSUS: Seeking the Seed

In verse 4, John <u>heard the number</u>, but in verse 9 he <u>looked, and behold, a great multitude which no one could count</u>. Why the difference? <u>The number</u> in verse 4 is proof that <u>The Lord knows those who are His</u> (2 Timothy 2:19, cf. Nahum 1:7) and "<u>I know My own</u>" (John 10:14). God intimately knows each of His people, and thus He can state a number (even though the specific number stated is symbolic). But when John <u>looked</u>, he saw an innumerable number of saints. If we look forward to Revelation 9:16, we see a demonic army of <u>two hundred million</u>, and despite John's admission, <u>I heard the number of them</u>, the staggering fact remains that the number of God's people throughout history is far greater than <u>two hundred million</u>.

## 2. Further proofs of the identity of the 144,000

There is no question that the <u>great multitude which no one could count</u> in verses 9-17 are Christians—spiritual Israel. But is there any way to prove from another text that the <u>one hundred and forty-four thousand</u> are also Christians—spiritual Israel?

Yes. Two ways. The first is in Revelation 14, and the second is in Revelation 21.

## a. The 144,000 are marked out as believers in Jesus (Revelation 14:1)

First, Revelation 14:1 says,

<u>Then I looked, and behold, the Lamb *was* standing on Mount Zion, and with Him one hundred and forty-four thousand, having His name and the name of His Father written on their foreheads.</u>

This is the same group mentioned in Revelation 7. Notice what John says about their foreheads: <u>Having His name and the name of His Father written on their foreheads</u>. Jesus promised the church—a Christian, not Jewish, gathering—at Philadelphia the following in Revelation 3:12,

<u>He who overcomes, I will make him a pillar in the temple of My God, and he will not go out from it anymore; and I will write on him the name of My God, and the name of the city of My God, the new</u>

Jerusalem, which comes down out of heaven from My God, and My new name.

If the one hundred and forty-four thousand has Jesus' name on their foreheads, then they must be Christians—spiritual Israel. It is further interesting that John describes the new Jerusalem, which comes down out of heaven in Revelation 3.

## b. The 144,000 are the bride of Christ (Revelation 21:9-11, 15-17)

Second, Revelation 21:9-11, 15-17 says,

> Then one of the seven angels . . . came and spoke with me, saying, "Come here, I will show you the bride, the wife of the Lamb."
> And he carried me away in the Spirit to a great and high mountain, and showed me the holy city, Jerusalem, coming down out of heaven from God, having the glory of God . . . The one who spoke with me had a gold measuring rod to measure the city, and its gates and its wall. The city is laid out as a square, and its length is as great as the width; and he measured the city with the rod, fifteen hundred miles; its length and width and height are equal. And he measured its wall, seventy-two yards.

The angel tells John he is going to show him the bride—the church (cf. Ephesians 5:32)—but then he shows him a city. Why?

The city is the bride. John also personifies a city as a group of unfaithful people (cf. the prostitute of Revelation 17). The bride—church, new Jerusalem—is the antithesis of the harlot in Revelation 17. But there's more!

In Revelation 21:16, John tells us that the city is fifteen hundred miles square. This is where English unit translations/conversions don't help. The inspired measurement in Greek is twelve thousand stadia. And then the height in 21:17 is not seventy-two yards, but one hundred and forty-four cubits tall. This is not to be taken literally. This is John connecting the church—explicitly—to those who were sealed, one hundred and forty-four thousand sealed from every tribe of the sons of Israel (Revelation 7:4).

# (Doxology)

To sum up, as Paul prophesied, all Israel will be saved (Romans 11:26), but this does not refer to national Israel either in Romans or in the book of Revelation.

> For he is not a Jew who is one outwardly, nor is circumcision that which is outward in the flesh. But he is a Jew who is one inwardly; and circumcision is that which is of the heart, by the Spirit, not by the letter; and his praise is not from men, but from God. [8]
>
> Are you so foolish? Having begun by the Spirit, are you now being perfected by the flesh? [9]
>
> So then, does He who provides you with the Spirit and works miracles among you, do it by the works of the Law, or by hearing with faith? Even so Abraham BELIEVED GOD, AND IT WAS RECKONED TO HIM AS RIGHTEOUSNESS. Therefore, be sure that it is those who are of faith who are sons of Abraham. The Scripture, foreseeing that God would justify the Gentiles by faith, preached the Gospel beforehand to Abraham, saying, "ALL THE NATIONS WILL BE BLESSED IN YOU." So then those who are of faith are blessed with Abraham, the believer. [10]
>
> Christ redeemed us from the curse of the Law, having become a curse for us—for it is written, "CURSED IS EVERYONE WHO HANGS ON A TREE"— in order that in Christ Jesus the blessing of Abraham might come to the Gentiles, so that we would receive the promise of the Spirit through faith. Brethren, I speak in terms of human relations: even though it is *only* a man's covenant, yet when it has been ratified, no one sets it aside or adds conditions to it. Now the promises were spoken to Abraham and to his seed. He does not say, "And to seeds," as *referring* to many, but *rather* to one, "And to your seed," that is, Christ. What I am saying is this: the Law, which came four hundred and thirty years later, does not invalidate a covenant previously ratified by God, so as to nullify the promise. For if the

---

[8] Romans 2:28-29.
[9] Galatians 3:3.
[10] Galatians 3:5-9.

inheritance is based on law, it is no longer based on a promise; but God has granted it to Abraham by means of a promise. [11]

For as many as are the promises of God, in [Jesus Christ] they are yes. [12]

Do you believe in the promise of God—Christ? Are you a child of Abraham? Are you a spiritual Jew due to the work of the Spirit in your heart?

If you've made it this far and the answer is still "no," then I beg you to place your faith in Him now! You have no hope apart from Him. John 3:18 says, He who believes in Him is not judged; he who does not believe has been judged already, because he has not believed in the name of the only begotten Son of God. And John further says in Revelation 20:12, 15,

> And I saw the dead, the great and the small, standing before the throne, and books were opened; and another book was opened, which is *the book* of life; and the dead were judged from the things which were written in the books, according to their deeds . . . And if anyone's name was not found written in the book of life, he was thrown into the lake of fire.

Believe today! Live! And escape judgment! I beg you!

## IV. Practical Applications

With all that said, though, what's the point? Why is it necessary to hold this view as opposed to one that sees Israel being nationally saved? I have five reasons.

### A. Pastors don't need to fear the Old Testament

First, pastors don't need to fear the Old Testament. As Paul said in 2 Timothy 3:16, All Scripture is inspired by God and profitable for teaching, for reproof, for correction, for training in righteousness. The all Scripture Paul refers to here is primarily the Old Testament. He knew nothing of a New

---

[11] Galatians 3:13-18.
[12] 2 Corinthians 1:20.

Testament—other than the one mentioned to in 1 Corinthians 11:25, "This cup is the new [testament] in My blood; do this, as often as you drink *it*, in remembrance of Me," quoting Jesus.

When we read the Old Testament, we are reading the story first described in Genesis 3:15, "And I will put enmity Between you and the woman, And between your seed and her seed; He shall bruise you on the head, And you shall bruise him on the heel." The Old Testament is a tale of two seeds.

If a handful of Galilean fishermen and other "nobodies" could preach Christ from the Old Testament, then seminary-educated pastors today have no excuse not to preach Christ from the Old Testament. And even if you are not seminary-educated, knowledge is so accessible today that any excuse is still absent. What is keeping you from preaching, studying, or reading the Old Testament?

It is profitable for teaching, for reproof, for correction, for training in righteousness.

## B. People can better love Christ

Second, people can better love Christ because there are sixty-six books about Him—thirty-nine more than the twenty-seven of the New Testament. I have often heard it said that the Bible is a love letter from God. If your significant other wrote you a letter, you'd read every word repeatedly; you'd do whatever it takes to make sure you understand your significant other's intended meaning. But for some terrible reason, we too often decide that we don't care about everything God has to say about His Son to us. We take a handful of memory verses or stories (often misinterpreted) from the Old Testament, and we praise God that we don't have to obey its rules anymore (which isn't even 100% true). We must love Jesus enough to see what the Old Testament has to say about Him.

Do you love Him? Do you want to love Him better? When was the last time you dove into your Old Testament?

Allow me to try to make Jesus a little more accessible in the Old Testament. Genesis 12:7 says,

> The LORD appeared to Abram and said, "To your descendants (seed) I will give this land." So he built an altar there to the LORD who had appeared to him.

This is one of the verses Paul was referring to in Galatians 3:16. God promised the land to Christ. Paul wrote in Romans 9:6-7, "For they are not all Israel who are *descended* from Israel; nor are they all children because they are Abraham's descendants." True Israel is Jesus; He said, "I am the true vine" (John 15:1). For this reason, the Old Testament is the story of "fake" (better: shadowy?) Israel. When we read Israel's story, we must ask the following questions:

1. How does this text eventually bring about Jesus? (genealogies, especially)
2. How does this text emphasize the perfection of Jesus (sin stories, especially)
3. How does this text mirror Jesus' life (least common, usually)

Are you eager to love Jesus more? What are you waiting for? Dive into the Old Testament!

## C. Evangelism must be a regular part of our lives

Third, evangelism must be a regular part of our lives. When every text (at least every logical section) is about Christ over and above everything else, then it is only natural for Gospel proclamation to flow from our lips. And this isn't just for pastors. Paul doesn't even mention pastors in Romans 10:13-15,

> "WHOEVER WILL CALL ON THE NAME OF THE LORD WILL BE SAVED." How then will they call on Him in whom they have not believed? How will they believe in Him whom they have not heard? And how will they hear without a preacher? How will they preach unless they are sent? Just as it is written, "HOW BEAUTIFUL ARE THE FEET OF THOSE WHO BRING GOOD NEWS OF GOOD THINGS!"

The only office Paul mentions is preacher. But don't let *How will they preach unless they are sent?* stop you. Jesus commanded the disciples (cf. Matthew 28:16) in Matthew 28:19-20,

> "Go therefore and make disciples of all the nations, baptizing them in the name of the Father and the Son and the Holy Spirit, teaching them

to observe all that I commanded you; and lo, I am with you always, even to the end of the age."

If the disciples (28:16) are commanded to make disciples and teach them to observe all that [Jesus] commanded [the eleven disciples], then it follows that all believers—as disciples of disciples going all the way back to the apostles of Christ—are commanded to go therefore and make disciples of all the nations.

This starts in your own nation/city. If you can't evangelize in your own hometown, why would you evangelize elsewhere? Jesus said the following in Acts 1:8, "You shall be My witnesses both in Jerusalem, and in all Judea and Samaria, and even to the remotest part of the earth." Evangelism must start locally.

Are you evangelizing? What keeps you from it? Love Jesus more by getting to know Him better, and then open your mouth and tell about the One your heart loves.

## D. The mantra, "We stand with Israel," is less than Biblical

Fourth, the mantra, "We stand with Israel," does not arise from the Bible (unless you're speaking of spiritual Israel). Now don't hear what I'm not saying. I'm not saying that we need to stand against Israel. Never! I'm saying that as believers, our hope is Christ, not the nation of Israel. As believers, we know that Israel's only hope is Christ. As believers, we know that IN HIS NAME THE GENTILES WILL HOPE (Matthew 12:21).

For this reason, befriending Israel in the name of Christianity isn't enough. We must also befriend Muslim nations, Hindu nations, Buddhist nations, Catholic nations, pagan nations, and atheist nations. We must stand with all these people in the name of evangelism because they are no better or worse than the nation of Israel. If they don't believe in Jesus, then they will perish. Just because someone is an Israelite means nothing: For they are not all Israel who are descended from Israel (Romans 9:6), and For there is no partiality with God. For all who have sinned without the Law will also perish without the Law, and all who have sinned under the Law will be judged by the Law (Romans 2:11-12).

Do you claim to stand with Israel? Why? Is it because they are commonly known as God's people? Are you a Christian?

If so, you are more rightly called one of God's people than any nonbelieving Israelite. Look to Jesus—true Israel—and not a faraway, hardened nation. And if you insist on being a friend of Israel—which is fine—I challenge you to be a friend of other nations too. They all need Jesus. You have Jesus if you are a Christian!

## E. Christ can return at any moment

Fifth and finally, Christ can return at any moment because nothing else needs to take place in the Middle East before He returns. If events in the Middle East had to happen before Jesus could return, then this verse would be false: <u>For this reason you also must be ready; for the Son of Man is coming at an hour when you do not think He will</u> (Matthew 24:44). He will return before any telltale signs occur in the Middle East, and many people will be desperately surprised.

Are you ready for His return?

Don't look at the news reports. Look at your Bible. Look at your friends. Look at your family. Are you and they ready for Christ to return if He came back right now? I hope so!

In conclusion, I hope you can see how these applications all tie together. It starts by recognizing the Old Testament as valuable. The more valuable we find the Old Testament, the more we will be able to love Christ. The more we can love Christ, the more eager we will be to evangelize. The more enthusiastic we are to evangelize, the more we will see all nations as needing the Gospel of Christ—including Israel. And the more we see all nations in desperate need of Christ, the imminent return of Christ spurs us into action.

Into which part of this process do you need to dive?

*Galatians 6:15-16 (NASB)*
*For neither is circumcision anything, nor*
*uncircumcision, but a new creation. And those who*
*will walk by this rule, peace and mercy be upon*
*them, and upon the Israel of God.*

EXCURSUS: Seeking the Seed

**Figure 1**
This table goes with the discussion in III.B.1

| | Revelation 7:4-8 *text in question* | Genesis 29-30, 35 *birth story* | Genesis 35:23-26 *birth order (wives)* | |
|---|---|---|---|---|
| | Judah | Reuben | Reuben | |
| | Reuben | Simeon | Simeon | |
| | Gad | Levi | Levi | Leah |
| | Asher | Judah | Judah | |
| | Naphtali | Dan | Issachar | |
| | Manasseh | Naphtali | Zebulun | |
| | Simeon | Gad | Joseph | Rachel |
| | Levi | Asher | Benjamin | |
| | Issachar | Issachar | Dan | Bilhah |
| | Zebulun | Zebulun | Naphtali | |
| | Joseph | Joseph | Gad | Zilpah |
| | Benjamin | Benjamin | Asher | |

| Genesis 46:9-27 *Trip to Egypt* | Genesis 49:3-27 *Jacob's blessing* | Numbers 1:5-15 *Tribal leaders* | Numbers 1:20-43 *First census* |
|---|---|---|---|
| Reuben | Reuben | Reuben | Reuben |
| Simeon | Simeon | Simeon | Simeon |
| Levi | Levi | Judah | Gad |
| Judah | Judah | Issachar | Judah |
| Issachar | Zebulun | Zebulun | Issachar |
| Zebulun | Issachar | Ephraim | Zebulun |
| Gad | Dan | Manasseh | Ephraim |
| Asher | Gad | Benjamin | Manasseh |
| (Joseph) | Asher | Dan | Benjamin |
| Benjamin | Naphtali | Asher | Dan |
| Dan | Joseph | Gad | Asher |
| Naphtali | Benjamin | Naphtali | Naphtali |

| Numbers 2:3-31 | Numbers 7:12-83 | Numbers 26:4-51 | Deut. 33:1-29 |
|---|---|---|---|
| *Camp arrangement* | *Dedication offering* | *Second census* | *Moses' blessing* |
| Judah (east) | Judah | Reuben | Reuben |
| Issachar | Issachar | Simeon | Judah |
| Zebulun | Zebulun | Gad | Levi |
| Reuben (south) | Reuben | Judah | Benjamin |
| Simeon | Simeon | Issachar | Joseph |
| Gad | Gad | Zebulun | Zebulun |
| Ephraim (west) | Ephraim | Manasseh | Issachar |
| Manasseh | Manasseh | Ephraim | Gad |
| Benjamin | Benjamin | Benjamin | Dan |
| Dan (north) | Dan | Dan | Naphtali |
| Asher | Asher | Asher | Asher |
| Naphtali | Naphtali | Naphtali | |

| Joshua 13-19 | 1 Chronicles 2:1-2 | 1 Chronicles 2-8 | Notes |
|---|---|---|---|
| *Tribal allotments* | *List of Israel's sons* | *Israel genealogy* | |
| Reuben (eastern) | Reuben | Judah | |
| Gad | Simeon | Simeon | |
| ½ Manasseh | Levi | Reuben | |
| | Judah | Gad | |
| Judah | Issachar | ½ Manasseh | |
| Ephraim | Zebulun | Levi | |
| Manasseh | Dan | Issachar | |
| Benjamin | Joseph | Benjamin | |
| Simeon (Canaan-dwellers) | Benjamin | Naphtali | |
| Zebulun | Naphtali | Manasseh | |
| Issachar | Gad | Ephraim | |
| Asher | Asher | Asher | |
| Naphtali | | | |
| Dan | | | |

# References

Aland, Kurt, ed. *The Greek New Testament*. 4th ed. New York: United Bible Societies, 1983.

Andy Mineo, "Every Word (feat. Co Campbell)," *Formerly Known* (Atlanta: Reach Records, 2013), Spotify.

Baker, David W. *Nahum, Habakkuk, Zephaniah: An Introduction and Commentary*. Tyndale New Testament Commentaries. Nottingham, England: Inter-Varsity Press, 1988.

Bunyan, John. *The Pilgrim's Progress*. 1678. New Kensington, PA: Whitaker House, 1973.

Calvin, John. *Commentaries on the Epistles of Paul to the Galatians and Ephesians*. 1548. Grand Rapids: Christian Classics Ethereal Library, 2009. Kindle.

Capes, David B., Rodney Reeves, and E. Randolph Richards. *Rediscovering Paul: An Introduction to His World, Letters and Theology*. Downers Grove, IL: IVP Academic, 2011.

*Chuck*. Created by Josh Schwartz and Chris Fedak. Burbank, CA: Warner Home Video, 2008-2012. DVD.

Cole, R. Alan. *Galatians: An Introduction and Commentary*. Tyndale New Testament Commentaries. Nottingham, England: Inter-Varsity Press, 1989. WORD*search*.

Conway, Tim. "Is Theology Your Idol?" *I'll Be Honest*. August 20, 2009. https://www.illbehonest.com/is-theology-your-idol-tim-conway.

Eaton, Sam. "59 Percent of Millennials Raised in a Church Have Dropped Out—And They're Trying to Tell Us Why." *Faith It*. April 4, 2018. http://www.faithit.com/12-reasons-millennials-over-church-sam-eaton.

Fitzmyer, Joseph. A. *Romans*. Anchor Yale Bible. London: Yale University Press, 2008. Logos.

Flame, "Read 'Em and Weep." *Royal Flush*. St. Louis, MO: Clear Sight Music, 2013. Spotify.

Hart, John F. "Paul as Weak in Faith in Romans 7:7-25." *Bibliotheca Sacra* 170 (July-September 2013): 315-43.

*Hitch*. Directed by Andy Tennant. Culver City, CA: Sony Pictures Home Entertainment, 2005. DVD.

Hillsong Music. "Christ Is Enough." *Glorious Ruins*. Sydney, Australia: Hillsong Music, 2013. Spotify.

Hoole, Charles, trans. *The Didache: The Teaching of the Lord to the Gentiles through the Twelve Apostles*. London: David Nutt, 1894.

Howard, Jeremy Royal, ed. *HCSB Study Bible*. Nashville: Holman Bible Publishers, 2010.

Kittel, Gerhard, and Geoffrey William Bromiley, eds. *Theological Dictionary of the New Testament*. 10 vols. Grand Rapids, MI: Eerdmans, 1964-1976.

Kruse, Colin F. *John: An Introduction and Commentary*. Tyndale New Testament Commentaries. Downers Grove, IL: InterVarsity Press, 2003. WORD*search*.

Lecrae. "Lecrae - Church Clothes (Music Video)." *YouTube*. May 10, 2012. https://www.youtube.com/watch?v=tlWvx0wdySk.

Lightfoot, J. B. *The Epistle of St. Paul to the Galatians*. Peabody, MA: Hendrickson Publishers, 1982.

# References

liL fytr. "Ammunition." *Welcome to da Faith*. Victorville, CA: FYTR records, 2017. Spotify.

_____. "Teach Me Some Respect (feat. Pastor Stephen Feinstein)." *Teach Me Some Respect*. Victorville, CA: FYTR records, 2017. Spotify.

Luther, Martin. *A Commentary on St. Paul's Epistle to the Galatians*. 1538. Grand Rapids: Christian Classics Ethereal Library, 1999. WORD*search*.

MacArthur, John. *Galatians*. MacArthur New Testament Commentaries. Chicago: Moody, 1987.

Morris, Leon. *1 Corinthians: An Introduction and Commentary*. Tyndale New Testament Commentaries. Downers Grove, IL: InterVarsity Press, 1985. WORD*search*.

Owen, John. *Sin and Grace*. Works of John Owen, Volume 7. 1689. Carlisle, PA: Banner of Truth, 2014. Kindle.

Plato. "Plato, Lysis (English)." *Greek Texts & Translations*. http://perseus.uchicago.edu/perseus-cgi/citequery3.pl?dbname=GreekFeb2011&getid=1&query=Pl.%20Ly.%20208c.

Platt, David and Tony Merida. *Christ-Centered Exposition – Exalting Jesus in Galatians*. Nashville: Broadman & Holman, 2014. WORD*search*.

Richards, E Randolph. *Paul and First-Century Letter Writing: Secretaries, Composition, and Collection*. Downers Grove, IL: IVP Academic, 2004.

Shai Linne, "Christ Crucified," *The Solus Christus Project* (Philadelphia: Lampmode Recordings, 2005), Spotify.

Staff Writer. "Spanked Children more likely to have low self-esteem." *Guelph Mercury Tribune*. January 7, 2011. http://www.guelphmercury.com/living-story/2685238-spanked-children-more-likely-to-have-low-self-esteem.

*Star Wars: Episode V - The Empire Strikes Back*. Directed by Irvin Kreshner. Beverly Hills, CA: Twentieth Century Fox, 2013. DVD.

*Star Wars: Episode VI - Return of the Jedi*. Directed by Richard Marquand. Beverly Hills, CA: Twentieth Century Fox, 2013. DVD.

Strong, James. *Strong's Talking Greek & Hebrew Dictionary*. Austin, TX: WORDsearch Corp., 2007. WORDsearch.

Taylor, Justin. "How Much Do You Have to Hate Somebody to Not Proselytize?" *The Gospel Coalition*. November 18, 2009. https://www.thegospelcoalition.org/blogs/justin-taylor/how-much-do-you-have-to-hate-somebody-to-not-proselytize.

Thayer, J. H. *Greek-English Lexicon of the New Testament*. New York: Harper & Brothers, 1889. WORDsearch.

Tolkien, J. R. R. *The Two Towers*. 1954. New York: Del Rey, 2012.

Twain, Mark. *The Prince & the Pauper*. 1882. Mineola, NY: Dover Publications, 2000.

Washer, Paul. "General Session 9." *Shepherd's Conference 2016*. March 11, 2016. https://www.gracechurch.org/sermons/11837.

Wingerd, Joshua. "Condemnation, Justification, and Federal Headship." *live in Love; find your true reward*. October 6, 2019. https://www.lilfytr.com/2019/10/06/federal-headship.

_____. "'God-Breathed Scripture' Necessitates It Be Inerrant." *live in Love; find your true reward* September 24, 2018. https://lilfytr.com/2018/09/24/mark1_2-3-and-inerrancy.

_____. "Living to Love (3 of 3)." *live in Love; find your true reward*. May 20, 2016. http://www.lilfytr.blogspot.com/2016/05/living-to-love-lil-fytr-explanation-3.html.

## References

Wingerd, Joshua. "Love Wins: Paul and the Content of the Earliest Christian Gospel." *Academia*. November 8, 2015. https://www.academia.edu/25063760/Love_Wins.

———. *Stranded*. Awakening, book 1. Victorville, CA: Wingerd Writings, 2017.

# Scripture Reference Index

(*Italicized* page numbers refer to footnotes)

## Old Testament
### Genesis

| | |
|---|---|
| 1:1 | 15 |
| 2:24 | 254 |
| 3:14 | 92 |
| 3:14-15 | 92 |
| 3:15 | 92, 173, 177, 292, 302, 319 |
| 3:21 | 292 |
| 12 | 263 |
| 12-21 | 86 |
| 12:1 | 253 |
| 12:1-3 | 79, 252, 253 |
| 12:3 | 79, 262, 263 |
| 12:7 | 90, 252, 254, 319 |
| 13:15 | 90, 252, 253 |
| 15 | 86 |
| 15-16 | 128 |
| 15:1-6 | 128 |
| 15:2-3 | 78 |
| 15:4-5 | 253 |
| 15:5 | 78, 79 |
| 15:5-6 | 78 |
| 15:6 | 78, 253 |
| 15:12 | 90 |
| 15:18 | 90 |
| 16 | 129, 267 |
| 16:15 | 253 |
| 17 | 253 |
| 17:8 | 90, 252, 253 |
| 18 | 267 |
| 18:14 | 269 |
| 18:25 | 83 |
| 19 | 274 |
| 21 | 128, 267 |
| 21:1-3 | 129 |
| 21:9 | 130 |
| 21:10 | 130 |
| 21:12 | 255, 268 |
| 24:7 | 90, 252, 253 |
| 29:31-35 | 306 |
| 29:32 | 306, 310 |
| 29:32-30:24 | 309 |
| 29:33 | 312 |
| 29:34 | 312 |
| 29:35 | 310 |
| 30:8 | 311 |
| 30:11 | 311 |
| 30:13 | 311 |
| 30:18 | 312 |
| 30:20 | 313 |
| 30:24 | 313 |
| 32:24-31 | 311 |
| 35:18 | 309, 313 |
| 35:25 | 306 |
| 35:26 | 306 |
| 41:51 | 311 |
| 41:51-52 | 309 |
| 48:13-14 | 306 |
| 48:17-19 | 306 |
| 48:21-22 | 309 |

### Exodus

| | |
|---|---|
| 2:8 | 301 |
| 5:1 | 112 |
| 9:16 | 271 |
| 12:38 | 112 |
| 16:3 | *55* |

| | |
|---|---|
| 19:18-20:21 | 257 |
| 20:2-17 | 164 |
| 20:3-17 | 103 |
| 20:12 | 98 |
| 20:14 | 98 |
| 33:19 | 270 |

## Leviticus

| | |
|---|---|
| 10:10 | 186 |
| 18 | 98 |
| 18:3 | 81 |
| 18:5 | 81 |
| 19 | 98 |
| 19:18 | 163 |
| 23 | 118 |
| 25 | 118 |

## Numbers

| | |
|---|---|
| 1 | 306, 308 |
| 1:5-15 | 308 |
| 1:47 | 308 |
| 2 | 306, 307, 309 |
| 3 | 308 |
| 7 | 306, 307, 308 |
| 11:4-6 | 55 |
| 14-26 | 257 |
| 14:2-4 | 55 |
| 15:17-21 | 289 |
| 23:19 | 83, 92, 254 |
| 26 | 306, 308 |
| 26:57-62 | 308 |
| 26:62 | 308 |

## Deuteronomy

| | |
|---|---|
| 6:4 | 98 |
| 10:9 | 308 |
| 18:1 | 308 |
| 19:15 | 17 |
| 27-28 | 84 |
| 27:26 | 80 |
| 33 | 307 |
| 33:1-29 | 309 |

## Joshua

| | |
|---|---|
| 1:12-15 | 306 |
| 2 | 259 |
| 2:10 | 271 |
| 13-19 | 307, 308 |
| 18:7 | 308 |
| 19:1 | 307 |

## Judges

| | |
|---|---|
| 1:1-2 | 309 |

## 1 Samuel

| | |
|---|---|
| 8:20 | 310 |

## 2 Samuel

| | |
|---|---|
| 11:1 | 310 |

## 1 Kings

| | |
|---|---|
| 12:16-17 | 307 |

## 2 Kings

| | |
|---|---|
| 24:6-16 | 274 |
| 25:27-30 | 274 |

## 1 Chronicles

| | |
|---|---|
| 2-8 | 306, 308, 309 |

## Esther

| | |
|---|---|
| 3:13-15 | 68 |

## Job

| | |
|---|---|
| 41:11 | 298 |

## Psalms

| | |
|---|---|
| 1:1 | 15 |
| 2 | 272 |
| 22:7 | 119 |
| 23:5 | 286 |
| 32:1-2 | 201 |
| 32:11 | 201 |
| 51 | 202 |
| 51:5 | 203 |
| 51:12 | 201 |
| 69:22-23 | 286 |
| 139:7-8 | 185 |

## Proverbs

| | |
|---|---|
| 1:8-18 | 247 |
| 13:24 | 246 |
| 14:12 | 80 |
| 16:18 | 218 |
| 16:25 | 80 |
| 22:6 | 246 |
| 30:18-19 | 302 |

## Isaiah

| | |
|---|---|
| 5 | 256 |
| 5:1-2 | 256 |
| 5:3-6 | 256 |
| 5:7 | 256 |
| 7-8 | 299, 300, 302 |
| 7:3 | 301, 302 |
| 7:9 | 300 |
| 7:10-16 | 300 |
| 7:14 | 300, 301, 302 |
| 7:16 | 300 |
| 8:1 | 301 |
| 8:1-8 | 300 |
| 8:3 | 301 |
| 8:4 | 301 |
| 8:8 | 301 |
| 28:16 | 279 |
| 40:13 | 298 |
| 40:28 | 298 |
| 55:8-9 | 297 |
| 55:11 | 274 |

## Daniel

| | |
|---|---|
| 8 | 303 |
| 9:27 | 303 |

## Hosea

| | |
|---|---|
| 11:1 | 257 |

## Joel

| | |
|---|---|
| 2:32 | 279 |

## Nahum

| | |
|---|---|
| 1:7 | 315 |

## Habakkuk

| | |
|---|---|
| 2:4 | 27, 80 |

## Zechariah

| | |
|---|---|
| 9:9 | 260 |

## Malachi

| | |
|---|---|
| 1:2-3 | 269 |

# Deuterocanonical Books

## Ecclesiasticus

| | |
|---|---|
| 23:16-17 | 186 |

# New Testament

## Matthew

| | |
|---|---|
| 1:1 | 15, 257 |
| 1:1-17 | 310 |
| 1:2 | 253 |
| 1:5 | 259 |
| 1:21-23 | 302 |
| 2:15 | 257 |
| 3:9 | 257 |
| 3:13-4:11 | 257 |
| 5 | 257 |
| 5:3-12 | 261 |
| 5:5 | 103, 204 |
| 5:21-26 | 280 |
| 5:22 | 68 |
| 5:27-30 | 98 |
| 5:44 | 248 |
| 6:19-21 | 51 |
| 7:1-5 | 102 |
| 7:12 | 164 |
| 7:15-20 | 200 |
| 7:20 | 200 |
| 8:5-13 | 258 |
| 8:20 | 51 |
| 9 | 258 |
| 9:10-11 | 57 |
| 9:12 | 110 |
| 10:2-4 | 258 |
| 10:7 | 258 |

| | |
|---|---|
| 10:17 | 261 |
| 10:17-18 | 258 |
| 11:6 | 119 |
| 11:28 | *101* |
| 11:28-30 | 141, 165, 217, 262 |
| 12:3 | 128 |
| 12:5 | 128 |
| 12:21 | 321 |
| 12:28 | 261 |
| 13:14-15 | 259 |
| 14:13-21 | 259 |
| 15:18 | 280 |
| 15:19 | *186* |
| 15:28 | 259 |
| 16:1-12 | 259 |
| 16:13-20 | 259 |
| 16:16 | 57, 259 |
| 16:17 | 259 |
| 16:22 | 57 |
| 17:1-13 | 260 |
| 17:5 | 260 |
| 18:16 | 17 |
| 19:4 | 128 |
| 19:17 | 204 |
| 19:24 | 261 |
| 19:26 | 260 |
| 21 | 256 |
| 21:5 | 260 |
| 21:13 | 260 |
| 21:31 | 261 |
| 21:33-44 | 263 |
| 21:33-45 | 260 |
| 21:37-39 | 260 |
| 21:38 | 263 |
| 21:42 | 276 |
| 21:43 | 260, 261, 262, 263, 276 |
| 21:45-46 | 261 |
| 22 | 261 |
| 22:31 | 128 |
| 22:37-39 | 257 |
| 24:2 | 262 |
| 23:2-4 | 261 |
| 23:14 | 261 |
| 23:16 | 261 |
| 24-25 | 304 |
| 24:44 | 322 |
| 25:1 | 262 |
| 25:14 | 262 |
| 25:31-46 | 262 |
| 25:32 | 262 |
| 25:34 | 313 |
| 25:34-36 | 262 |
| 25:35-36 | 263 |
| 25:41-43 | 263 |
| 25:42-43 | 263 |
| 26-27 | 263 |
| 26:41 | 193 |
| 26:63-66 | 265 |
| 27:25 | 263 |
| 27:38 | 51 |
| 27:57-60 | 51 |
| 28 | 263 |
| 28:16 | 320, 321 |
| 28:19 | 263 |
| 28:19-20 | 280, 320 |

## Mark

| | |
|---|---|
| 1:1 | 313 |
| 4:3-8 | 229 |
| 4:14-20 | 229 |
| 7:20-23 | 184 |
| 7:21-22 | *186* |
| 9:42 | 156 |
| 10:18 | 204 |
| 14:29-31 | 57 |
| 14:66-72 | 57 |
| 15:34 | 83 |

## Luke

| | |
|---|---|
| 2 | *202* |
| 2:21-24 | 110 |
| 3:23-34 | 310 |
| 3:23-38 | 310 |
| 10 | 164 |

## Scripture Reference Index

14:13-14 .................................................. 50
18:19 .................................................... 204
21:1-4 ................................................... 226
23:12 .................................................... 189
24:27 .................................................... 251
24:44 .................................................... 251

### John

1:17 ...................................................... 203
1:29 ...................................................... 295
3:16 ...................................................... 292
3:16-18 ................................................... 83
3:18 ...................................................... 318
5:39 ............................................... 99, 251
6:1-13 ................................................... 259
6:22-58 ................................................. 259
8:11 ............................................... 157, 194
8:33 ...................................................... 112
8:34 ............................................... 144, 162
8:36 ....................................... 138, 144, 162
10:14 .................................................... 315
11:25 .................................................... 166
13:3-15 .................................................. 163
13:16 ...................................................... 51
13:35 ...................................... 50, 163, 201
15 .......................................... 255, 290, 292
15:1 ..................... 255, 256, 260, 294, 320
15:1-8 ................................................... 255
15:2-8 ................................................... 256
15:5 .......................................... 99, 138, 256
15:15 ...................................................... 33
17 .......................................................... 40
20:29 ..................................................... 40
21:3 ....................................................... 57

### Acts

1:8 ....................................................... 321
7 ........................................................... 40
7:53 ....................................................... 98
9:4-5 .................................................... 239
9:15-16 .................................................. 36
9:19a ..................................................... 37

9:19b ..................................................... 37
9:19b-20 ................................................ 37
10 .......................................................... 59
11:27-30 ................................................ 46
11:30 ............................................... 45, 56
12:6-17 .................................................. 56
12:17 ..................................................... 56
13-14 .................................................... 109
13:46 .................................................... 289
15 ............................................. 45, 46, 58
15:1 ...................................................... 151
15:23-29 ................................................ 46
15:24 ..................................................... 57
17:1-2 ................................................... 266
22:3b-5 .................................................. 35
26:9-11 .................................................. 34

### Romans

1:16 ........................... 266, 268, 303, 310
1:16-17 ................................................. 277
1:18-20 ................................................. 281
1:20 ...................................................... 303
1:26-27 ................................................. 187
2:4 ........................................................ 203
2:11-12 ................................................. 321
2:14-16 .................................................. 70
2:28 ....................................................... 79
2:28-29 .............................. 293, 294, 317
3 .......................................................... 276
3:12 ...................................................... 204
3:15 ...................................................... 280
3:21-30 ................................................. 277
3:23 ...................................................... 178
4 .......................................................... 276
4:1-8 ..................................................... 277
5:1 ....................................................... 202
5:8 ....................................................... 142
5:10 ...................................................... 202
6:1-2 .............................. 144, 172, 291
6:13 ...................................................... 173
7 ................................ 38, 174, 175, 176, 177
7:7-12 ................................................... 175

| Reference | Pages |
|---|---|
| 7:7-25 | *38*, 173 |
| 7:7-8:17 | *171* |
| 7:12 | 77 |
| 7:13-25 | 176 |
| 8 | 176 |
| 8:7 | 189 |
| 8:12-15 | 174 |
| 8:13 | 70 |
| 8:14-16 | 314 |
| 8:28 | 299 |
| 8:28-30 | 71 |
| 8:28-39 | 36 |
| 8:30 | 288 |
| 8:37-39 | 288 |
| 8:38-39 | 72, 283, 291 |
| 9 | 276 |
| 9-11 | 264, 267, 279, 287, 288, 302 |
| 9:1 | 264, 266 |
| 9:1-2 | 264 |
| 9:1-3 | 247, 270 |
| 9:1-5 | 27, 264, 273 |
| 9:2 | 265 |
| 9:3 | 265, 266, 296 |
| 9:3-5 | 265, 310 |
| 9:4 | 265 |
| 9:4-5 | 265 |
| 9:5 | 265, 293 |
| 9:5-8 | 296 |
| 9:6 | 260, 268, 270, 275, 283, 293, 309, 321 |
| 9:6-7 | 320 |
| 9:6-8 | 265, 266, 267 |
| 9:6-26 | 267 |
| 9:6-11:26 | 293 |
| 9:6a | 267 |
| 9:6b | 267 |
| 9:6b-7 | 267 |
| 9:6b-8 | 267 |
| 9:7 | 268 |
| 9:7b | 268 |
| 9:8 | 268 |
| 9:9 | 269 |
| 9:9-13 | 268 |
| 9:10-11 | 269 |
| 9:11 | 269, 275, 284 |
| 9:12 | 269 |
| 9:13 | 270 |
| 9:14 | 270 |
| 9:14-18 | 270 |
| 9:15 | 270 |
| 9:16 | 270 |
| 9:17 | 270, 271 |
| 9:18 | 271, 275, 285 |
| 9:19 | 271 |
| 9:19-26 | 271, 275 |
| 9:20 | 270, 273 |
| 9:20-21 | 272 |
| 9:22 | 203, 272 |
| 9:22-23 | 272, 283 |
| 9:22-24 | 272 |
| 9:22-26 | 272 |
| 9:23 | 273 |
| 9:24 | 272, 273, 283 |
| 9:25-26 | 272, 273 |
| 9:26 | 273 |
| 9:27-29 | 273, 275 |
| 9:28 | 274 |
| 9:29 | 274 |
| 9:30-33 | 275 |
| 9:30-10:21 | 274, 275 |
| 9:30b-31 | 275 |
| 9:31-32 | 285 |
| 9:32-33 | 275, 276, 286 |
| 9:32a | 275 |
| 10 | 275, 276 |
| 10:1 | 266, 283 |
| 10:1-2 | 277 |
| 10:1-4 | 276, 277 |
| 10:2 | 277 |
| 10:3 | 277 |
| 10:3-4 | 277 |
| 10:5-8 | 278 |
| 10:5-13 | 277, 278 |
| 10:5-17 | 277 |
| 10:6-7 | 278 |

## Scripture Reference Index

| | |
|---|---|
| 10:6-8 | 278 |
| 10:8 | 278 |
| 10:9 | 142 |
| 10:9-10 | 279 |
| 10:9-13 | 278 |
| 10:11 | 279 |
| 10:12 | 279, 281 |
| 10:13 | 279 |
| 10:13-15 | 320 |
| 10:14-15 | 274, 278, 279, 280 |
| 10:14-15a | 279 |
| 10:14-17 | 280 |
| 10:15 | 280 |
| 10:16 | 281 |
| 10:16-17 | 278, 281 |
| 10:17 | 281 |
| 10:18-21 | 281 |
| 10:18a | 281 |
| 10:18b | 282 |
| 10:19 | 282 |
| 10:19a | 282 |
| 10:19b-21 | 282 |
| 10:21 | 282, 283 |
| 11 | 256, 270, 276, 277, 287 |
| 11:1 | 283 |
| 11:1-6 | 282 |
| 11:1a | 283 |
| 11:1b | 283 |
| 11:2a | 283 |
| 11:2b-5 | 283 |
| 11:3 | 284 |
| 11:5 | 287, 288, 294, 309, 310 |
| 11:5-7 | 291 |
| 11:6 | 270, 284, 285 |
| 11:7 | 282, 285, 287, 288, 293, 294, 297, 309 |
| 11:7-10 | 285 |
| 11:7-26 | 274 |
| 11:8-10 | 285, 286 |
| 11:9 | 286 |
| 11:10 | 286, 287, 294 |
| 11:11-12 | 289 |
| 11:11-16 | 288, 295, 297 |
| 11:11-24 | 287, 288 |
| 11:11a | 287 |
| 11:11b-12 | 288 |
| 11:11b-16 | 288 |
| 11:13-14 | 266, 289 |
| 11:15 | 289 |
| 11:16 | 289, 290 |
| 11:17 | 290 |
| 11:17-18a | 290 |
| 11:17-24 | 288, 290, 296 |
| 11:18 | 294 |
| 11:18b | 290 |
| 11:19-21 | 290 |
| 11:20 | 291 |
| 11:22 | 291 |
| 11:23 | 290, 292 |
| 11:24 | 291, 292 |
| 11:25 | 290, 293 |
| 11:25-26 | 287, 296 |
| 11:25-27 | 293 |
| 11:25-32 | 264, 293 |
| 11:26 | 294, 309, 317 |
| 11:26-27 | 295 |
| 11:28 | 295, 296 |
| 11:28-29 | 295 |
| 11:29 | 296 |
| 11:30-31 | 297 |
| 11:30-32 | 296 |
| 11:32 | 271, 297 |
| 11:33-36 | 297, 298 |
| 11:34 | 298 |
| 11:35 | 298 |
| 13:9-10 | 164 |
| 15:30 | 311 |
| 16:25 | 303 |

## 1 Corinthians

| | |
|---|---|
| 1:10 | 217 |
| 1:10-25 | 25 |
| 5:6-8 | 156 |
| 6:9-10 | *186* |
| 6:9-11 | 69 |

| | |
|---|---|
| 6:19 | 188 |
| 10:1-2 | 257 |
| 11:19 | 191 |
| 11:19-21 | 191 |
| 11:25 | 319 |
| 14:6 | 47 |
| 14:16 | 240 |
| 14:25 | 47 |
| 14:29-31 | 47 |
| 15 | 304 |
| 15:22-23 | 289 |

## 2 Corinthians

| | |
|---|---|
| 1:20 | 91, 240, 253, 263, 266, 318 |
| 5:7 | 81 |
| 5:21 | 29 |
| 6:17 | 307 |
| 8:8-9 | 226 |
| 10:1 | 205 |
| 11:23-25 | 119 |
| 11:28 | 121, 239 |
| 12:9-10 | 119 |
| 13:1 | 17 |

## Galatians

| | |
|---|---|
| 1-2 | 151 |
| 1:1-2a | 15 |
| 1:1-5 | 13, 107, 140 |
| 1:1-2:21 | 33 |
| 1:2 | 17 |
| 1:2b-3 | 17 |
| 1:3-4 | 18 |
| 1:4-5 | 17 |
| 1:5 | 40 |
| 1:6 | 16, 23, 24, 120, 247 |
| 1:6-7 | 25 |
| 1:6-10 | 21, 107, 140 |
| 1:7 | 26, 240 |
| 1:8 | 245, 247, 248 |
| 1:8-9 | 26 |
| 1:9 | 67 |
| 1:10 | 25, 27 |
| 1:11 | 6 |
| 1:11-24 | 1, 31, 33, 107, 140 |
| 1:11-2:10 | 238, 239 |
| 1:12 | 35, 36, 40, 46 |
| 1:13-14 | 33 |
| 1:15-16 | 35, 69, 71, 118 |
| 1:15-16a | 35 |
| 1:16 | 46 |
| 1:16a | 36 |
| 1:16b-24 | 36 |
| 1:17 | 37 |
| 1:18-20 | 39 |
| 1:21-24 | 39 |
| 2:1 | 39 |
| 2:1-2 | 39 |
| 2:1-2a | 45 |
| 2:1-5 | 140 |
| 2:1-10 | 43, 45, 56, 107 |
| 2:1-14 | 151 |
| 2:2 | 46, 47, 48 |
| 2:2b | 47 |
| 2:3-5 | 46, 47 |
| 2:4 | 45 |
| 2:4-5 | 48 |
| 2:5 | 50 |
| 2:6 | 49 |
| 2:6-9 | 48 |
| 2:6-10 | 48, 140 |
| 2:9 | 49 |
| 2:10 | 49, 51 |
| 2:11 | 55, 56 |
| 2:11-14 | 140 |
| 2:11-21 | 53, 107, 238 |
| 2:11-4:7 | 237 |
| 2:12 | 57 |
| 2:12-13 | 56 |
| 2:13 | 59 |
| 2:14 | 58, 59 |
| 2:14-21 | 58 |
| 2:15-16 | 59 |
| 2:15-21 | 140 |
| 2:16 | 3, 58, 59 |

## Scripture Reference Index

2:17 .................................................. 59
2:18 ............................................ 82, 111
2:18-20 ............................................. 60
2:19 .................................................. 61
2:19b-20 ........................................... 61
2:19b-21 ........................................... 85
2:20 ............................................. 60, 82
2:21 ............................. 58, 61, 69, 285
3 ................................................ 97, 99
3-4 ................................................. 152
3:1 ................ 7, 29, 67, 68, 130, 140, 155
3:1-5 .......................................... 65, 107
3:1-5:1 ............................................. 33
3:2 ........................................ 16, 69, 71
3:2-3 ........................................ 176, 215
3:2-4 ............................................... 67
3:2-14 ............................................ 141
3:3 ..................................... 69, 285, 317
3:4 ................................................. 71
3:5 ................................ 67, 71, 77, 82
3:5-9 .............................................. 317
3:6-14 ...................................... 75, 107
3:6-26 ............................................... 1
3:6-7 ............................................. 253
3:6-9 .............................................. 78
3:7 .................................................. 79
3:8 .................................................. 79
3:9 ............................................ 79, 230
3:10 ..................................... 80, 230, 278
3:10-12 ........................................... 79
3:10-14 .......................................... 237
3:10-29 .......................................... 130
3:11 ................................................ 80
3:12 ................................................ 81
3:13 ................................................ 19
3:13-14 ..................................... 78, 82
3:13-18 .......................................... 318
3:13a .............................................. 82
3:14 ............................................... 157
3:15 ........................................... 89, 91
3:15-18 ........................... 79, 87, 107, 141

3:16 .... 79, 89, 237, 238, 252, 253, 254, 257, 263, 264, 267, 268, 294, 320
3:16a .............................................. 90
3:16b ........................................ 90, 251
3:16c .............................................. 91
3:17 ................................................ 91
3:18 ................................................ 91
3:18b .............................................. 92
3:19-20 ........................................... 97
3:19-24 ........................................... 97
3:19-26 .......................................... 141
3:19-29 ..................................... 95, 108
3:21-24 ........................................... 98
3:22 ................................................ 99
3:24 ..................... 100, *101*, 108, 175, 278
3:25-26 .......................................... 101
3:25-29 ..................................... 97, 101
3:27-4:7 ......................................... 141
3:28 ........................... 77, 104, 202, 237
3:28-29 .......................................... 254
3:29 ............................. 253, 254, 257, 268
4 ................................................... 108
4:1-2 .............................................. 108
4:1-7 ....................................... 105, 108
4:3 ................................................ 109
4:3-5 ............................................. 108
4:6-7 ............................................. 110
4:7 ................................................ 111
4:8 ................................................ 117
4:8-10 ........................................... 117
4:8-11 ........................................... 141
4:8-20 ........................................... 115
4:8-6:10 ........................................ 236
4:9 ................................................ 118
4:11 .............................................. 118
4:12 .............................................. 141
4:12-15 ......................................... 118
4:12-20 .................................... 117, 141
4:13 .............................................. 119
4:15 .............................................. 120
4:16 .............................................. 122
4:16-20 ......................................... 120

| Reference | Pages |
|---|---|
| 4:17 | 68, 236 |
| 4:20 | 127 |
| 4:21 | 127, 141 |
| 4:21-31 | 125, 138, 141 |
| 4:22-23 | 128 |
| 4:24-27 | 128, 129 |
| 4:25 | 37 |
| 4:26 | 130 |
| 4:28-31 | 128, 130 |
| 4:29 | 237 |
| 4:30 | 245, 247, 249 |
| 5 | 28, 48, 77, 108 |
| 5-6 | 24, 62, 236 |
| 5:1 | 3, 55, 135, 137, 138, 140, 141, 144, 151, 153, 154, 161, 209, 237, 247 |
| 5:1-12 | 1 |
| 5:2-4 | 151 |
| 5:2-5 | 155 |
| 5:2-12 | 147, 161, 245, 249 |
| 5:2-6:10 | 33 |
| 5:4 | 153, 156, 247 |
| 5:5 | 154 |
| 5:6 | 50, 154, 155, 161, 236 |
| 5:6-6:15 | 154 |
| 5:7 | 68 |
| 5:7-12 | 155 |
| 5:9 | 156 |
| 5:10 | 68, 156, 239, 248 |
| 5:12 | 68, 247, 249 |
| 5:13 | 139, 154 |
| 5:13-14 | 50 |
| 5:13-15 | 155, 159, 161 |
| 5:13-6:10 | 155, 224, 236, 237, 238 |
| 5:13a | 161 |
| 5:13b-14 | 163 |
| 5:13b-15 | 161 |
| 5:14 | 157, 207 |
| 5:15 | 164, 189 |
| 5:16 | 171, 172, 174, 199 |
| 5:16-18 | 48, 169 |
| 5:17 | 173, 174, 184 |
| 5:18 | 174, 176 |
| 5:19 | 184, 192 |
| 5:19-21 | 172, 181, 202, 205, 206, 208 |
| 5:19-23 | 104 |
| 5:19b-21a | 185 |
| 5:20 | 188, *190* |
| 5:21 | 173, 177, 184, 194, 206 |
| 5:22 | 199 |
| 5:22-23 | 208 |
| 5:22-24 | 172, 197, 199 |
| 5:23 | 206, 219 |
| 5:23-24 | 200 |
| 5:24 | 207, 237 |
| 5:25 | 215, 219 |
| 5:25-6:5 | 199, 211, 214 |
| 5:26 | 215 |
| 5:26-6:10 | 215 |
| 6 | 174 |
| 6:1 | 165, 217, 218, 219, 225 |
| 6:1-2 | 216 |
| 6:1-5 | 216, 225 |
| 6:2 | 174, 217, 218, 239, 240 |
| 6:3 | 218 |
| 6:3-5 | 217 |
| 6:4-5 | 218 |
| 6:5 | 239 |
| 6:6 | 224, 225, 226 |
| 6:6-10 | 221 |
| 6:7-8 | 225 |
| 6:9-10 | 227 |
| 6:10 | *99*, 177, 228 |
| 6:11 | 235 |
| 6:11-18 | 231, 234, 236 |
| 6:12 | 68, 240 |
| 6:12-13 | 236 |
| 6:14 | 237 |
| 6:14-15 | 237 |
| 6:15 | 155 |
| 6:15-16 | 322 |
| 6:16 | 237, 294 |
| 6:17 | 238, 239 |
| 6:18 | 240 |

## Scripture Reference Index

### Ephesians

| | |
|---|---|
| 1:3-5 | 36 |
| 1:3-6 | 71 |
| 1:4 | 298 |
| 1:13 | 72 |
| 1:14 | 208 |
| 2:1 | 203 |
| 2:7 | 203 |
| 2:8 | 284 |
| 2:8-10 | 99 |
| 2:11-22 | 273 |
| 2:12-13 | 298 |
| 2:20 | 49 |
| 4:2 | 217, 218 |
| 5:3-5 | 186 |
| 5:22-32 | 239 |
| 5:31-32 | 313 |
| 5:32 | 316 |

### Philippians

| | |
|---|---|
| 2:5-8 | 204 |
| 2:10-11 | 203 |
| 2:14-15 | 187 |
| 3:4b-6 | 35 |

### Colossians

| | |
|---|---|
| 1:1 | 314 |
| 2:20-23 | 98 |
| 3:5 | 186 |

### 1 Thessalonians

| | |
|---|---|
| 4:3 | 186 |

### 2 Thessalonians

| | |
|---|---|
| 3:17 | 235 |

### 1 Timothy

| | |
|---|---|
| 1:2 | 258 |
| 1:8 | 77 |
| 1:9-10 | 186 |
| 1:15 | 35 |
| 3:15 | 49 |
| 5:19 | 17 |

### 2 Timothy

| | |
|---|---|
| 2:19 | 315 |
| 3:16 | 128, 318 |
| 3:16-17 | 252 |
| 4:8 | 312 |

### Titus

| | |
|---|---|
| 1:2 | 254 |
| 1:13 | 248 |
| 2:11-14 | 99 |
| 3:9-10 | 58 |
| 3:10-11 | 27 |
| 3:14 | 99 |

### Philemon

| | |
|---|---|
| 1:19-21 | 236 |

### Hebrews

| | |
|---|---|
| 5:12-14 | 165 |
| 6 | 153 |
| 6:18 | 254 |
| 6:20 | 312 |
| 7:14 | 312 |
| 7:15 | 312 |
| 10:1-10 | 312 |
| 10:12 | 313 |
| 11 | 204, 310 |
| 12:1 | 172 |
| 12:2 | 157, 239 |

### James

| | |
|---|---|
| 1:27 | 51 |
| 2:10 | 70, 83, 153 |
| 2:24 | 17 |
| 3:1 | 27, 156 |

### 1 Peter

| | |
|---|---|
| 2:9 | 312 |
| 3:16 | 71 |
| 4:3 | 312 |

### 2 Peter

| | |
|---|---|
| 1:3 | 72 |

| | |
|---|---|
| 1:5-7 | 206 |
| 3:9 | 202 |

## 1 John

| | |
|---|---|
| 2:1 | 162 |
| 3:9 | 162 |
| 3:16 | 201 |
| 4:17 | 155 |
| 5:21 | 187 |

## Revelation

| | |
|---|---|
| 1 | 304 |
| 1:1 | 299, 303, 304 |
| 1:1-20 | 304 |
| 1:1a | 15, 303 |
| 1:3 | 303 |
| 1:4 | 304 |
| 1:9 | 311 |
| 1:19 | 304 |
| 2-3 | 304 |
| 2:1-3:22 | *304* |
| 2:1-16:11 | 304 |
| 2:7 | 304, 312 |
| 2:10-11 | 312 |
| 2:11 | 304 |
| 2:17 | 304, 307, 312 |
| 2:26 | 304 |
| 2:26-28 | 312 |
| 3 | 316 |
| 3:5 | 304, 312 |
| 3:12 | 304, 307, 312, 315 |
| 3:21 | 304, 312 |
| 5:5 | 309 |
| 5:8 | 311 |
| 5:9 | 287 |
| 7 | 299, 302, 303, 304, 305, 308, 309, 310, 313, 315 |
| 7:4 | 314, 315, 316 |
| 7:4-8 | 305, 306, 309, 314 |
| 7:5 | 310 |
| 7:9 | 314, 315 |
| 7:9-10 | 314 |
| 7:9-17 | 314, 315 |
| 7:13-14 | 314 |
| 9:16 | 315 |
| 9:21 | 188 |
| 14 | 315 |
| 14:1 | 315 |
| 16:12 | 305 |
| 16:12-22:9 | 304 |
| 17 | 316 |
| 17-22 | 304 |
| 18:4 | 307 |
| 18:23 | 188 |
| 19:7-8 | 254 |
| 20:12 | 318 |
| 20:15 | 318 |
| 21 | 315 |
| 21:9-11 | 313, 316 |
| 21:14 | 49 |
| 21:15-17 | 316 |
| 21:16 | 316 |
| 21:17 | 316 |
| 22:10-21 | 304 |
| 22:14-15 | 185 |
| 22:15 | *186* |
| 22:20 | 311 |
| 22:20-21 | 157 |

## Early Christian Writings
### Didache

| | |
|---|---|
| 11:10 | 240 |

## Greco-Roman Literature
### Plato's *Lysis*

| | |
|---|---|
| 208c | 101 |

www.ingramcontent.com/pod-product-compliance
Lightning Source LLC
Chambersburg PA
CBHW021831220426
43663CB00005B/203